T0244351

Tell Mother I'm in Paradise

Tell Mother I'm in Paradise

Memoirs of a Political Prisoner in El Salvador

Ana Margarita Gasteazoro

Edited by **Judy Blankenship** and **Andrew Wilson**
Introduction by **Erik Ching**

THE UNIVERSITY OF ALABAMA PRESS
Tuscaloosa

The University of Alabama Press
Tuscaloosa, Alabama 35487-0380
uapress.ua.edu

Typeface: Arno Pro

Cover image: Ana Margarita Gasteazoro in Cuenca, Ecuador, 1992; photo by Judy Blankenship
Cover design: Lori Lynch

Cataloging-in-Publication data is available from the Library of Congress.
ISBN: 978-0-8173-2121-5
E-ISBN: 978-0-8173-9397-7

To all women currently imprisoned for their political beliefs, to the mothers who worry about them, and to the daughters who are inspired by them

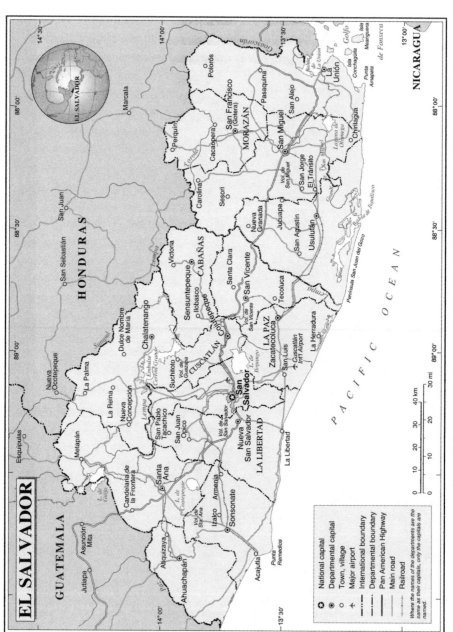

Figure 1. Map of El Salvador (Based on United Nations Map No. 3903, Rev. 4, May 2003)

Contents

~

Part I. A Nice Girl like Me

Part II. A Nice Country like El Salvador

Part III. A Nice Prison like Ilopango

Figures

Preface

⁓

When we first met in San José, Costa Rica, Ana Margarita Gasteazoro was just 36 years old—beautiful, vibrant, intelligent, curious, full of life. It was late in 1986, and she was working as a translator and Spanish teacher at a private school. I had come to Central America the year before with a Canadian nongovernmental organization to work as a photographer and adult educator. We connected when a cooperant from the same NGO, Andrew Wilson, met Ana Margarita and invited us all to a dinner party where she and I found we had a lot to talk about. The friendship and collaboration between the three of us—four actually, with my new partner Michael—endured until her death, seven years later.

In those first months, as I got to know Ana Margarita, she told captivating stories of her life: from her childhood in an upper-class Salvadoran family, with a religious mother and liberal father who insisted she be educated at the American School in San Salvador, to her turbulent adolescence and awakening social consciousness (ironically, through the influence of Maryknoll nuns in Guatemala), to her young adult years of political activism, including an underground life in war-torn El Salvador. She revealed that she was a political refugee in Costa Rica documented with the United Nations High Commissioner for Refugees. In El Salvador, she had been "disappeared" for 11 days in a clandestine jail cell of the National Police before she was imprisoned without charge for two years in Ilopango, the notorious women's prison. She told these stories with exquisite detail and humor, but an underlying melancholy suggested a deeper narrative. (One benefit of her refugee status was the services of a psychiatrist who helped her deal with the trauma of her arrest and two years in prison.) When I proposed we get together regularly and tape her life story, she readily agreed.

In the small house in San José where I lived with Michael, we met in my darkroom-cum-office on evenings and weekends, with my Sony cassette recorder on the desk between us. Her English was perfect and my Spanish was not, so we recorded in English. As I reviewed the tapes, I was struck by the timeliness of her stories. In 1986 the war in El Salvador was still raging, and much of my documentary photography work was related to human rights groups in Central America. The United States was still providing military aid worth hundreds of millions of dollars, despite flagrant human rights abuses, including the assassinations of four American churchwomen by the Salvadoran military in 1980. (US aid to El Salvador in 1987 marked a milestone, as for the first time the total amount of US aid exceeded the national budget of the receiving country.)[1]

After a few meetings, I suggested to Ana Margarita that we make a real oral history; I would transcribe the tapes, and we'd schedule additional sessions to fill in details and gaps. We asked Andrew if he would join us as a fellow transcriber and editor. He and I both had some background in journalism, and I think we saw the potential for—well, at that point we weren't thinking beyond the pleasure of working together. Ana Margarita loved to talk, I loved to ask questions, Andrew loved to shape written narratives, and Michael loved to cook. Listening to the tapes, I can hear him banging about in the kitchen, singing, or calling us to the table for dinner. We were a happy team.

Everything changed in 1988 when Ana Margarita came back from a holiday in the Caribbean coastal town of Puerto Viejo and announced she was going to act on a dream to open a restaurant. She wanted to bake bread and make pizza—simple as that (well, not quite so simple at first, but a loan from Andrew to buy the pizza oven certainly helped). Never alone for long, Ana Margarita soon met a local man called Smokey (Adolfo Stewart) who owned land near the beach, and they decided to build an open-air café with living quarters above. Café Coral was opened later that year, and Ana Margarita happily settled into a very different life from that of San José, her "hippy-café" attracting surfers and backpackers with her famous homemade granola (which I still make today) and Smokey's lobster and fresh green peppercorn pizzas. Forever the organizer, Ana Margarita was soon chairwoman of the community of Puerto Viejo, pushing hard for ecologically friendly development in the surrounding area. By this time, Andrew had

Figure 2. Portrait of Ana Margarita in Cuenca, Ecuador (Courtesy of Judy Blankenship)

finished his NGO contract and returned to Canada, where he freelanced as a writer and editor.

Then in 1990 came Ana Margarita's diagnosis of breast cancer. After surgery and some time recovering in El Salvador, she returned to Puerto Viejo, to Smokey and Café Coral. Life seemed to return to normal, and although our recording sessions were now sporadic, Andrew and I continued to transcribe the tapes. By now we three were in agreement that this was to be a book, and we began to shape chapters and think about a narrative thread for English-language readers. Shortly after, in 1991, Michael and I moved to Ecuador. After six years in Costa Rica, I was eager to begin a new photography project in the Andes.

Andrew continued to edit and made a few trips to Puerto Viejo for fill-in recordings. In July 1992, family connections permitted Ana Margarita to arrange some medical appointments at a Los Angeles hospital. Andrew flew to LA, having interested the late Mike Hamilburg, a well-known Hollywood agent, in Ana Margarita's story. I still have a letter in which Andrew described meeting with the agent after first driving Ana Margarita to an appointment:

> In the UCLA Medical Centre parking lot Ana and I were winked through by a Salvadoran parking attendant—but then Ana, even with her hair reduced by chemotherapy and her neck in a brace and pilled-up on Valium, is a warm, wonderful presence.
>
> I felt that presence work its magic as we talked with the agent. They liked each other; they connected; they "did lunch" without having lunch. I mostly sat back and passed over manuscripts and fed Ana bits of her own extravagantly interesting history when I felt she was playing herself down. Totally straight exchange of information about her health: she might die, but she doesn't intend to. The agent told her, "You can't! Authors have to publicize their books you know," and she thanked him. The connection was personal: he'd read the outline and said he would read the chapters.

Hamilburg liked what he read and sent query letters to major publishers. But time was running out.

A bit later in 1992, Ana Margarita and Smokey came to Cuenca, Ecuador, for a long-planned visit. Michael and I hadn't seen her since we'd left San José. Her magnificent dark hair had grown back but was still short. And she was still beautiful. But what should have been a joyful reunion of old friends was steeped with sadness. Just before the trip, Ana Margarita, feeling tired and achy, had gone for tests that revealed her breast cancer had metastasized to her

Figure 3. Ana Margarita with Smokey in Cuenca,
Ecuador (Courtesy of Judy Blankenship)

bones. After she mentioned this to me, and we silently acknowledged what we both knew it meant, nothing more was said about it during the week-long visit. I'm not even sure that Smokey knew at that point. Instead, we spent a day and night in Cañar, the indigenous town where I was beginning a documentary project that continues to this day. We shopped at the *antigüedades* stores in Cuenca where Ana Margarita bought a multistrand coral necklace, and I made a last portrait of her wearing it. In the evenings, we sat by the fireplace making the last recordings of the oral history that is the basis of this book.

With unspoken regret, Ana Margarita talked about a future that could have been. The El Salvador peace accords had just been signed, after 12 years of war and 75,000 deaths. She had been invited by the leaders of her party, the Movimiento Nacional Revolucionario (National Revolutionary Movement, MNR), to come back and run for office. Had she been healthy, she would have done so, she said. She could not continue running a small restaurant in Costa Rica while her country was rebuilding.

We said goodbye, Michael and I promising to come to Costa Rica for Christmas, which we did. But by then Ana Margarita was in too much pain to do much beyond endure the hours between morphine shots, which she gave herself while living in a friend's house in San José. Smokey came and went from Puerto Viejo, mostly silent, stoically trying to come to terms with losing Ana Margarita. Her mother was there too, waiting to take Ana Margarita back to El Salvador to die. Andrew, back in Canada, made one last trip to see Ana Margarita during her finals days in San Salvador. She died there in January 1993 as the country laid the groundwork for its first democratic elections.

Back in Ecuador, grieving at the news of Ana Margarita's death and wondering what I could do to honor her memory, I recalled a story she'd told during one of our recording sessions. She'd said that as much as her father loved her and recognized her intelligence, he told her that he could not afford to send her to university because he had three sons: "Your brothers will marry and have to support families, so I will educate them, but you will marry and your husband will support you." Ana Margarita did not get her university education, she never married, and she never forgot the injustice of her father's decision.

That year, I started the Ana Margarita Gasteazoro Fund for Women's Education (now the Cañari Women's Education Foundation). Since then, 38 indigenous women from Cañar Province have received full scholarships to state universities in Ecuador. The foundation's graduates include some of the country's first Quichua-speaking physicians, dentists, lawyers, agronomists, economists, nutritionists, nurses, and accountants. Ana Margarita would have been pleased; a born teacher, she believed strongly that the education of women was one of, if not the, most important tools for social and political progress in Latin America.

I miss her still.

JUDY BLANKENSHIP
PORTLAND, OREGON, 2021

Introduction

Erik Ching

What follows is the life story of Ana Margarita Gasteazoro, a member of a "good" family in El Salvador who chose an alternative path, that of political activist and militant revolutionary during that country's 12-year civil war (1980–1992). For her choice, the Salvadoran government declared her an enemy of the state, and eventually the Salvadoran military captured her and jailed her for two years (1981–1983). Many people captured by the Salvadoran military did not survive, but Gasteazoro did, and when she was released in 1983 in a general amnesty, she went into exile in Mexico, Cuba, and finally, Costa Rica.

There she met and befriended a young woman from the United States, Judy Blankenship, who was in Costa Rica working for a nongovernmental organization, Canadian University Service Overseas (CUSO). As their friendship grew and as Gasteazoro began to open up about her life, Blankenship realized the need to preserve her remarkable story. They began recording their conversations in 1987, gradually realizing the weekly sessions were creating a narrative for a book. They were joined by another friend and CUSO cooperant from Canada, a young journalist named Andrew Wilson, who eventually took the lead in crafting the interview transcripts into a readable narrative. This book is the fruit of their collective labor, finally coming to light, nearly three decades after Gasteazoro's untimely death from cancer in 1993.

The main setting for Gasteazoro's story is El Salvador's civil war, a brutal, bloody trauma that cost upward of 75,000 lives and placed that tiny nation of five million people at the center of Cold War geopolitics. Gasteazoro participated actively in that conflict, first as a member of a small social democratic political party and later as a ranking member of the political wing of a militant guerrilla organization. Consequently, much of Gasteazoro's story revolves around the politics of that war and the mobilization leading up to it in the 1970s.

But Gasteazoro's story is about much more than that. It is a multidimensional tale that allows readers to see the world in new and complex ways. It's a coming-of-age story; it's a story about family bonds and the dramas that strain them; it's a story about gender, patriarchy, and religious conviction; and of course, it's a survival story.

Not all life stories are as multidimensional as this one; in fact, few of them are. To tell a multidimensional tale, the storyteller has to be able to see their lived experiences in complex ways, from a perspective of emotional depth, and with an eye to nuance. Perhaps most of all, the storyteller has to be willing to risk exposure, to open up and share their inner feelings. I have read a lot of life stories in my career. In fact, as part of my research for my 2016 book, *Stories of Civil War in El Salvador*, I read every life story that has appeared in El Salvador since the end of the war in 1992, and there are a lot of them. I have found it to be rare to encounter a storyteller who possesses the necessary traits to tell a transcendent tale.[1]

Tell Mother I'm in Paradise is an exception to that norm, and the reason is its protagonist, Ana Margarita Gasteazoro. She was a self-reflective, empathetic, and insightful person who experienced extraordinary things extraordinarily. The title to Gasteazoro's story reveals its multidimensionality. The phrase "tell Mother I'm in paradise" was the message Gasteazoro sent to her mother from prison to assure her that not only would she survive, but she intended to thrive as a person. She was confident of finding a community among her fellow political prisoners, of working collectively to defend themselves against their jailers and to make demands based on their human rights. The title reveals to us that this story is set squarely within a family drama, told by an activist woman who was jailed by a regime that her family supported.

El Salvador's Civil War

El Salvador had a civil war because a militant opposition took up arms against the Salvadoran state. It did so because its members and supporters believed that a repressive clique of military officers and economic elites who had violently suppressed all demands for peaceful change was ruling their country.

The war had terrible consequences. In addition to 75,000 or more deaths, it resulted in hundreds of thousands of injuries and more than one million people displaced from their homes. The number of people who were tortured, jailed, sexually assaulted, or generally terrorized is beyond measure—all in a nation of five million people, not even the size of Massachusetts. Salvadorans will bear a deep psychological scar for decades to come because of what transpired in their country in the 1980s.

In basic terms, the war consisted of two opposing sides. On the one side was a guerrilla army, the Farabundo Martí National Liberation Front (FMLN), named after an activist who was murdered by the Salvadoran army in 1932 during an earlier example of the Salvadoran state using brutal violence to suppress popular dissent. The FMLN comprised five rival guerrilla organizations that had formed in the 1970s and united in October 1980. At any given moment throughout the war, the FMLN had between 3,000 and 10,000 fighters in the field. They were hunkered down in rural enclaves with a widespread network of civilian support. The FMLN also had a highly successful political wing that had a diplomatic and fundraising presence throughout the world, including in the United States and Western Europe.

On the other side was the Salvadoran government and its armed wing, the Salvadoran military, which consisted of anywhere between 50,000 and 100,000 soldiers. The formal military was assisted in its operations by a variety of paramilitary organizations, some of which served as its eyes and ears, and others that were shadowy death squads specializing in extralegal abductions, torture, and assassinations. Often the death squads left the corpses of their victims in conspicuously public places to deliver a message about what happens to suspected opponents. The government and military too had their base of popular support, much of it from poor, rural people who were either apolitical or genuinely opposed to the guerrillas because they considered them communists and atheists. The primary financial backer of the Salvadoran government was the United States.

Each side in the conflict claimed to be defending the civilian population from the other side. The government and military claimed to be the rightful defenders of the sovereign national state, protecting the population from insurgent communist terrorists who wanted to sow seeds of chaos and destruction so that they could create a power vacuum and sweep in and take control. They claimed that the insurgents' goal was to create a totalitarian dictatorship and ally El Salvador with supposedly similar nations, such as Nicaragua, Cuba, and the USSR.

The guerrillas claimed that they were defending the population from a predatory elite and a repressive state that had for decades exploited poor peoples' labor and built a system of exclusive authoritarianism that benefited only a small segment of the population. The guerrillas and their supporters claimed that for decades the populace had made repeated requests for change, almost all of them nonviolent, only to be met each time with violence and intransigence. They contended that by the 1970s a growing percentage of the population had reached its breaking point and decided that the only way to effect change was by taking up arms. Thus, the guerrillas were merely the armed wing of a people seeking justice.

Ana Margarita Gasteazoro fell into the latter camp. Even though she came from an affluent, conservative, religious family, she chose the path of political radicalism and religious agnosticism. How she came to that conscience, why she joined the opposition, what she did in her capacity as a leader of that opposition, and how she endured two years of incarceration are the essence of her story.

So who was right? The guerrillas and Ana Margarita Gasteazoro, or the Salvadoran government and military? Each of us has to answer that question for ourself. We should do so by assessing the evidence presented by each side and analyzing the interpretive methodologies their proponents employ to advance their arguments. As an example, consider the events that transpired in the village of El Mozote in northeastern El Salvador on December 11, 1981. One version is that an elite combat battalion of the Salvadoran army intentionally massacred as many 1,000 unarmed civilians, many of them children, as part of its scorched-earth counterinsurgency campaign. A second version is that a battle occurred between guerrillas and the army, and the victims were either guerrilla fighters or civilians caught in the crossfire. If I tell you that the first version is accurate and the second version is bogus, I do so because I find the evidence for the first argument, including eyewitness testimony and forensic analysis, to be sound, whereas the second argument either has no evidence or its advocates employ unsound approaches to interpret the existing evidence.[2]

Unfortunately assessing evidence and interpretive methodologies is hard work that requires time and expertise. We can't all become experts on every contested issue, so we have to trust reliable professionals to guide us through the morass. The University of Alabama Press has chosen me to serve in that capacity for you here. To that end, I say to you that Gasteazoro's version of events is fundamentally more accurate than that of her adversaries in the Salvadoran government and military. In fact, one of the things that surprised me when reading her life story was how much I agreed with her. I am used to reading life stories as sources, as things to be dissected and studied, not necessarily as places to look for reliable sources of information. But *Tell Mother I'm in Paradise* was a different experience for me. I was impressed with Gasteazoro's insights and the accuracy of her analysis. As readers, we should remain ever-critical analysts, but to the extent my word means anything, I assure you that you can place a lot of trust in Gasteazoro as your guide through El Salvador.

As just one piece of evidence to support my claim, consider the Truth Commission for El Salvador. As part of the negotiated settlement to the civil war, the United Nations was allowed to investigate as many of the killings and human rights violations as possible, especially some of the more notorious cases like the El Mozote massacre, the assassination of Archbishop Romero in March 1980, and the murder of six Jesuit priests in November 1989. The Truth Commission revealed that the Salvadoran military and its paramilitary allies were responsible for the overwhelming number of deaths and human rights violations throughout the war. Specifically, it attributed 85 percent of human rights violations to them and only 5 percent to the guerrillas, with the remaining 10 percent undetermined. Critics of the Truth Commission claim that the investigators did not dig down sufficiently into the guerrillas' activities; there is a modicum of truth to that accusation.[3] But it does not change the simple facts: only one side perpetrated mass killings of civilians and widespread torture and other human rights violations. The Truth Commission exposes the fallacy of a common rhetorical tactic used by supporters of the government and military. They say, in effect, "We did some bad things, they did some bad things, so let's just put it all in the past and move on." Evidence like that of the Truth Commission exposes this type of claim as a false equivalency.[4]

Gasteazoro was not an armed combatant. Rather, she was a member of a small, left-wing political party, and then later she served in the political and logistical wing of one of the clandestine guerrilla organizations. But the fighting and dying on the battlefield defined everything she did. In broad terms, the military aspect of the war can be divided into two periods: 1980–1983 and 1983–1992.

A decade of mass mobilization preceded the outbreak of war and brought together the two insurgent forces that would make up the FMLN: a militant urban guerrilla organization, with affiliated mass-front organizations, and an insurgent rural peasantry. At one time, the former was credited for giving rise to the latter, a storyline that guerrilla leaders, not surprisingly, found agreeable. Since then, the extent to which the peasantry came to militant consciousness autonomously, in no small part due to the influence of liberation theology and the wing of the Catholic Church that embraced the preferential option for the poor, has been revealed.[5]

The war is widely recognized as starting in 1980 because so much fighting was occurring by then. The "official" start date is January 10, 1981, when the recently formed FMLN launched its first Final Offensive. The goal of the offensive was to deliver a quick blow to the Salvadoran military and take control of the state before Ronald Reagan was sworn in as US president on January 20. The offensive failed, forcing the guerrillas to more or less abandon the cities, where the military's counterinsurgency tactics were more effective, and move their command structures to the countryside. It was at this moment that the war became a protracted rural insurgency fought by a peasant army led by a coterie of guerrilla commanders, most of whom were college-educated urbanites.

The first three years of the war were its most brutal, and in fact, in per capita terms, they may constitute the most violent phase of any of the civil conflicts in 20th-century Latin America. On average, 1,000 people died per month, most of them civilians killed in gruesome ways by the military or paramilitary death squads. When the war began, the Salvadoran military was not prepared for counterinsurgent warfare. Its historic mission had been to protect the nation from hostile neighbors like Honduras, with which it fought a war in 1969. So even though the FMLN was poorly armed and outnumbered, it stood up to the Salvadoran military and within two years controlled 25 percent of Salvadoran territory, mostly in the northern, rural zones along the mountains bordering Honduras. Relatively quickly, and with substantial support from the United States, the military ramped up its counterinsurgency capabilities, which included the creation of four new combat battalions that did most of the actual fighting. They were also the units responsible for most of the mass killings that were part of the military's scorched-earth counterinsurgency campaign, including but hardly limited to the massacres at Sumpul River (May 1980), El Mozote (December 1981), El Calabozo (August 1982), and Copapayo (November 1983).

By 1983 it looked like the Salvadoran military was at a breaking point. But the United States stepped in and changed the trajectory. President Reagan doubled down on his administration's claim that El Salvador was the front line of the Cold War. The problem was opposition within the United States, particularly from Democrats in Congress who questioned ongoing support for a regime so compromised by human rights violations. Reagan officials responded by striking a deal with the Salvadorans: they would minimize the mass killings, reduce the human rights violations, and purge the officer corps of the most egregious abusers, and the aid would continue to flow from the United States. And flow it did, to the tune of $1 million per day on average and a total of $4 billion over the span of the war—only Egypt and Israel received more financial aid from the United States during that period. As long as advocates for the Salvadoran government could frame the civil war as a component of the Cold War, rather than as a popular insurgency based on decades of inequity and abuse, then even the critics would have to relent, because no one could weather the political fallout of appearing to appease the USSR or to be soft on communism.[6]

In response to a rejuvenated enemy, the FMLN had little choice but to make a strategic shift—from a war of position, in which it stood up to the

Salvadoran military with battalion-sized units, to a war of attrition, in which small units were dispersed throughout the country in hopes of bleeding the regime to death. At that point, the war became a stalemate. The military could not dislodge the FMLN or drain its support among the population, and the guerrillas could not defeat the military on the battlefield. After a failed but spectacular second Final Offensive in 1989, in which FMLN units attacked multiple cities throughout the country, and even held portions of the capital city of San Salvador for up to three weeks, the war wound down to a negotiated settlement in 1992.

Gasteazoro and the Role of Women in the Civil War

Women made up as much as 20 percent of the FMLN's combatants. They made up a similar percentage of its leadership and a majority of its support staff. Some of the more well-known female commanders are Ana Guadalupe Martínez, Nidia Díaz, and Lorena Peña. Both Martínez and Díaz, like Gasteazoro, were captured and jailed by the military. They too survived and went on to write memoirs about their experiences. Peña served as a field commander for the Fuerzas Populares de Liberación Farabundo Martí (FPL). She avoided capture, survived the war, and wrote a memoir about her experiences as well.[7]

El Salvador in the 1970s was a patriarchal society with an inchoate feminist movement. Women did not even gain the right to vote until 1950. It would seem that all this female participation in the FMLN would constitute a significant advance for women's rights. After all, women fought alongside men, they commanded troops, including male combatants, and they more or less were the backbone of the entire oppositional infrastructure, not only within the FMLN, but also within a whole range of other human rights and labor organizations.

This substantive presence of women has drawn increasing attention from scholars. There is an emerging debate among them as to what these high levels of female participation meant for women's rights. Some scholars argue that the high level of participation by women during the war was a boon to women's rights, yet those advances dwindled after the war as society returned to its patriarchal norms. Other scholars argue that patriarchy persisted during the war, because opposition leaders prioritized the class struggle over gender equity, but then after the war women used their organizational experience to launch a vigorous women's rights movement that carries on to the present day. We need not resolve this debate here, but acknowledging its existence reveals the important role of women in the civil war.[8]

Gasteazoro's life story reveals a great deal about sexism and patriarchy and about women's various coping mechanisms. Affluent families like Gasteazoro's, especially ones that subscribed to conservative Catholic values, adhered to traditional social norms. They expected women to be dutiful daughters and nurturing mothers whose main preoccupation was their family's domestic sphere. As a young woman, Gasteazoro was outgoing and precocious, and she chafed under these rigid expectations. When she was in high school, her parents sent her to a finishing school in Guatemala run by Maryknoll nuns, expecting them to straighten her out and convince her to accept her assigned role. Instead, the Maryknolls were open-minded intellectuals who had embraced liberation theology. They exposed Gasteazoro to a new reality and therein nurtured her growing political radicalism.

A Salvadoran friend of mine, who also hails from an affluent family, felt compelled to share with me his reaction to this part of Gasteazoro's story. He said that it offers a rare glimpse into the world of elite Salvadoran families and the bubbles they placed around their children, especially the girls, to shield them from Salvadoran reality. He said that one of the reasons elite families came to despise certain religious orders, like the Maryknolls in Guatemala and the Jesuits in El Salvador, was because when these groups gained access to their children, they pierced the bubbles. Some family members felt betrayed and responded with outrage.[9]

As an adult, Gasteazoro's relationships with men were a mixed bag. She was an attractive, outgoing person who drew a lot of male attention, much of it unwanted and uninvited. She describes some of her relationships with men as positive and life affirming, and others not, including one boyfriend who subjected her to significant emotional abuse. In her professional life as an activist, she was often the only woman among the delegates on the various political and diplomatic missions to which she was assigned. Her descriptions reveal that she experienced many gendered microaggressions, as we now call them, as well as harassment and even outright sexual assault. But Gasteazoro's story also reveals a capable, resilient woman who garnered widespread respect among her peers, regardless of gender norms.

All women within the FMLN confronted patriarchal norms, but not all women experienced them equally; class status divided them. As I mentioned, most FMLN leaders, including the women, were college-educated urbanites from middle-class or lower-middle-class families, whereas the rank and file hailed from poor families, mostly in rural areas. These divisions caused tensions, which reveal the disproportionate privilege of the *comandantes* and their occasional inability to recognize it in their relations with the rank and file. The editors of the book *Mothers in Arms/Madres en armas*, a compilation of five life stories of female members of the FMLN, discovered this divergence. They interviewed three former female commanders and two female members of the rank and file. They found many commonalities based on gender issues but also discovered the discord that resulted from the women's divergent backgrounds. As they put it: "Could Nidia the *comandante* ever truly be a peer with Claudia the conscripted cook?" They went on to observe that after the war, "Nidia has armed bodyguards around her because of assassination attempts . . . [but] that is not an issue for the likes of Claudia and Julia [the other rank-and-file interviewee]."[10]

Gasteazoro fell into the category of an urbanite leader from an affluent background. But what distinguishes her is the extent to which she retained self-awareness about her status. She knew where she came from and she recognized her privilege relative to other women. That awareness is perhaps most clearly on display in her description of her relationships with her fellow inmates in prison. Most of them came from much different circumstances than she did, and we are aware of that as readers because Gasteazoro was aware of it and tells us about it as she openly grappled with the issue.

Tell Mother I'm in Paradise as a Text

Tell Mother I'm in Paradise was born of the friendship between Ana Margarita Gasteazoro, Judy Blankenship, and Andrew Wilson. Its origin imbues the text with distinct characteristics. It is not a memoir or autobiography in the traditional sense, because Gasteazoro did not write the manuscript herself. Rather she provided the raw material for the narrative in a series of recorded interviews, and then Blankenship and Wilson, primarily the latter, took that information and crafted it into the present narrative. They did so in direct consultation with Gasteazoro, who read and approved every word; but technically, the text is not her own written expression.

In Latin American Studies, a text like this is sometimes classified as a testimonial, or *testimonio*, that is, when a person delivers their story in the form of an interview to another person who then writes it up and oversees its publication. However, the term "testimonial" is reserved for cases when the interviewee is a poor or otherwise marginalized person in their society, often illiterate, who has no other way to get the story out except through an outside interviewer, often an academic with contacts in the publishing world. As an educated, literate, urbanite from a relatively affluent family, Gasteazoro does not fit that category. Therefore, her narrative is a "life story," a catchall term that refers to any and all forms of expression by individuals seeking to share some part of their lived experience.

One of the great qualities of *Tell Mother I'm in Paradise* is its explanatory clarity. El Salvador's civil war was nothing if not a sprawling, convoluted series of events that involved a host of individuals and organizations. Those people who were enmeshed in it, like Gasteazoro, often speak in a dizzying array of acronyms and pseudonyms, almost like a second language, or, as Fidel Castro once reportedly described it, "the alphabet soup of El Salvador."[11] *Tell Mother I'm in Paradise* does not suffer from that problem. A main reason for this is, once again, its origins in friendship. By their own admission, Blankenship and Wilson knew little about El Salvador when they became friends with Gasteazoro in Costa Rica. So when Gasteazoro began telling them about her life, she had to explain things. As they made the transition to formal recordings, they preserved this aspect of their exchange. When Gasteazoro assumed too much or moved too quickly through a complex event, Blankenship and Wilson would ask her to clarify. The ultimate beneficiaries of this process are we the readers of *Tell Mother I'm in Paradise*.

The interview sessions were conducted in English, because Gasteazoro's English was better than Blankenship's and Wilson's Spanish at the time. As Wilson describes it, "Her English was both educated and idiomatic. It came from years in San Salvador's American School as a student, a year with her Anglophone cousins in Los Angeles at age 11, English as the lingua franca during her years in Europe, and finally the two years she lived with Anthony Abrahams [her boyfriend] in Jamaica." Thus, this text's native language is English, although Gasteazoro's native language is Spanish. This fact avoids some of the interpretive complexities caused by translated texts. Translation is a sophisticated art, and in analyzing translations, we have to ask some difficult questions: Who did the translation? What were the person's qualifications? Under what conditions was the translation done? Why was it done at all? Think here of all the debates over the varying translations of the Bible. Fortunately, these questions need not be asked of the English-language version of Gasteazoro's story.

That is not necessarily the case with the Spanish version, which ironically appeared before this English-language original. The Spanish translation was published in El Salvador in 2019, under the title *Díganle a mi madre que estoy en el paraíso: Memorias de una prisionera política*. According to Blankenship and Wilson, the original goal of the interview sessions was to produce a book for North American audiences. However, as their interviews were winding down, Gasteazoro felt a growing desire to have her story available to Salvadorans, and she expressed some regret that the interviews had been conducted in English.

Had she lived to see the day, she would have been happy to know that her story did appear in Spanish, appropriately published by the Museo de la Palabra y la Imagen (Museum of Word and Image, MUPI), which is dedicated to keeping alive the memory of El Salvador's civil war.

The Spanish translation came into existence as an act of beneficence, from a Salvadoran exile Blankenship met in a solidarity group in Portland, Oregon, and who volunteered to do the initial draft. It took nearly five years of intermittent work to complete, during which time Blankenship met the director of MUPI, Carlos Henríquez Consalvi, who committed to publishing Gasteazoro's story. Later, Eva Gasteazoro, Ana Margarita's cousin, who grew up in neighboring Nicaragua and knew Ana Margarita since childhood, and who coincidentally works as a professional writer and editor, volunteered to give the text an additional round of editing. Wilson and Blankenship say that they were always captivated by how similar Eva is to Ana Margarita in her speech pattern and mannerisms, and that she did an excellent job of "recovering Ana's voice." It is an interesting and atypical case to have a native Spanish speaker tell her story in English and then have it translated back into Spanish by one or more third parties.

The interviews that provided the raw material for *Tell Mother I'm in Paradise* consist of roughly 25 recorded hours. Gasteazoro narrated her story more or less chronologically. When Wilson and Blankenship found gaps or holes in the story after reviewing their transcriptions of the recordings, they went back and conducted a handful of "fill-in" interviews, as they describe them.

Tell Mother I'm in Paradise is Gasteazoro's story, but Blankenship and Wilson have a definitive presence in the text. Most notably, it was they, and particularly Wilson, who took the raw transcripts and crafted them into a final narrative, albeit in direct collaboration with Gasteazoro. Wilson estimates that the transcripts total some 200,000 words, and the final version published here with the University of Alabama Press is roughly half that length. Obviously, Wilson and Blankenship (and Gasteazoro) made a significant number of editorial choices about what to include and how much space to dedicate to any given topic. According to Wilson, much of the discarded material came from Gasteazoro's early life, which, although interesting, was deemed less germane to the central storyline of her activism and incarceration.

Wilson also says that many of the words from the transcriptions needed to be cut because they were extraneous. He notes that interviewees rarely, if ever, narrate in perfectly linear form; they pause, loop back, repeat themselves, and sometimes speak in run-on sentences. The process of crafting all that into a coherent, linear narrative requires a lot of editorial decision making, about diction, sentence length, and even the location of paragraph breaks. Wilson and Blankenship say the ultimate goal was to capture Gasteazoro's voice, which they describe as "a very warm voice, not a literary voice." In the end, in collaboration with her, they believe they succeeded in doing so.

Questions of editorial choice matter when it comes to analyzing a life story, because those choices can define a text. For example, I and two Salvadoran scholars, Héctor Lindo and Rafael Lara, studied another transcribed life story from El Salvador and found evidence to suggest that the editorial choices of the interviewer (the famed Salvadoran poet and revolutionary Roque Dalton) may have changed the meaning of the story from his interviewee (Miguel Mármol).[12] I am not suggesting that such a process occurred here between Wilson, Blankenship, and Gasteazoro, especially because Gasteazoro reviewed and approved the text. Nevertheless, such questions always need to be asked when analyzing a life story. The original interview recordings are housed at the University of Texas Libraries, in the Benson Latin American Collection, in Austin. Just as readers can compare the Spanish version with the English version of Gasteazoro's story, so too can they compare the interviews with the published text.

Another factor to consider when analyzing a life story as text is the nature of the interview process. For example, did the interviewer(s) allow the interviewee to tell the story more or less as they wished, or did the interviewer intervene, even perhaps challenging some of the claims? In the present case, it was a little bit of both. Blankenship, who did the bulk of the interviews, describes herself as a more passive interviewer, whereas Andrew says he was more interrogative but still largely deferential to Gasteazoro. Thus, we should interpret this life story as Ana Margarita Gasteazoro's version of herself.

A notable aspect of *Tell Mother I'm in Paradise* is the length of time it took to appear in print. The first draft of the manuscript was completed in the early 1990s, before Gasteazoro's death. Yet, here we are, nearly three decades later, finally able to read the finished product. The main reason for the long delay was, first, Ana Margarita's death and, later, hesitance within the Gasteazoro family. Some members believed, understandably so, that the story and its intimate details should not be shared publicly. It was only after a lot of internal family discussion, the passage of much time, and the passing of the family matriarch that Gasteazoro's siblings approved publication. These types of behind-the-scenes affairs, including such things as editorial decisions by publishers, can define any text. In the end, Gasteazoro's life story was a long time coming, but we can be grateful that it has finally arrived.

Abbreviations

~

AGEUS	Association of Students of the University of El Salvador
ANDES	National Association of Salvadoran Educators
ANEP	National Association of Private Enterprise
ANTEL	National Telecommunications Administration
BPR	Popular Revolutionary Bloc
CEDAL	Latin American Center for Democratic Studies
COMADRES	Committee of Mothers of the Disappeared
COPPES	Committee of Political Prisoners of El Salvador
COPREFA	Press Committee of the Armed Forces
DRU	Unified Revolutionary Direction
ERP	People's Revolutionary Army
FALANGE	Armed Forces of Anti-Communist Liberation–Wars of Elimination
FAPU	Unified Popular Action Front
FARN	Armed Forces of National Resistance
FDR	Democratic Revolutionary Front
FMLN	Farabundo Martí National Liberation Front
FPL	Farabundo Martí Forces of Popular Liberation
JLP	Jamaica Labour Party
LP-28	Popular Leagues of February 28th
MIPTES	Independent Movement of Professionals and Technicians of El Salvador
MNR	National Revolutionary Movement
MPSC	Popular Social Christian Movement
NDP	New Democratic Party (Canada)
NGO	nongovernmental organization
OAS	Organization of American States
ORDEN	Nationalist Democratic Organization
PNP	People's National Party (Jamaica)
PRTC	Revolutionary Workers Party of Central America
PSOE	Spanish Socialist Workers Party
RN	National Resistance (see also FARN)

SI	Socialist International
UCA	University of Central America
UDN	Nationalist Democratic Union
UNO	National Opposition Union

Prologue

⁓

"Do you want us to send a message to your mother?"

The secretary of Ilopango Prison for Women sat at her desk, impatient. I stood uncomfortably before her holding a newspaper in one hand and a plastic bag in the other. The newspaper's front page had a two-column photo of me under the headline TERRORIST CONFESSES. In the plastic bag were all my possessions: a comb, a bar of soap, a roll of toilet paper, and the clothes I had worn for 11 days in the Guardia Nacional headquarters during my interrogation.

"We can call her and tell her you're here," said the secretary.

Perhaps Mother knows already, I thought. I'd seen her the day before, along with my brother Javier. Somehow my endlessly energetic brother had got one of his highly placed friends, maybe Vides Casanova himself, the commander of the Guardia Nacional, to allow them into the headquarters to see me. It was absolutely unheard of, but they'd managed it.

Since the morning of my arrest, the Guardia had been telling me that my family had abandoned me as a traitor and didn't care if I was alive or dead. Though I'd never really believed it, I now had proof it wasn't true, and my heart was full of love for them both as I prepared to be admitted to prison. Even if Javier had spent the entire visit scolding me for not accepting my interrogator's offer of exile. Even if Mother had spent the visit crying and telling me to be strong, to believe in God. Their family solidarity, offered unconditionally across a huge chasm of ideology and past argument, gave me strength.

Did they know I had already been moved to Ilopango? After Javier had finished telling me what an idiot I was, he'd said that at least the Guardia couldn't kill me now, not if he and Mother had seen me alive. So I was going to prison, which he said I deserved. I wondered if he would think I'd deserved the final beating I got after they'd left, the one to make me sign my confession.

My ribs and legs and the rest of my body still ached from the Guardias' boots and fists. Yet I found myself feeling strangely optimistic as I thought about what I wanted to say to Mother.

If I'd been in a spiteful mood I might have sent her a revolutionary slogan like "Cada momento, cada situación es tu trinchera." *Every moment, every situation is your trench in the war.* As I'd often said before when we were arguing, she had her catechism and I had mine. But she didn't deserve that from me, not now, not after what she and Javier had done for me. Even so, the slogan rang truer than ever. In this new moment, this new situation in my life, I was actually looking forward to digging a new trench and continuing the war against the Salvadoran government.

I'd thought about it a lot in my cell in the Guardia Nacional headquarters. During the long hours between interrogations, especially the three days they'd kept me tied to my cot, there had been nothing to do but think. And I hadn't spent much of it wondering what a nice girl like me was doing in a place like this. Unlike the authorities, I knew exactly what my role had been in El Salvador's civil war. The Guardia knew only half of it—the public and entirely legal half that they'd arrested me for, not my clandestine work with the guerrilla.

As far as I was concerned, neither the war nor my role in it was over. I knew that the male political prisoners at Santa Tecla prison had already organized themselves into the Committee of Political Prisoners of El Salvador (COPPES). Before I was arrested, one of my many jobs for the legal opposition had been to receive and publicize COPPES's smuggled communiqués to a world that was becoming increasingly disgusted with the abuse of human rights in El Salvador. There were very few women political prisoners in the country, and so far as I knew they were not yet organized. Well, now there was one more female political, and she was eager to help dig a new trench.

The thought of the male prisoners in Santa Tecla made me think of Sebastián, the man I had lived with for the past year. I wondered if his feet had recovered from the electric shocks the Guardias had given him when we were arrested—two wires plugged into our living room wall and attached directly to his feet. His moans had torn me apart as I stood by helplessly, forced to listen while they tortured him. But he was alive, I was sure of that. While they were beating me into signing my confession yesterday, they'd shown me his signature on a similar document. Sebastián was a strong man and a tough, disciplined revolutionary. To get him to sign his confession they must have . . . Better not to think about it.

The Guardia had driven me to Ilopango that morning. Very odd: During most of the trip I'd chatted with the sergeant who had sat through most of my interrogations, typing everything that was said on an old black Underwood. He'd even stopped the car on the way and bought me the newspaper with my face and the trumped-up charges on it. Then he'd shaken my hand, said goodbye, and delivered me to the prison guards.

The guards had taken my name and particulars and escorted me to the office where they'd handed me over to the secretary. From now on I would be among women, both jailers and prisoners, commons and politicals. No trial, no sentence. There was no telling how long I'd be here.

"Well?" the secretary asked. "Do you have anything you want us to say to her?"

I thought about the Guardia troopers who had fixed the wires to Sebastián's toes. About the goon with the mirrored glasses who had alternately felt me up and kicked me around in my cell in the Guardia Nacional headquarters. About Enrique Barrera, my rotund and easygoing colleague whose mutilated body I had identified the day after his arrest six months ago. Then I turned my mind to the organizing that was going on in Santa Tecla and my plans to carry on the struggle in Ilopango. *Cada momento, cada situación.* I was alive, my family still loved me, life was beautiful, even concrete-walled Ilopango was beautiful.

"Yes," I said. "Tell Mother I'm in paradise."

Part I

A Nice Girl like Me

1

My Family and Other Contradictions

Mothers everywhere wonder where they "went wrong" with their kids, but I'll bet mine has done more wondering than most. Four of her five children turned out reasonably normal by upper-class Salvadoran standards. Javier, the oldest brother, is now a successful businessman; José Francisco (known as Chico) became a priest; Eva María, a nun; and Ricardo Antonio is a chemical engineer. With all of that respectability and achievement in the family, why should one of her children—and a girl at that—have managed to get herself arrested as a political subversive, splashing the family name across the newspaper front pages for all to see?

It would make things so much simpler if there were some particular incident, some clearly marked fork in the road of my growing up that would explain why I landed in Ilopango prison. But it's hardly ever that simple in people's lives, and I'm no exception.

Without being too facetious, I could say that I come from a family of 14: a mother, a father, five children, and seven servants. We might best be described as a well-connected, upper-middle-class Salvadoran family. In economic terms that would easily put us in the top 5 percent of Salvadorans, but still not into the oligarchy. The term used to just mean *las catorce*, the 14 families that owned and ran most of what was worth owning and running in the country. In the early days, that basically meant coffee and cattle. While things are more complex now, it's still true that economic power is highly concentrated in El Salvador. There's the oligarchy at the top, a small middle class, and a lot of people both urban and rural who are poor.

So our family was in the upper reaches of the social pyramid, if not at its summit. My paternal grandfather, Augustín Gasteazoro, came to San Salvador as an exile from Nicaragua in the early part of the 20th century. He was a Liberal and had to leave around the time that the Liberal president José Santos

Zelaya was forced into exile under pressure by the United States. Grandfather was a doctor who had trained in Germany. He had been a big landowner in Nicaragua, with a large cattle farm in Conseguina, across the Gulf of Fonseca from El Salvador. When he went into exile he lost it all. But he did very well for himself and his family in El Salvador, because he became the favorite doctor of the oligarchy.

Grandfather died when my father was 18 and so I never met him, but I knew his wife, my grandmother, quite well. She was only 16 when she married my grandfather, who was 56. Like many well-off Central American parents, Grandfather wanted all his children (especially sons) to be educated. Accordingly, my father began his university career at Stanford in California and finished it at Louisiana State University. Those years at school in the United States were very intense for him. He belonged to a fraternity and the university bridge club. There is a yearbook photo of him in his boxer shorts, playing cards. With his fraternity cronies he made several trips to Cuba to party—a common thing for Americans to do in the 1940s, and indeed up until the Cuban Revolution in 1959. He graduated as an engineer and was about 26 when he met and married my mother in 1944.

I'm sure everyone thought it a good match, even though she was a head taller. My father was an eligible professional man and Mother was (and still is) a good-looking woman.[1] She was in her early 20s, the daughter of an upper-class

Figure 4. Gasteazoro family portrait (Courtesy of Elizabeth Fujimori)

family from San Miguel in the east of the country. Her father, a prosperous farmer, was twice mayor of San Miguel. In such families, the male offspring could expect to receive land or an education, but the women got neither; they were expected to get what they needed by marrying well. My mother learned shorthand and typing in high school and worked as a secretary for four years after the family moved to San Salvador, but once married she didn't work again until her children were grown.

I was the second of five children, arriving four years after my older brother Javier. Before my birth Mother had two miscarriages and lost another child after only seven days, so I was very anxiously awaited. Perhaps those worries and expectations are where some of our continuing problems come from. After me came Chico, Ricardo, and my sister Eva María.

In addition to the family, our household included two inside maids, a cook and a washerwoman, a gardener, and a chauffeur. We also had a seamstress at times, so as a young girl all of my clothes were made by hand—shirts, blouses, school uniforms, everything. That made it all the bigger an event when my father traveled abroad and brought back a dress for me. The most important person of all was my nanny, who took care of the whole house and brought us all up. While Nana would bring us to our mother to be breastfed, it was she who took care of us during the night, and who bathed and dressed us. In fact, she took over from the moment we were born. Forty years later she is still with my mother.

Until I was five years old, we lived in a house in the city of San Salvador. Then we moved to Las Terracitas, the Little Terraces, a small farm 20 minutes from the city because my mother wanted more space to grow flowers. It was actually a *quinta*, a country house, with a swimming pool and a couple of terraced acres full of fruit trees and flowers. The house was quite new and built of brick and wood in a U shape, with a patio in the middle and bedrooms on all sides. Las Terracitas was beautiful, with a wonderful view of the city below.

When I was little my parents often invited the daughters of friends to play with me and sometimes the children of the farm laborers came as well. However, that was a bit feudal, less an invitation than a summons. At lunchtime I would be called to the table with my parents, and the farm kids were sent home. They could never stay for lunch as my "peers" would.

My father was very interested in politics, and in order to stay informed he used to get up in the morning and listen in to the international bands on his enormous shortwave radio. I remember watching him search the frequencies for news and information, especially on Sunday mornings.

I also remember waiting for the world to end when I was 10, at the time of the Cuban Revolution. In my mind, there was a relationship between the end of the world and the communists taking over. That was probably because the press reported the Cuban Revolution as if it *was* the end of the world for Latin America. At the same time, I had another source of information in Father, who often told stories about Havana from his student days. While he distrusted the communists, he also listened to Radio Rebelde, the insurgents' station from within Cuba. It impressed him that this group of men in the mountains was taking over the repressive Batista regime. He talked about it sometimes, and the mixed messages left me with strange, confusing conceptions about the political world that took a long time to clarify.

My mother's domain was the house. She loved to cook and grow flowers in her gorgeous garden. Every morning she went out with her gloves and shears and walked around cutting flowers, followed by the gardener carrying a basket. Afterward she spent a half hour or more arranging them. The house was always full of flowers and every room was decorated. I can still picture the ginger at the house's entrance, roses in the bedrooms, zinnias and dahlias in other rooms. That was Mother's life: Mass every morning and flowers afterward, followed by picking up the kids at school and, as we grew older, taking us to swimming classes, dance classes, and piano classes.

When I was 12 or 13, she started making trips to Europe with a group of rich, elderly Central American ladies who belonged to Opus Dei. Opus Dei, or "the Work of God," is a Catholic lay organization begun in Spain in the late 1920s. Its members dedicate themselves to working quietly and secretly for God within their own professions or activities. Members are supposed to avoid having political leanings, but they are reputed to be very powerful in the political and economic lives of many countries. In Spain, for instance, many of the men in General Franco's cabinet were members of Opus Dei. There are Opus Dei schools, residences, and even universities like the University of Navarra, one of Spain's biggest. Because of the Spanish connection, it's not surprising that Opus Dei is powerful in Central and Latin America.

In the early 1960s two Opus Dei priests came to El Salvador from Spain. At first, Don Fernando and Don Javier stayed in the residence of the archbishop, but my mother got involved in finding a house for them and in otherwise organizing their lives and work. She did that for a number of years, before actually becoming a member of the organization. And as we grew up, all of us children got involved.

Opus Dei is a class-ridden but very complete organization. It runs clubs for children, for instance, but if you come from an upper-class family, you go to an upper-class club and never have to mix with people from the working class. My nanny's daughter went to a different club. The classes never mix, just as men and women never mix. The Opus Dei line is that if you are born a street cleaner, you stay a street cleaner and you work to sanctify your street cleaning. And you should never try to be more. As I grew older I came to look upon it as a Catholic caste system, and at its heart a fascist one.

When Mother joined Opus Dei she became a supernumerary, which is the category most married people fall into. Supernumeraries are supposed to aim for sanctification of daily life, to become saints in their day-to-day lives. Since their task is essentially to perfect their lives, many are prominent professionals in their fields. But Opus Dei is also a very secretive organization, so no one is supposed to know that you are a supernumerary.

I grew up with two opposing ideas of life—very liberal and anti-religious from my father, and very narrow and dogmatic from my mother. Of course, El Salvador being a profoundly Catholic country, my father went to church on Sunday. But he would stay outside or stand in the back, and there would always be a big fight between my parents because I wanted to stay with him.

Another source of tension was school, though that argument too had a religious overtone. My father wanted us to grow up in a liberal environment and to speak English, so he sent us to San Salvador's American School, the Escuela Americana. American Schools are found in capital cities all over the world and provide typical North American educations for the children of the American foreign service and businesspeople. That meant I grew up with North American kids, but there were also Jews, Arabs, and other recent arrivals, as well as a few other Salvadorans from the more liberal-thinking families.

The school was the most expensive one in El Salvador, but Father was adamant about sending us there and stood fast against all of Mother's objections. I sometimes think it was one of the reasons my mother involved us so much in Opus Dei, to counteract the lack of Catholic religious training at the American School.

The middle class in El Salvador considered the girls in the American School "loose," and my mother thought so too. "Nice" girls went to convent schools, where they stayed under the watchful eyes of nuns and weren't allowed to even dance with boys until they were 15. By contrast, the American School was coed and some of us started having boyfriends and girlfriends in the sixth grade. Eventually, Mother was able to convince Father to put my brothers in a Jesuit school called the Colegio Externado de San José, or Externado.

The Jesuits and Opus Dei don't get along, so Mother wasn't entirely happy with the arrangement. The Jesuits are an intellectual and progressive order of priests, while Opus Dei is deeply conservative. The Jesuits educated many boys from the oligarchy and upper-middle class. Freddy Cristiani, the current president of El Salvador, was a classmate of my brother Javier while he was at the American School.[2] Actually, Cristiani's mother and my mother grew up together in San Miguel and are still good friends.

It's ironic but typical of El Salvador that a lot of El Salvador's revolutionaries went to the Externado too. Fermán Cienfuegos and Héctor Silva are among the leaders of the FMLN who studied there as children. El Salvador is so small and there are so few good schools that "everybody who's anybody" knows everybody else, or is related to them, or went to school with them.

In any case, with the exception of two years—one in Los Angeles and one in Guatemala—I was at the American School from kindergarten through to my high school graduation.

When I was 11, I was sent to Los Angeles, to improve my English. I stayed with my mother's oldest sister, Isabel, who was married to an Irishman, my uncle Jack. Their daughter, Liz, is just a year and nine months older than me, and during my year there we became best friends, telling each other secrets and discussing absolutely everything. It was a total change for me, and a very

Figure 5. Ana Margarita, ca. 10 years old (Courtesy of Elizabeth Fujimori)

happy experience, to live with a typical North American middle-class family. I had been so protected in El Salvador, where I was never allowed to go out to the street on my own unless I was with my nana. In Los Angeles I could take a bike to school or go out for a walk without having to answer to anybody. I was even left alone in the house occasionally, whereas up till then I had never been alone in a house in my life. It was important to me to make my own bed, help with the dishes, and just be part of the family.

In Los Angeles I went to a public school, while my Catholic cousins went to the parochial school where, for some administrative reason I never quite understood, I was not admitted. So I was on my own, which made me feel very important and independent. Unlike in El Salvador, where the cook prepared my lunch and had it ready when I left my house for school, in Los Angeles I fixed my own lunch.

My year in the United States was also the first time I saw Black people. For many years Black people were not permitted to even visit El Salvador, unlike other Central American countries where they were brought in from the Caribbean islands to work in the banana plantations. Perhaps I had seen them before on a couple of trips to Nicaragua with my father, but until I was 11 I had never actually talked to a Black person.

I had got my period in Los Angeles, and I couldn't stand sanitary napkins. When I read in a magazine that you could wear tampons even if you were a virgin, I went out and bought tampons all on my own. That was okay in LA, but back in El Salvador my mother just about died when she found them in my room—what was an 11-year-old doing buying tampons!

Mothers can be very destructive without wanting to be, but the clash was inevitable because we had such different outlooks on life. She was so contained, so traditional, and so controlled. And I was like my father—extroverted and curious, wanting to know everything, wanting to try out everything.

Mother's influence was very strong and amplified by the Opus Dei clubs all we children belonged to. There is a strict policy within the organization to segregate men and women, and it begins with the children's clubs. During the summer holidays the activities at the Opus Dei houses kept us busy all day long, but separately. My brothers got to do all sorts of interesting things, from hiking to photography. My sister Eva María and I belonged to a girls' club, where we learned cooking and crafts and had classes in etiquette. Needless to say that the cooking class didn't cover rice and beans, the Central American staples; we learned how to make fancy appetizers and gourmet meals.

The focus for girls was preparation for marriage, but there was never ever any discussion of sex or marriage itself. The themes were purity and modesty, and that created a lot of confusion for me, as I'm sure it did for the other girls. We were taught that anything you did with your body, and especially anything that your body enjoyed, was a mortal sin. It could take you to hell. Even "bad thoughts" were sinful, but I had a lot of trouble figuring out exactly what bad thoughts were, because they never told us. Instead, religious ritual permeated all the club activities: saying the rosary, going to Mass, communion, and "circles," which are talks from the "numeraries" who were the top lay members of Opus Dei. Circles are the main tool for indoctrination into Opus Dei, especially through study of *El Camino*, or *The Way*, a book of 999 reflections on life by the organization's founder, Monseñor Josemaría Escrivá de Balaguer.

Both my brother Chico and sister Eva María became numeraries while they were at school, around the age of 16. Numeraries are akin to priests and nuns, but in the place of vows they make vows such as chastity, poverty, and obedience. They remain laypeople and can choose to work either outside the organization or within it. Within it, they can teach at schools and clubs, or run the residences. Chico originally planned to stay a layman and studied for many years to become an engineer, like Father. But when he was 29 he decided (or the organization decided for him) that he would become a priest in its Order of the Holy Cross. Eva María remains a numerary, a lay nun, and works at a hospital in Honduras.

I too felt the pull of Opus Dei as a teenager, but it was always a conflict. I was aware of the difference in treatment that the organization gave to boys, to my brothers in my own family. It all seemed so unfair.

When I was 15, my mother "didn't know what to do with me." I was always in trouble. I smoked. I went out with boys. All too often I would come back at 1:00 a.m. when I was supposed to be back at 11:00 p.m. She wanted to put me in a convent school in El Salvador, and of course this caused a fight between her and my father. His position was that I would lose my English if I went to a nun's school, and furthermore that the nuns in El Salvador were retrograde and neurotic. He conceded to my mother on many issues, but on this one he wouldn't budge. The two of them finally managed a compromise when my father heard about an upper-class girls' school in Guatemala called Monte María, run by Maryknoll nuns. Though attended by well-to-do girls from all over Central America, the language of study was English, and the academic standards were high.

The year at school in Guatemala was a deeply important experience that indeed did change me—but not in the way my mother had intended. Mother had arranged for me to live in the Opus Dei residence at the University of Guatemala, and although I was too young, they accepted me because my mother had become one of the pillars of Opus Dei in Central America.

At first glance the arrangement might have been exactly what Mother wanted, and the exact opposite of what I would enjoy. I had to wear a school uniform for the first time in my life. Almost all of my teachers were nuns and the curriculum was avowedly Catholic. I was living in a residence run by one of the world's most conservative religious organizations, where Mother had arranged for me to take religion classes and all my meals. So while it probably seemed to her that she had blocked off all the possible roads to temptation, in reality I ended up with more freedom than ever before. Since it was a university residence, I could leave at 6:00 in the morning and didn't have to be back until 9:00 at night. That's terribly strict for a college student, but after living under the watchful eyes of Mother and Nana, it was wonderful for a 15-year-old.

As the youngest person there, I had an immediate identity as everyone's "little sister." People wanted to spoil me and applauded anything I did. Everything was discreetly genteel, right down to the *tertulia*, the get-together, after dinner. Everyone from the students to the Opus Dei ladies who ran the residence (though not, of course, the cleaning staff) came together for coffee and sweets and polite conversation about the day's events. We even danced together, women with women.

Most important of all was my friendship with María Cristina Arathon, whom everyone knew as "Titina." She was a 25-year-old psychologist and social worker who had graduated years before from the Maryknoll school but was then taking a couple of courses at the university. Her mother lived only three blocks away but the two of them didn't get along, so Titina stayed at the residence. She was beautiful, a tall woman with dark eyes. But she had lupus, a disease that often caused terrible sores to break out on her legs. Her only relief was to lie on her back for long periods of time, and when that happened I sat on the floor beside her and kept her company.

We talked a lot. Much of what we talked about was the social work she did in the poor communities of Guatemala City. Actually, she didn't really tell me much about her own activities so much as describe the conditions where she worked. I didn't know until long after that she was leading a double life, but I was fascinated by her stories of the communities, especially a barrio called La Limonada. She talked about her cases, about mothers who had to leave their children tied up to a bedpost during the day while they went to work. She also let me talk and listened carefully to me. It was a very special, rich friendship that wasn't impaired by the difference in our ages. I looked up to her; I wanted to be a psychologist, everything she was.

Through her I met Sister Marian Peter, a Maryknoll sister who had stopped teaching a year before to dedicate herself to the poor. Her name is now Marjorie Melville, and during the 1970s she became quite well known in the United States as an antiwar activist. But when I met her she was in her late 20s and still a nun. Though she lived at Monte María, much of her time was spent working outside so the students saw little of her. All of the older students felt it was a great loss to the school that she was no longer teaching. They called her "Mighty Mouse" because she was small and energetic, always striding through the halls in her gray habit. But she was also loved because she was so accessible when anyone had a problem.

The Monte María girls went out to the poor barrios once a week to distribute food, work in the clinics, and look after children, but because of my separate status I wasn't involved. Instead, Titina took me on Saturdays to La Limonada, where Sister Marian Peter was the driving force behind a clinic and community center. The barrio was a shantytown with houses thrown together from whatever the residents could find or buy cheaply. You find them all over Central America, and I had already seen them in El Salvador. But now I had contact with the people who lived there. The sister and Titina put me to work helping in the clinic, washing, taking care of kids, and even giving literacy classes. Again, I was the only student and was surrounded by older women who accepted me.

A couple of times a week Titina took me along to work at a downtown drop-in center called The Crater. It had a dining room that sold very cheap meals, or occasionally gave free meals, to penniless university and high school students. It also had a study room and activities like darts and ping-pong, so there were always 30 or 40 young people there. Mostly I washed dishes and felt pleased to be contributing.

With my newfound freedom and my friendship with Titina and Sister Marian Peter, I got involved in all kinds of activities that would not have been possible at home. It was a great privilege to be close to these women, to eat and talk with them. They were my friends or as we say in Spanish *mi gente*, my people. And in fact they were something new to me, women who seemed to be in control of their own lives. I wanted to be like them, not necessarily doing the same things, but being independent and responsible for myself.

As summer approached I was invited by Sister Marian Peter to spend three months up in the mountains working in a *cursillo de cristiandad social*, a Christian retreat aimed at building awareness of your responsibility toward society. These were the precursors of the Christian base communities that supported the revolutionary movement. Very Catholic, but they served as springboards for people who got more involved in the struggle later on. I was captivated by the idea of spending my vacation doing community work up in the mountains near Huehuetenango. Sister Marian Peter insisted that I get my parents' permission, but for some reason I didn't think it would be a problem and didn't ask them immediately.

During that year I had met a guy who was studying veterinary science at the university. His name was Jorge and we started seeing each other, even though he was about 10 years older. So by the time I turned 16, I felt I had it all: a boyfriend, community work, and of course my friendship with these two wonderful women, Titina and Sister Marian Peter.

It was too good to last. One day while I was at home for a visit, I brought about the end in my usual enthusiastic way, dropping two bombshells at once on my parents. The first was my announcement that Jorge and I had decided to get married. Perhaps I was reassured by the fact that his family had agreed to the match, not surprising since girls often get married very young in Central America. But when I said that not only was I going to get married but that I intended to spend the summer in the Guatemalan mountains, their reaction was swift and conclusive: goodbye to Jorge, goodbye to Monte María, and goodbye to Guatemala. They let me finish my exams and get my report card, and that was it.

Since the American School in El Salvador kept to the American schedule, I found myself back in school almost immediately. But my year in Guatemala, one of the most influential experiences in my life, had awakened my social conscience. Since I had got used to walking in the poor barrios and sitting at the same table with working-class people, I couldn't understand why we had to have such gulfs between rich and poor in El Salvador. It made me quite belligerent in school, and although I didn't have the historical or political background to know what I was talking about, I was quite vocal.

Luckily, I wasn't totally alone in this, because there was another girl in my class who also demonstrated the beginnings of a political consciousness. Her name was Carmen Elena, and her parents were friendly with mine. Actually, she was more advanced than I was, and we talked often about inequality and socialism, and about the Cuban Revolution. The two of us made a pretty spirited showing in history class, where we first learned about social problems in the United States. The American textbooks we used were rabidly anti-communist, so it was easy for us to take the opposite point of view and defend Cuba's system.

Sometimes I also spoke about these subjects with my father. I would say, "You see, Father, within 10 years there's going to be a revolution in this country," and he would say, "Nah, the country's too poor and controlled by the rich and the military. The conditions aren't there yet."

Still, I had no sense of what was really going on in El Salvador. That may seem strange, but you have to take into account that the political reality of El Salvador was not common knowledge. We young Salvadorans were very ignorant of recent history in El Salvador, and most of us remained so as adults. I remember a party in Jamaica when I was in my 20s where someone mentioned that El Salvador had had a military dictator for many years. I was offended. "But El Salvador has always had elections," I said. "How could there be a military dictator?"

My ignorance was easily explained: the newspapers were totally aligned with the oligarchy. Salvadorans who could read (a minority for most of our history) were kept in the dark, and many didn't want to see anyway. You got better information if you bought foreign newspapers, but for that you had to read foreign languages. It was only with the birth of the popular organizations and with their activities in the 1970s that it became known that the political situation was incendiary and volatile.

On the social side of my life, I spent my junior and senior years at what was pretty close to a normal American high school. All of the teachers were Americans who had come to El Salvador expressly to teach at the American School. Most were youngish men in their late 20s or early 30s. Some of them went out with girls in the school, which was totally against the rules. But that crowd was pretty relaxed, and after all it was the latter half of the 1960s. We smoked marijuana at a lot of the parties. One of my best friends was an American girl whose father was the US military attaché. I used to go with her to the marine base, where they had parties pretty frequently.

It was confusing: the parties, the attraction and repulsion of Opus Dei, my political concerns, and the weight of the various conflicts at home. I still wanted to get away and be free of my parents.

The only real calm I found during my last two high school years was with Titina. I saw her every couple of months when she came to San Salvador for treatment of her disease. She always stayed with an aunt in San Salvador, and when I came to visit she would sit in a rocking chair with her feet up on a stool to take pressure off the circulation. I remember pulling up my dress and sitting on the floor, feeling the coolness of the ceramic tiles on my legs and listening to Titina tell me that she envied me because I could be on the floor. It was always a treat to see her. As before, we talked a lot about where she worked and what she had seen, but very little about what she actually did.

When I did finally find out, more than a year after her last visit to El Salvador, it was from the front page of the newspaper. Titina and others in her group had been involved with the revolutionary forces, though they were not guerrillas themselves. The Guatemalan authorities had finally discovered this involvement, but she and her *compañero* Juan managed to escape to Mexico before they could be arrested. They were married by Arthur Melville while in exile, and eventually returned to Guatemala where they joined the guerrilla. Titina died in 1969 of lupus complicated by pregnancy. She had always wanted to have a child, though she knew that it was risky because of the disease. She was 25 when she died.[3]

In the same year, Sister Marian Peter and the Melville brothers—Thomas and Arthur, both Maryknoll priests—were expelled from Guatemala for their involvement with the guerrilla organizations. Another big scandal. I found out that all during the year I'd been going to The Crater, it had been a meeting place for the guerrilla.[4] Some of the leaders, like Turcios Lima, had been there frequently. Almost all of them are dead now, killed in the struggle. But at the time Titina and Sister Marian Peter had been careful not to let me know.

After they were expelled, the Melville brothers and Sister Marian Peter went first to Mexico and then to the United States, where they joined the anti-draft movement. In May 1968 they and other Catholic activists known as the Catonsville Nine stole and burned draft records from the Selective Service office in Catonsville, Maryland. Sister Marian Peter spent time in prison and eventually married Thomas Melville. The two of them wrote a book called *Whose Heaven, Whose Earth?*[5]

2

Wanderings of a Salvadoran Black Sheep

After I graduated from high school in 1968 I was sent to school in Boston. It was my father's decision. I wanted to be a landscape architect, or possibly a psychologist, but my father said I had to be realistic.

"You're going to end up getting married at 20 or 21," he said, "so you don't need a profession. What you need are skills to work until you meet the right fellow." The best thing for me, in his opinion, was to train as a secretary. This was my "progressive" father—which was kind of confusing for me.

So I ended up at Bay State Junior College on Commonwealth Avenue in Boston. Mother arranged for me to live in an Opus Dei residence for college students. It was very beautiful, and very fashionable, full of women students like me from Central and South America.

This was 1968 and college life in the States was probably a lot different than my parents imagined. And in some ways I was a lot different than they imagined. I had already smoked a little dope and dropped acid with friends in San Salvador. My dress had become more hippie-like.

I guess the most important thing that happened to me that year in Boston was that I met a man. Jack was an American and quite a bit older than I—almost exactly double my 18 years. He spoke Spanish well because he had worked as an accountant with the United Fruit Company in Honduras and Colombia, and he hung around the Colombian crowd. He dated mostly Latin girls, and I think his image of women was very Latino, meaning that of virginal, sweet, submissive women.

Jack had never married. At 39 it seemed a bit weird, but also attractive. Looking back on it, I can see clearly that Jack was a stereotypical father figure for me—very Catholic, very serious, and very square. His parents lived in a little town on Cape Cod called Green Harbor, and I got to like them and became part of the family.

I thought I wanted to get married, and I pushed him for this. Eventually, and reluctantly, Jack agreed. I was very confused and divided within myself. On the one hand, I had said more than a few times, to myself, that I would never get married because I didn't want to have a life like my parents. But on the other hand, if I never married, what was I? In El Salvador, women are brought up to marry and have children. If you don't get married, you are a failure as a woman. According to my upbringing, there was only one alternative to celibacy or marriage: being a *puta*, a whore.

After Jack and I finally decided that we would marry, I went home for summer vacation. Soon after arriving, I announced my intention to my parents. Inevitably, they were upset. They didn't know this man. They wanted me to marry into a nice family in El Salvador, to someone they approved of. They'd been looking forward to arranging all the details.

Most of all, they objected to any guy I went out with if they didn't know his family. I suppose that's fairly typical of parents, not just in El Salvador. The first thing my mother would ask after I came home from a date was, "Who's his father? Who's his mother? Where do they live? What do they do?" It all had to do with status.

Still, short of tying me up, there wasn't much they could do about it. I was adamant that I was going back to get married. Not only that, I was going to study landscape architecture. Before going home, I got a transfer to Northeastern University, also in Boston. After a lot of argument, Father finally gave in to my demands. But then the war between Honduras and El Salvador broke out, and that changed everything. Like many Salvadorans, my father had business interests in Honduras and he lost a lot of money because of the war. So he said no more schooling for me.

Father wasn't broke, of course, but Javier was already in college in Vermont and my younger brother was just about to graduate from high school. Since he was a man, he "needed" a college education to take on family responsibilities in later life. Whereas I didn't need an education because I would be getting married soon and would be taken care of by some man. And Father couldn't pay for a US college education for the three of us at the same time. It was as simple as that.

So I had to stay in El Salvador and go to school there. I registered in a general course at the UCA, the Jesuit university of El Salvador. I didn't like it much; I was there just to be in school.

At that time my father was maintenance engineer for the American embassy and this brought our family into contact with the American community. Father was usually very critical of the Americans, but around this time he made friends with a marine guard at the embassy. I remember him saying, "At last, there's one marine that's worth something. The others don't know their toes from their head."

As if that wasn't unusual enough, the marine, Jerry, was Black, perhaps the only Black man in El Salvador at the time. Most Black people in Central America came as slaves from the Caribbean to the Atlantic coast, or in a second wave starting in the late 1800s, when they worked on plantations owned by British and North American companies.[1] But El Salvador does not have an Atlantic coast, just the Pacific, and, historically, there were relatively few Black people in El Salvador compared to its neighbors. There was actually a law prohibiting the entrance of Black people into the country. They could come only if they were connected with sports or the entertainment business. I think the American embassy was trying Jerry out to see if he would be allowed to stay in El Salvador.

Every Friday there was a happy hour at Marine House, which was a private American club. Students from the American School could go and meet the embassy crowd and the rest of the American community there, so one Friday I went along, and that's where I met Jerry. He was 21 or 22, and I fell for him. (I guess I had sort of forgotten about Jack in Boston.)

Figure 6. Ana Margarita, ca. 20 years old (Courtesy of Iván Montecinos)

Another scandal in the house. When she found out, my mother forbade me to see Jerry, but I found ways to meet him. Finally, after I was "caught" seeing a movie with him, my mother decided to take drastic action and send me to college in Spain. Opus Dei runs a large and very conservative university in San Sebastián called the University of Navarra (my younger brother later studied there to become a priest). My mother actually saw her decision as a miracle. God had filled her with light and showed her the way. So, being the energetic and organized woman she was, she called the university and arranged to have me accepted without any formalities—no transcripts, no application, no entrance exams, nothing. She even got some high official of the school to meet me at the airport when I arrived. And why not? I was the daughter of one of the most important Opus Dei representatives in El Salvador. I was to study to become a kindergarten teacher.

In the next three days she organized everything else: clothes, tickets, passport, and a thousand other details. That's how efficient she was. Of course I didn't want to leave, but because I was underage and still under my parents' control I could do nothing. They couldn't afford to maintain me in Boston, but while the trip to Spain was expensive, the maintenance once there was practically nothing. The exchange rate at that time was 70 pesetas to the dollar. I could live on an allowance of 25 dollars a month, compared to monthly expenses in Boston of about 500 dollars. I suspect that my mother and father negotiated something—she had a store by then, and perhaps she offered to pay some of my expenses.

The year in San Sebastián was one of the saddest and most confusing years of my life. It is a beautiful town, but it's in Basque country and the people of the region are very formal and conservative. This was the height of the Franco regime, when Spain was probably the most reactionary country in Europe. The students in my program were almost all women and they all dressed alike: wool kilts, Shetland sweaters with a little pin, and loafers with high knee socks—everything perfect. Coming from an American School in El Salvador, my style was miniskirts or long hippie skirts, hot pants, long hair, makeup, and dangling earrings. So from the day I arrived it was clear I didn't fit in.

The college atmosphere was quiet and subdued, with a sort of cultured formality. But it wasn't only the school—the whole city was like that. Boys and girls didn't go out together alone except to promenade in public, not even to the movies. Boys couldn't even go into a girl's house. So if you displayed any of the normal North American or European signs of freedom, like wearing a miniskirt—*fatal!* as we say in Spanish.

In early November we were let out on holiday for All Saints' Day. Two friends and I took a day trip together to a nearby beach. Around 5:00 we decided to walk back over the hills to San Sebastián, so we bought a couple of bottles of brandy and some olives and started walking. It grew cold, and after a few kilometers we were freezing. But we didn't have any money, so we pushed on.

Around 3:00 in the morning we arrived exhausted at a tiny train station, which luckily was open all night. We went in, pulled some benches together, and huddled to keep warm. All of a sudden the doors burst open and in came about eight civil guards in their old-fashioned tricorn hats. We were terrified. They threw us against the walls and searched us abusively, putting their hands inside our panties and roughing us up. We were very scared of getting raped.

The guards accused us of having contraband, but wouldn't let us explain ourselves. They were going to take us to jail, they said, and we could spend the rest of our lives in prison. After about an hour they left us alone. We never knew how they knew we were there, whether they had been watching us or if someone had reported us. That was my first actual experience of police repression.

We reported the incident when we got back to San Sebastián. But the response we got was typical. The school said it was our fault for having done something so foolish—we were looking for trouble.

Everything in me rebelled against San Sebastián. But I hadn't long to wait before this part of my life finished abruptly. In June 1968 I went with a school group to see the running of the bulls at Pamplona. Actually, the bulls weren't the only attraction for me. I had met four American boys a week earlier on the beach in San Sebastián. We discovered we were all going to be in Pamplona, so we agreed to meet. As soon as my group arrived from school, all I wanted to do was meet these guys and leave the group. They were camping out in a van and asked me if I wanted to stay with them. Of course I said yes. So I sent word back to my group that I was not going back with them, and that I wouldn't be back for two days. And that got me expelled from the university.

That was the way my life in San Sebastián ended. The university authorities told me that I was not fit for their school. Nonetheless we reached an agreement that I would leave and that they would not tell my mother about Pamplona. When they notified my mother, they simply told her that my background was too different and I could not adapt. But I had finished the year and received a certificate in teaching English as a second language. Mother had said I only had to go to this university for a year, so she more or less accepted it. She flew over to take charge of me, and we took a trip through Europe for a month. We visited friends in Geneva and in England, and she shopped for antiques to sell in her store.

We ended our trip in Madrid, and there I convinced her to let me stay in Spain for another year. Mainly I argued that I hadn't seen enough, that there was more for me to learn. I went further: following her own strategy of efficient organizing, I enrolled in a computer course. When I showed her the registration papers as proof that I had already arranged everything, she agreed I could stay one more year. She arranged for me to live with a family, then she kissed me goodbye and flew back to El Salvador.

But Mother's arrangements weren't perfect, for once. Another girl named Turka was living with this family. By January it was clear there wasn't room for us all to live comfortably in the same house. So Turka and I decided to find an apartment together.

She worked and I was still going to school. My parents were not happy about my move when I wrote them; they wanted me to move in with another family. But I had decided that the time was ripe to become independent of my parents, so I started looking for a job. After a short while, Turka found me a job as a secretary with a Hungarian, Mr. Finale. He was a count who had left Hungary after the Soviet invasion of 1956 and sought refuge in Franco's Spain.

Mr. Finale owned condominiums on the island of Ibiza. I worked in his tiny office five hours a day, from 4:00 p.m. to 9:00 p.m., with my desk crammed in alongside his. We managed all the administrative details of the condos, from time-sharing arrangements to straight rentals.

Mr. Finale taught me how to do office work, and I became a real secretary. After I typed letters he would carefully inspect them against the light; if I had made one error or a messy erasure, he would give it back to me to type over. So I learned to type very well, and be careful and orderly with accounts.

One day he had to make a sales trip to Ibiza with a group of North Americans and asked me if I would accompany him since the young German woman in charge of the company office in Ibiza had quit. Of course I said yes, and the moment I set foot on Ibiza I knew that was where I wanted to be. It was beautiful. The earth was a clay-red color; there were pink and white almond blossoms all over, and small white-washed houses and people dressed in black. I fell in love with it, and I started my campaign that very day to convince my boss to let me take over the German girl's job.

At the end of the summer I asked Mr. Finale to give me a permanent job in Ibiza. He was a little upset to lose his secretary in Madrid, but I convinced him, and in September I moved to Ibiza. A few months later Mr. Finale sold all his properties to a German named Schmelzer, who already owned many development properties in Spain including hotels, apartments, and houses. Mr. Schmelzer offered me a job with his company, and soon after starting work, I became his private secretary and girl Friday. I took care of his personal accounts, his reservations, his house and office expenses, and details relating to his mistress in Munich. I also traveled with him often. I wasn't sure at that time if his business was legitimate—and it was only after I'd left that I found out it wasn't. It didn't look like a scam; everything seemed to be in the open and there was certainly a lot of building going on, especially of model houses.

Part of my job was arranging for all the dinner parties, business breakfasts, and business lunches. Sometimes I would be sent to Dusseldorf in Mr. Schmelzer's plane with hundreds of marks to buy sausages, breads, cheeses, and wine. Or he would send word that he had invited 10 people over to lunch, and I would get on my motorbike and rush into the village and buy 10 rabbits.

I learned to cook for up to 60 people. I worked for him the rest of the almost three years I was in Ibiza.

By that time violence was rising again in El Salvador but I wasn't really very aware of what was going on. Then in 1971 Ernesto Regalado Dueñas was kidnapped. That was a direct blow at the oligarchy; both Regalado and Dueñas are oligarchy family names. So it was big news, so much so that I even heard about it in Ibiza. The operation was claimed by an organization called El Grupo. They kidnapped him for ransom, but in the course of the exchange they killed him. Most of the kidnappers were arrested, and it was one of the first big scandals because some of the kidnappers were children of well-known political figures. One was a daughter of Fabio Castillo, a rector of the National University of El Salvador and one of the grand old men of the Salvadoran intellectual Left. Another came from a diplomatic family, Jorge Cáceres. He was the only one to go on trial. Some were held in jail without trial while others were sent into exile. A couple still live in exile in Costa Rica.

El Grupo grew out of a number of organizations at the National University, including people from the Christian Democrats, the Communist Party, and even Christian religious organizations. Joaquín Villalobos, future leader of the People's Revolutionary Army (ERP), was in it. Basically they were just young people who saw the impotence of traditional politics to bring about change and were turning to the lessons of the Cuban Revolution. Despite the arrests, El Grupo continued to exist and the ERP was created in 1970.

But not a lot of that filtered over to me in Spain. There were long periods during which I didn't write my parents or hear anything from them.

In mid-1973 I went to Munich to study German and my father came to visit me in October. He spent a month there, and we became good friends. He found a little apartment in a motel near me, and we spent the month walking, reading, visiting factories, and looking at photographic equipment. He would meet me at school when my classes were over, and we would have lunch or dinner together, or go to museums, or sit in the park. All my friends liked him, because he was a very charming guy. So charming that in the course of the month he spent with me in Munich, he convinced me to come back to El Salvador and try life out there.

3

Jamaica

Once I was back in El Salvador, I got several job offers. One was managing a very chic boutique. That was what my parents wanted me to do, but I didn't want to help women try on shoes and clothes all day. I was determined to work in hotels and tourism because of all the experience I had built up in Ibiza. The only thing I could find in that line was as head waitress of the night shift at the cafeteria of the Hotel Camino Real.

My parents were really annoyed and even ashamed when I took that job as a waitress, but I calculated that before too long I would go much farther. So I took the night shift job, working from 4:00 to 12:00. My calculations were right: six weeks later I got promoted to an executive post in charge of conventions, with responsibilities in running the restaurant, which made me part of the management team of the hotel in one jump.

The hotel was one of the most important in the country, and I had to be there for all the big governmental events. One day I organized a dinner for about 20 people, including the foreign minister Mauricio Borgonovo and the businessman Roberto Poma. The guest of honor was Eric Anthony Abrahams, minister of tourism for Jamaica, who had come to advise El Salvador's tourism industry on behalf of the Organization of American States.

Anthony was from an upper-middle-class banking family, the light-skinned class that dominates industry and finance. His father was president of the biggest bank in Jamaica. Anthony was an extremely bright student, and he ended up at Oxford University in England studying political science as a Rhodes Scholar. In his second year he became president of the Oxford Union, the debating society, where the future leaders of Britain and the Commonwealth get their debate training. At the end of his term, in 1964, he exercised his right to choose a guest to address the Oxford Union, and he chose Malcolm X. He also led some serious demonstrations against apartheid. After he left Oxford, he became the BBC's first Black television reporter before going back to work in media and tourism in Jamaica.[1]

I was fascinated by him. He was tall and good-looking, a beautiful man with dark skin and an Afro. He wore impeccable white suits and had the ability to talk to anybody. Although he was only 40, he'd been minister of tourism for four years, since 1970. He was married with two children but was in the process of a very messy divorce.

Anthony and I started seeing each other during the month he spent doing his advisory work in El Salvador, and it turned into a very intense relationship. He charmed my parents when I first took him to meet them, but that was before the relationship was in the open. Once again, I had a partner my parents found impossible to accept, particularly my poor mother. I started flying to Jamaica to be with Anthony on weekends, and eventually I left my job altogether and went to live with him in his house outside Kingston.

He had moved there after separating from his wife, and the place was a mess. My first task was to put the house in shape for him, so I became a housewife for the first time in my life. When people asked me, "What do you do?" I would reply that I was a woman of leisure, a kept woman. It wasn't strictly true, because I started giving Spanish lessons and selling African violets that I grew at home in a greenhouse, but it was close enough. For his part, Anthony introduced me in his professional and social life as his future wife, saying that we were living together until he got his divorce. So I was very official from the start with his parents and all of his friends: the almost-wife.

The love affair continued at the same intensity all the way through. It never stopped. I was going through a stage in my life when I believed in open marriage and absolute honesty. Or, not believed, but I wanted to work toward those things. Be open about other relationships, about other sexual relationships. Heavy-duty: I didn't know what kind of a swamp I was getting into. Or quicksand. That part of me fascinated Anthony. That and my energy and ability to stay up all night and listen to his ideas. And I came from a very bourgeois family—I knew how to cook and to set the table and to be a hostess, even at 24. I was extremely young, and he was the minister of tourism for all of Jamaica.

Being with him introduced me to politics in a serious way because he knew everybody. Michael Manley was president of Jamaica at the time, and I quickly met him and other prominent people in the People's National Party like P. J. Patterson.

The deputy prime minister, David Core, was one of Anthony's best friends, and his wife Mirth and I became very good friends right from the start. She was very high up in the organizational committee of the PNP, and she got me involved, first by giving Spanish lessons to people who did international work for the party. Manley was a social democrat, very much to the left. He had been to Cuba. Jamaica was the first country in all of the Americas to declare itself social democratic and the Cubans now had a big mission in Jamaica. He and Mirth and P. J. Patterson were all a generation older than me, but I liked them and they had a great influence on my political thinking.

Both Manley and Edward Seaga of the Jamaica Labour Party wanted Anthony to run with them as a member of parliament. He had been neutral for a long time. Because I was getting quite involved with the PNP, Anthony used to tease me that I was becoming too much of a socialist and would end up as a *guerrillera*. At first it was like a joke that I didn't know anything about El Salvador. But little by little I started informing myself. As for himself, he started flirting with politics again, drifting toward the right and getting closer to Seaga. He took me everywhere, to meetings with Seaga and Manley and I used to listen quietly, like a little sponge soaking it up.

At the same time, Mirth was showing me what the PNP was. I started wanting to read more, study, go back to school. I also got more involved with Mirth in social work, attending a clinic, doing a lot of party work like typing.

Anthony had not made up his mind about who he was with. This cost him his job as minister of tourism, because when his contract was over in 1975 it was not renewed. It was Manley's way of punishing him. And yet Anthony remained friends with Manley and Mirth and the others in the PNP. Jamaica is a very formal and civilized country in lots of ways.

They didn't stop inviting Anthony to dinner just because he was getting closer to Seaga; people could laugh about Anthony being the conservative and me being the socialist in our household.

In the streets it was a different matter. Racial and political violence really started breaking out. Most of the country's white and Chinese people were leaving, and enormous numbers of ordinary Jamaicans were going to Toronto and Canada as refugees. It affected us directly in several ways. The first was about property. Anthony still owned the house where he had lived with his wife and kids before his separation and had rented it to the First National City Bank of Jamaica. It was an enormous, beautiful plantation house in another part of the city, but it had been empty for a while after its occupants left Jamaica. One day we went by and found that it had been looted and wrecked. Supposedly there had been a watchman, but it was entirely possible that the watchman had something to do with it. This was happening all over the country.

Eventually the racial violence started affecting me more directly. I was white and I stood out like a sore thumb as I went around the city in my little red Mini Morris. The first incident was when I was at the supermarket with Anthony's mother. Mrs. Abrahams was an admirable woman who did a lot of charity work, including the management of five homes for the elderly. She bought all their food and medicines, and I used to help her with it. We went to different places in a carefully planned route—the big warehouses and distributors first, and finally a supermarket for little things. At the supermarket we collected three or four carts full of things and then divided the carts according to the specific needs of each home. We were checking the last cart through and there was quite a line behind us when she remembered that we needed a special type of sanitary napkin for one of the old ladies in one home. She said, "Hold it, I'll go get them and you stay right here," and she rushed off.

There was a Black woman getting very impatient behind us. She said, "Jesus Ras, why doesn't this woman hurry up with her things!" I turned around and said, "Listen, we're almost through, can't you be patient?" And she slapped me. "You white trash, don't you dare talk to me like that." It was a really heavy moment. Everyone in the supermarket was paralyzed because Mrs. Abrahams was a VIP, someone you didn't fool around with, much less her daughter-in-law that everybody in the supermarket knew. The cashier and the manager came immediately to calm down the woman and opened another cashbox.

It was followed by other incidents. Once, when I was sitting in the front seat of a friend's car, a woman passed by and spat at me, right on the car window, saying, "You white trash!"

Race also came up in other ways. I had been thinking about continuing my education for some time, but when I tried to get into the University of the West Indies the authorities made it very difficult for me. I was a qualified teacher already, with proof of it, but they wanted me to do the British proficiency levels and redo the final year of high school. Even with Anthony's support and face-to-face meetings with university officials, the university wouldn't budge.

These experiences brought home for me that fact that however much I worked for the PNP, I was not Jamaican, and my struggle was not in Jamaica.

But what really broke us up was my need to go back to school and to know more about El Salvador. I started to think about my life with Anthony in Jamaica. Life was very easy, and I thought maybe we could make it work but only if I could get some schooling. By this time he had joined the JLP and I was working hard with the PNP.

At the end of the year, I went to spend Christmas with my family in El Salvador. Father had visited Jamaica but he never stayed with us. He used to say, "I understand the situation that you're in but I do not accept it or approve. Therefore I want to stay in a hotel." Mother was totally against it, but Father and Tono both came to visit. When I told my father how disappointed I was that I couldn't go back to school, he said, "Go talk to Padre Gondra and see what you can do."

Padre Gondra was the director of admissions at the University of Central America. I was too late, and I didn't have any of my credentials on hand, but since I was a Gasteazoro, they permitted me to start in the middle of the school year. I decided to try studying for a semester and would travel to Jamaica as much as I could.

By this time Anthony was running for election in Port Antonio, a very beautiful part of the country. I went to visit him once a month, staying for the weekend. But after just a few months in El Salvador my political views were hardening. I couldn't understand how Anthony could be on the right, speaking against all the social programs that Manley had installed and denouncing the country's relationship with Cuba. For his part, Anthony resented that I wasn't there to support him when he was campaigning. There were other issues between us as well that drove us apart, but the political one was insurmountable. He lost that election, but eventually won the constituency in 1980 and became minister of tourism under Seaga. He later split with Seaga and formed his own party.

But by that time our relationship was over. We'd had a huge argument during one of the weekend visits, and I simply left the house without even packing my clothes. I never went back and we never talked again.

Part II

A Nice Country like El Salvador

4

~

Getting Involved

B ad news in El Salvador always seems to be delivered first by radio. As I think
back over the deaths of so many colleagues and *compañeros* during my years
in political opposition, the trebly sound of a transistor radio carries their names
and that first word of their murder, or kidnapping, or arrest, or disappearance.
María Magdalena Henriquez, Enrique Barrera, Martín Espinosa—I should warn
you that from here on, many of the names you read will be followed by "he/she
was killed by the army/national guard/death squad in 1978/79/80/81." That
was the reality of the El Salvador I returned to, and the price people paid for
their opposition.

The first name I heard in one of these radio bulletins was that of the Jesuit
priest Rutilio Grande.

When Padre Grande was murdered, I was studying part-time at the University of Central America. The date was March 12, 1977. It was a Sunday and
I was working with a group of female classmates on a paper for a psychology
course. I was 27, working with 17- and 18-year-olds and feeling very grown up.
It was an exciting period for me, when for the first time I was putting down on
paper things I believed to be correct.

We were at one girl's home in an upper-middle-class neighborhood called
Colonia Escalón when her parents told us to listen to the news. They were very
upset. I was amazed that people from such a bourgeois neighborhood should
be so touched by the death of a priest who had dedicated himself to working with peasants in the countryside. They also knew he was one of the big
promoters of the Christian base communities, and they knew about liberation
theology.

Essentially, Christian base communities are a way for poor people to participate and make the Church applicable to their own lives, rather than just
having a priest take them through the rituals once a week. It's a more flexible,

grassroots approach to spirituality. Some places in the country are too small or isolated to have a priest visit them regularly, so the Christian base communities often had lay leaders, something Padre Grande had been promoting since 1972. But like everything that increases the poor's control over their lives, the base communities were seen as a threat to the established power structure, and they were attacked as subversives. There was much fighting in the area, and many of the lay leaders had been threatened or killed by ORDEN, the semi-official rural vigilante organization.

The radio gave a brief account. Early that morning Padre Grande had set out from the capital in a jeep with his young acolyte and his sacristan, who looks after the church and rings the bells. The acolyte was 16 and the sacristan was 72. They were driving to celebrate Mass in the town of Aguilares, about 35 kilometers (22 miles) north of San Salvador and had almost arrived in town when they were ambushed. Their jeep was hit by machine gun fire from the cane fields by the road, and all three were murdered. Padre Grande, the sacristan, and this boy. It was terrible.

Padre Grande was the first important religious leader to be murdered. Many more have been assassinated since then. Between his death in 1977 and the time I was arrested in 1981, 10 priests were killed and some 60 forced into

Figure 7. Mural dedicated to Padre Rutilio Grande, ca. 1995, El Paisnal, El Salvador (Courtesy of Rachel Heidenry)

exile. There was the assassination of Archbishop Romero in March 1980 while he was saying Mass for the nuns in the chapel of the Divina Providencia hospital. At the end of the same year came the murder of four American churchwomen. And it hasn't stopped: as recently as November of 1989 six Jesuits of the UCA, including the rector, Padre Ignacio Ellacuría, had their brains blown out at close range by the armed forces. But Padre Grande's murder was the first, and it was especially significant because the Jesuits are an important institution in El Salvador and Aguilares is one of the Salvadoran towns hit hardest by government repression.

The base communities movement grew out of the Catholic reforms of Vatican II in 1963 and the Medellín Conference in the late 1960s.[1] My Maryknoll friend and mentor in Guatemala, Sister Marian Peter, was deeply involved in this movement.

I didn't know Padre Grande personally, but like most people, I had heard a lot about him. He had taught at the Externado, the Jesuit school where my father and brothers were educated. And it turned out that the family in whose house I was working with my classmates had a couple of kids in the Externado. No wonder they felt personally touched by the news that day.

It's yet another irony of El Salvador that it was the oligarchy families who supported the creation of the Jesuit university in the first place. They thought the National University was a *vivero de comunismo*, a greenhouse of communism. So they donated the land to the Jesuits and helped get the new university started so the Jesuits would give their children a "proper" Catholic education. And of course, it backfired. By the mid-1970s, the Externado too was seen as a greenhouse of communism.

Jesuit teachers from the UCA have been a progressive influence in the country, frequently acting as consultants to governments, political parties, and economic groups. They were heavily involved with President Arturo Molina's agrarian reform initiative of 1976. The reform was supported by a progressive sector of the bourgeoisie because they thought it was the way to avoid a communist revolution in the future.

But in El Salvador the controlling economic interests have never seen the point of sharing power. They accused the reform initiative of being communist-inspired and ignored the fact that it mostly affected public lands. They were not even impressed that the reforms had the official blessing and financing of the American government through the US Agency for International Development. Quickly, the elite mobilized through ANEP, an employers' alliance that included the coffee growers' association, the sugar cane growers' association, the cattle producers, the industrialists, and the Salvadoran and the American chambers of commerce. With massive publicity and political pressure, they managed to sabotage the agrarian reform.

The killing of Padre Grande simply confirmed my understanding of what was going on in El Salvador and my resolve to get involved. It didn't scare me, although it should have. Though I had no deep understanding, still less a plan or program, I was 27 and full of enthusiasm.

On my return to El Salvador, in addition to my part-time studies, my priorities were to get a job and get out of my parents' house. I got a job almost immediately teaching English at the Centro Cultural Salvadoreño Americano. It was part-time work, paid by the hour, and convenient, but I needed more work than was available, so I kept my eyes open for something else.

One day an ad appeared in the newspaper for an English-language scriptwriting job with El Salvador's educational TV station, and I applied. The TV station was called Televisión Educativa de El Salvador, and it was an experiment in the distance education movement, financed by the Japanese, the British, and the Americans. At the time it just sounded like an interesting job. I didn't know how handy that TV experience would come in shortly after my arrest in 1981, when I went through the toughest press conference of my life.

At the interview I was sitting in the station's waiting room when a little old man with a big nose and a shock of white hair came in. He was definitely not Salvadoran. In halting Spanish, with a heavy Eastern European accent, he asked what I was doing there. I replied in English that I was interviewing for the scriptwriting job.

"No, no, no, you're all wrong for this job," he said. "Come with me." He led me to his office and made me read out loud from the newspaper. Then he summoned a makeup woman and had her do my face. He said I would be perfect as the presenter, the person who says good morning when the channel first goes on air and then announces the agenda for the day. Finally he took me to the station director's office and said they'd have to find someone else for the scriptwriting job. I was now working in television.

This gentleman was a BBC expert working in El Salvador under a UN program, teaching presentation, locution, and structural linguistics for writing scripts. He drove me up the wall, but I learned a lot from him: how to write scripts, how to read them, and how not to be afraid of the camera. I worked the cultural section rather than the educational side, dealing with films and plays and books and so on. I loved it, but the pay wasn't great and I kept getting horrible colds because the studios were so cold.

About 10 months after joining the TV station, I got a call from the Institute for Foreign Trade[2] offering me a job showing Salvadoran crafts and goods at international fairs, with twice the salary I was making at the TV station. I accepted and spent the next few months traveling to trade fairs in Germany, the US, Panama, and Guatemala. The work was interesting and allowed me to meet a lot of people, but it was also exhausting because the institute didn't have sufficient resources for all the work that had to be done. In the end I only stayed a few months.

One of my last assignments was the first Trade Fair of the Americas, held in Miami in March 1978. It was important not only because it was the first but because Rosalynn Carter, the new American first lady, was going to inaugurate it. My memory of Mrs. Carter was that she was very kind and accessible, even while trying to visit all these stands on a tight schedule. I was wearing a lovely *típico* embroidered dress, and she commented on it.

But that was my last assignment for the institute. The work was so hectic that I didn't have time to study, and I felt I deserved a holiday. But when I got back to El Salvador, I found I had a new boss, a military type, and he didn't agree. I took the holiday anyway and got myself fired. Luckily, the TV station wanted me back, so I had a job to go to. This time I stayed there until my political work took over my life.

Having a job meant that I didn't have to live at my parents' house. I found a pretty little house in a neighborhood called Las Delicias. It was an interesting *colonia* made up of workers' housing built in the early 1950s under the presidency of Oscar Osorio. The houses were built on a hill, and they were small but very well planned, with no angles, only curves. All of them were painted in pastel colors like dark turquoise and yellow, with lots of bougainvillea in the narrow streets. It was not what you'd call a marginalized barrio; most residents owned their houses. Many were factory workers and teachers. I paid 125 colones (about 50 dollars) rent.

Although I lived very cheaply, I felt bad living alone in this house. It was a tiny two-story house with one door and one window. On the bottom floor was a kitchen, dining room, patio with a big sink, a bathroom, then two tiny rooms for my living room and my closet. Upstairs was a half-room attic under the eaves that was the bedroom. I soon had the house full of plants and put in a bamboo hedge outside. I was all too aware that while I had 22 square meters (about 237 square feet) to myself, the family next door had about 10 people in the same space: grandparents, cousins from the country, five children, two parents.

Housing was and is an important issue in El Salvador. It is a small country to begin with, about the size of Massachusetts, with about five million people. During my lifetime the population has grown rapidly, especially the urban population—but at the same time fewer and fewer people could make a living farming, the country's traditional economic activity. In the year I was born, 1950, a little over 10 percent of the population was landless. But by the time I returned to El Salvador, it was over 40 percent.[3] About 2,000 large landowners controlled almost 80 percent of the usable land, compared to 230,000 small landowners with less than 100 hectares each. These are the kind of statistics that result in civil wars.

Many of the landless streamed into the capital city, some into properly planned *colonias* like mine but far more into squatters' communities with no electricity, sewage, or drinkable water. Over half of the population was illiterate. Calorie intake, the measure of how well people eat, was one of the lowest in Latin America, and it remains so today. So many people existed (and still exist) on beans and rice and tortillas, day in, day out. Of course there's a small, better-off class of industrial workers, like many of my neighbors in the *colonia*, and a small middle class, but for every one of those people, there are three with next to nothing. So I knew how lucky I was.

My mother disapproved of my living alone and never came to visit. Now that I'm 40 she still disapproves, but it was much worse when I was 27 and should have been looking for a man to marry rather than a house to live alone. She used to say, "I'm not going to visit *un antro de perdición*"—a den of perdition, as if it were a bar or a brothel. But my father thought it was great and found excuses to visit me, usually to help me out in some way or another. He even installed a shower for me when he heard I was going to do it myself.

Once I had a job and a place to live, I started investigating the different political groups that made up the Salvadoran opposition. There were three approaches to choose from. One was through the legally constituted political parties who were trying to bring change through elections. A second was through the mass organizations, which were essentially alliances of trade unions and peasant associations. And finally there were the guerrilla groups, whose activities in the mid-1970s were quite limited compared to the extensive military operations that came later.

Essentially, I was pulled in two directions, one by experience and the other by intuition. Until then my only political experience had been with the social democrats of Jamaica, Michael Manley's People's National Party. But I felt that the reformist approach of the political parties, even the social democrats, wasn't enough. Looking at the structure and history of Salvadoran society, it seemed to me that there had to be a violent overthrow of the system. That meant the guerrilla groups, and so I asked around about them.

The oldest guerrilla group was the Forces of Popular Liberation or FPL (actually, the full acronym was the Farabundo Martí Forces of Popular Liberation or FMFPL). It was started in the late 1960s by Cayetano Carpio, a long-time member of the Communist Party who left because the party was not in favor of armed struggle. In 1972, a second group, the People's Revolutionary Army (ERP) was formed by a mix of younger Communists and impatient Christian Democrats. They were the ones who kidnapped Roberto Poma in 1977. In the mid-1970s a group called the Armed Forces of National Resistance (FARN) split from the ERP after Roque Dalton was executed, but it wasn't very large. By 1981 there were a total of five guerrilla groups that united to make up the Farabundo Martí National Liberation Front (FMLN). But when I came back to El Salvador, there were only three, and they weren't working together in any coordinated fashion.

In my heart, though, I still didn't believe in armed struggle, and in any case I didn't think I had the guts to join those groups. Nor did I have the guts to join the trade union movement or peasant organizations in existence at the time.

That left the legal parties of the opposition. There were only three: National Revolutionary Movement (MNR), Christian Democrats, and National Democratic Union (UDN), which was the Communist Party's political front.

When you came right down to it, there really wasn't much of a choice. Because of the conflicts in my youth, I rejected completely anything that had to do with the Church, and I did not like the idea of a political party with avowedly Christian tendencies. So the Christian Democrats were out of the running.

Nor were the Communists ever a serious option for me. I didn't know much about them, but they followed the ideological line of the Soviet bloc, and I had negative feelings about a party controlled by the Soviet Union. Like most Salvadorans, I associated them with the bloodiest single event in my country's history, one so traumatic that it's still just referred to as La Matanza, the Massacre.

It happened in 1932, when there was a *campesino* uprising in the central and western parts of the country. One of the leaders was Augustín Farabundo Martí, a communist labor leader and revolutionary who during the 1920s had fought alongside Sandino against the US Marines in Nicaragua.[4] He and Sandino split over communism because Sandino wanted to stay independent of foreign ideologies. So Farabundo Martí returned to El Salvador and helped organize the peasants against the terrible living conditions and repression of the landowners. The uprising was planned for January 22, but it was inadequately organized and quickly put down by the troops of General Hernandez Martínez. There was nothing new about that in Central American history, which is full of unsuccessful peasant uprisings. But then the authorities went crazy: they killed an estimated 32,000 people, almost all of them dirt-poor *campesinos*. Most were buried in common graves. El Salvador has never really recovered from the memory. Partly because of this and partly because of decisions of the Comintern in Europe during the 1930s, the Communist Party of El Salvador gave up the armed struggle and concentrated on organizing within the trade unions and universities.

My analysis was sophisticated enough to equate the Salvadoran attachment to the United States with the Cuban attachment to the USSR. There was no denying that the Soviet Union helped the revolutionary movements in Latin America. The parties in Guatemala and El Salvador were all originally soviets.[5] El Salvador was one of the first countries in the Latin world to have a soviet. Farabundo Martí was secretary-general in a little town called Armenia. They had all rallied to the call "Workers of the world unite."

But at the time I got involved, the Salvadoran Communist Party said that the conditions in El Salvador were not yet right for revolutionary change. They supported electoral politics and didn't take up arms again until 1979, when they created a guerrilla organization that is now part of the FMLN.

So my only option was the MNR—Movimiento Nacional Revolucionario. The MNR is a legal party working within the system but it's also a revolutionary party, philosophically based on the recognition that any real change in El Salvador will require a complete shift in political and economic structures. At the same time, it is a social democratic party, not so different from the German Social Democrats, the French Socialists, or Canada's New Democratic Party.

Figure 8. Augustín Farabundo Martí (Wikipedia)

Not long after registering at the university in late 1976, I went directly to the campus to speak to Guillermo Ungo, the secretary-general of the party. When I arrived he was talking with a very fat man named Enrique Barrera, whom he introduced as the party secretary. I'd never heard of Enrique and I couldn't have imagined that in three years' time I would be identifying his tortured corpse after he was kidnapped with several other MNR leaders.

I poked my head in through Ungo's open door, and when he looked up,

I said, "I want to work for your party." His reaction surprised me. Far from welcoming a new recruit to the cause, Ungo tried to dissuade me from joining his party!

As I look back on it, I have to laugh. First, this being El Salvador, Ungo and my mother had known each other from early childhood. My mother was a good friend of his mother, Doña Mercedes, and they had even traveled to Europe together a couple of times. Secondly, my mother still blames Ungo for the past 15 years of my life. I can still hear her saying, "He was your teacher, he influenced you!"

Ungo coolly asked me why I wanted to join the MNR. I replied that I wanted to contribute in some way to my country's struggle. I said I thought it was very important to be in a political organization, that things had to change in El Salvador, and that in my case the social democrats were the correct party. I said I had checked out all the alternatives before I came to him.

He asked me, "Do you know how we work? Do you know what it involves to be in a political party? Do you think you can stand the repression?" There was no suggestion that I try some small task and see if it worked out. It was more like a cross-examination. "Do you understand the implications? Are you being a romantic?" he continued.

Ungo is a kind man but he's also realistic and tends to be pessimistic. Not that it's any surprise. Over his years in the MNR, he has suffered the deaths of his closest colleagues and friends, seen his own name appear on death lists, and been forced into exile numerous times. He has even had election victories stolen from him.

So there I sat, not believing that this man was trying to convince me that I was making a mistake. He tried to tell me that I didn't know what I was doing, that I was naive. In fact, 15 years later, Ungo still believes that I'm naive; he once said that anybody can dab honey on their finger and I'll follow. But I insisted that I knew what I was doing and that I wanted to work for the MNR. Luckily, Enrique Barrera was there, chuckling throughout the cross-examination, and at the end he argued in my favor.

"Let her try," he said to Ungo. "She'll make her decision afterward."

Like Ungo, Enrique was a founder of the MNR, and over the next few years he became one of the men I most liked and respected. But unlike Ungo, who can come across as arrogant and cold, Enrique was big and jovial and warm. After the interview he took me for a coffee and told me not to worry about Dr. Ungo's aloofness. I loved Enrique immediately, and he became a mentor, friend, and comrade. I called him Gordo, or Fatty.

I usually enjoyed telling my father about what was going on in my life, but this was something different. When I told him about the interview with Ungo and Enrique, he grabbed his mane of hair in exasperation.

"Ana," he said, "why do you have to get into these things?"

"But Father, you've been a member of a political party."

"Yes, but now it's different," he said. "You're going to get yourself killed."

He understood the implications better than I did. The rest of my family didn't say anything. My mother just thought I was as crazy as ever and ignored it. By that time I wasn't living at home, and whenever I went to visit, we never talked politics or religion because it meant serious fighting.

Although I was glad to have finally joined the political struggle, my first encounters made me suspect that the MNR was elitist. The members were mostly university students and teachers. There were a few trade unionists, but no *campesinos* and no high school students.

But I didn't mind and enthusiastically took on whatever work they gave me. It came in bits and pieces. One week might find me organizing a women's group or analyzing the political reality of El Salvador with a student study group. The next week I'd be working like crazy putting out an edition of the party's newsletter. And there were always meetings to arrange. It was all legal work, done entirely in the open. I don't know if I was watched by the authorities, but certainly I was never harassed in those days.

Enrique Barrera and I became very good friends. We both liked to cook so we started cooking together, particularly for parties. He made a delicious beef stroganoff, and sometimes we would spontaneously invite people at meetings back to my house, where we would cook stroganoff or something tasty for them.

Everybody kidded Enrique about being in love with me, but we were just great friends. It used to frustrate me that people in the MNR treated me as "the girl" or "that woman." In any case, I had come to the decision that politics and relationships had to be kept strictly apart. I was fighting to be taken seriously in the party with half these men relating to me as a sexual object and half as a political colleague. If I started sleeping with political colleagues, I would lose my status in our political work—that's part of machismo.

The MNR was so small that it was not hard for someone willing to work hard to advance quickly in the ranks. Only a few weeks after joining, I was elected secretary of youth and had also become a sort of political secretary doing much of the party's administrative work. That included running the party headquarters, which was nothing more than a rundown little room downtown, abandoned since 1972. It was a mess, and I could never get it totally clean. But it worked well for us during the presidential election of 1977.

The voting took place on February 20, 1977. Again, the MNR campaigned for the Unión Nacional Opositora (UNO) alliance,[6] although we ran our own candidates for the National Assembly. We backed the Christian Democrats' presidential candidate Ernesto Claramount, an ex-colonel from the army. It was hoped that having a former military man as the UNO's candidate would calm the military's fears about the opposition and prevent a fraud or another coup. His vice-presidential running mate was José Antonio Morales Ehrlich, also from the Christian Democrats, whose son Tono became a very important person later on in the organization of political prisoners.

The election ended with another fraud. As in 1972, crowds of people flooded the streets to protest; in fact, the whole city of San Salvador was practically paralyzed by protests. But almost immediately there was serious repression. On the evening of February 28, thousands of people were protesting in front of the Church of the Rosary, in the Plaza de la Libertad. The demonstration was peaceful, a vigil really, but at 11:30 large numbers of soldiers and police arrived, and the shooting started. Hundreds of people were killed. No one was ever charged or disciplined for the massacre of February 28. But one result was that a new and very aggressive mass organization called the Popular Leagues of February 28 (known as the LP-28 or simply the Ligas) was formed, and the polarization of Salvadoran society deepened.

When I went to lunch with my family the day after the massacre, no one brought it up or acknowledged it. My father only brought it up with me later in private.

Stolen elections are something that American presidents can easily understand, as opposed to ongoing repression. The United States reacted to the fraud by cutting most of its aid to El Salvador (this was the Carter administration and Nicaragua had not yet had its revolution). But the aid cutoff had no effect. The United States has less influence than it seems to think, because even right-wing Latin Americans have their pride. When Carter had first tried to tie military aid to human rights during General Molina's presidency, Molina rejected the aid altogether.

The repression had serious effects on the MNR, however. The party never was very big, but in the wake of these killings, it lost a lot of members. In fact, it almost disappeared from the political landscape within the country.

Paradoxically, it was around that time we started doing quite well outside of the country.

5

International Work

The MNR joined the Socialist International in 1978, and that plugged us into the network of social democratic parties all over the world. Many were in power with leaders with international weight, such as former German chancellor Willi Brandt (who was the president of the SI at the time), François Mitterrand of France, and Sweden's Olaf Palme. Directly or through the Socialist International, they were generous with their support for small struggling parties like ours.

Since I spoke English, I was often sent out of the country for international meetings or conferences. My first trip representing the MNR was to a political propaganda course in Costa Rica run by CEDAL, the Latin American Center for Democratic Studies. Most of CEDAL's funding comes from the German Social Democrats through their Friedrich Ebert Foundation supporting training programs and workshops for trade unions and organizations of peasants, women, students, and social democratic parties. So, this course brought together people from social democratic parties in all of Latin America, including Guatemala, Nicaragua, Costa Rica, the Dominican Republic, and Jamaica.

The course was held in CEDAL's study center, La Catalina. It's in the small town of Barva de Heredia, a pretty place with an old church and red-tiled roofs on the buildings.

The course was a 15-day workshop. There were about 30 of us, and I was the only woman. Half of the participants were experienced politicians like Enrique, while the other half were neophytes like me.

We learned the basics of writing a newspaper article, layout, and the details of press work. I did not know anything systematic about propaganda, and even though the curriculum was very elementary and general, it made me realize how many skills you need in this type of work, and how crucial it is to know how to plan a print or publicity job. Common sense is great but when you get down to details—estimates, scheduling, quality control, and so on—it's not enough. On the other hand, often the only thing that political groups have is enthusiasm and the will to get things done. You need to write a newsletter? Okay, you just do it, and so what if you don't know a damn thing about style.

It was wonderful to meet all these people and realize how many countries had social democratic parties like ours. In the small workshops on topics like how to plan a newsletter and designing a newspaper, the differences between the Latino and the Caribbean delegates really showed when it came to designing front pages. The Latin Americans' front pages were heavy on text, with a standard and very orderly headline-subhead-couple-of-pictures format. The Caribbean people,

Figure 9. Ana Margarita, ca. 35 years old (Courtesy of Elizabeth Fujimori)

who were mostly young men in their 20s, produced showy layouts with masses of pictures and even headlines set diagonally.

I wasn't ready for this, but luckily I had two mentors for my international work: Héctor Oquelí and Vera Matthias. Vera was general secretary of Socialist International Women. She is Brazilian-Swiss, a journalist, and a wonderful woman with a tremendous capacity for lobbying. I met her the first time I went to London for a meeting, which is where I also really began to know Héctor.

I liked Héctor from the beginning. About seven years older than me, he was Salvadoran middle class like I was, though perhaps less acquainted with the oligarchy. He was thin and medium height, with gray eyes behind thick glasses, crooked teeth, and a little mustache. He was the dean of students at the UCA when I was first trying to enter the university, but by the time I joined the MNR, he had accepted a scholarship to the London School of Economics. Very soon after arriving in London, Héctor became the Socialist International's secretary of the Latin America and Caribbean Committee. Even away from El Salvador, Héctor was a strong presence within the MNR, and many people thought he would have made a better leader than Ungo. He had a capacity for organization that I've seen in very few people. He'd been in charge of the MNR's trade union sector, and when he left, many things he'd set up fell apart.[1]

Vera and Héctor pushed me into anything they thought I could handle. Often they took me along to meetings or events just to see how they worked.

By this time I had an additional connection to the MNR, in the form of a new boyfriend. Richard was a Canadian teacher from Victoria, British Columbia. While in Canada, he'd seen an announcement on a bulletin board saying that the Montessori school in El Salvador was looking for a grade 2 teacher. He applied and got it. Although the Montessori school was for rich kids, it had a kindergarten in the afternoon for poor people, and we met because I used to help there. I was struck by his gentleness, his hippieness: clogs, jeans, full reddish-blond beard, and clear blue eyes behind thick granny glasses—totally North American. It impressed me that a man would come to teach second-grade Montessori.

Richard was a year older than me and more sophisticated politically, having been an activist in Canada's New Democratic Party. He knew the party's higher ranks in British Columbia, people like Dave Barrett and Rosemary Brown whom I met later at Socialist International meetings. When we started living together, I had already joined the MNR, and it didn't take long before Richard became a member too. As a social democratic party, the MNR had a lot of similarities to the NDP, so Richard was quite comfortable with its ideology and programs. And he was a hard worker, very responsible. One of the wonderful things about him was that he began to learn Spanish immediately. He never just "stayed" in El Salvador; he became involved with the culture. When he left after four years, he was completely fluent in Spanish. He had all the idiomatic expressions—much more than me, really, in the way he spoke. My family really liked him, and it was wonderful to have someone like him to talk to and discuss politics, as well as all the other things that go with living together. Not that everything was perfect. We were competitive about our political work, for instance, and unfortunately for him, I was always the star, being given more of the high-profile international activities because of my native Spanish and because I was a woman (an advantage for some things at least).

In the summer of 1978 I was sent to the Eleventh International Youth Festival in Havana. All the Salvadoran opposition groups had been invited, with two tickets for delegates from each participating organization: the Christian Democrats, the Communist Party, and each of the different mass, political, and military organizations and so on. There were two places reserved for the MNR, and the party chose two women to go, though in the end I was the only one.

The festival was one of the most beautiful and exhausting experiences of my life. It was a meeting of all the progressive youth movements of the world. Held every four years, usually in Eastern Europe, the previous one had been in East Berlin, and the one before that in Bulgaria. This year's festival was in honor of the 20th anniversary of the Cuban Revolution so the Cubans made it even more open than usual to non-communist movements in other countries. Fidel Castro was president of the Non-Aligned Countries that year, so its congress was also held in Havana. It was the first time Cuba would be opened to so many people from so many other countries.

In the beginning, the power behind the festival organization in El Salvador

Figure 10. Poster for the 11th World Festival of Youth and Students, Havana, Cuba, 1978 (Hoover Institution Library and Archives, Digital Collections, Poster collection, record no. XX343.9940, https://digitalcollections.hoover.org)

was the Communists because, logically, they were aligned with the Soviets and Cubans. So they considered themselves the coordinators of the festival and decided that they would choose whom to invite. In political organizing, fairness doesn't count. The important questions are who has contacts with whom, who controls transportation, who has the biggest budget, and so on. Since the 1932 massacre, the Communists had remained behind their legal front, the UDN. It was a small, reformist party, far closer to the MNR and the Christian Democrats than to the guerrilla organizations. It did not support the guerrilla groups, most of which were made up of former Communists who had split to take up the armed struggle. So the armed groups were not included in the original plans for the festival.

But what about the mass organizations, who were so clearly in the forefront of the struggle? Another mass organization, the Bloque Popular Revolucionario, considered that they, not the timid reformists of the UDN, were the legitimate representatives of the Salvadoran people. They controlled the greatest number of organizations, while the Communists didn't even have a popular organization of their own. So, during the months leading up to the festival, there were parallel activities, one set controlled by the Communists and the other by the Bloque. What made things even more difficult—to prevent the police or army from knowing—all the organization activities had to be underground, had to be held in different locales such as trade union halls, with participation only by invitation.

The first stage was a mini-festival in San Salvador, which we held in November of 1977. It was supposed to be a replica of the big one in Havana with politics, sports, music, human rights and women's rights sessions, and trade union activities. All this effort was aimed at financing our participation in Havana. The main event of the mini-festival was a public concert in San Francisco Park in the downtown. I was involved because the MNR was in charge of organizing the concert, with the help of the Christian Democrats and the Communists. It was to start at 4:00 in the afternoon and our planning was so meticulous that we arrived at 20 minutes to 4:00 with our banners and equipment and set it up fast. It seemed the safest way to do it. But the police had found out somehow, and when we arrived, the park was filled with the military, including small tanks. Legal parties or not, with OAS observers or without OAS observers, that's the kind of repression we were up against.

Later in the day was a public meeting in front of the Hotel Camino Real. The main speakers were Ungo from the MNR and Mario Aguiñada from the Communist Party. A pathetic little crowd of maybe 80 people turned out for that, and even so there were police everywhere.

The second stage was a larger regional festival for all of Central America, held in Costa Rica in March and April of the following year. The parallel organizing activities continued, so two buses left for Costa Rica, the official one organized by the Communists and the other organized by the Bloque. The official group with the legal parties was very well organized and disciplined, with banners and slogans and everything. The Bloque's bus, which had people from about 15 different organizations, couldn't have cared less about nicely lettered banners. I couldn't go because I couldn't get time off from work, nor could Richard. The whole thing fell apart once they got to Costa Rica. There were big arguments. For example, when an all-countries concert was scheduled, there were two competing musical groups from El Salvador fighting about who would get up on stage. That sort of thing is very disruptive, and very embarrassing for the hosts. Nonetheless, despite the better organization and discipline of the Communists, the Bloque dominated the activity in Costa Rica. Their delegation was bigger and had more to offer in acting, singing, debates, speeches, sports, everything.

Once the Costa Rican festival was over and the delegations had returned to El Salvador, the focus was on one question: Who controlled the tickets to the Cuban festival? Theoretically each party, popular organization, and clandestine group had the right to two tickets. Cuba provided the transport, but each delegate had to contribute 60 dollars for food and maintenance in Cuba.

There were maybe 50 tickets in all allotted to El Salvador, but in the end only 28 of us went to Cuba because the Bloque and the other mass organizations decided to boycott the festival. They felt they were the legitimate representatives of the people's struggle, and if they couldn't all go, then it was an inherently revisionist festival and they wouldn't participate.

So the smaller organizations went: some trade unions, the Christian Democrats, the MNR, the student Christian movement, and two from the PRTC (the Revolutionary Workers Party of Central America, which was a guerrilla group). But the larger popular organizations such as the teachers' union ANDES, the *campesino* groups, and the Bloque stayed out. In the end, the Communist Party sent very few people. It's not surprising: people were simply scared, and with good reason. If the authorities found out, going to Cuba could mean your arrest or even a visit from the death squads once you got back to El Salvador.

Even the woman who was supposed to lead the Salvadoran delegation couldn't go. She was the general secretary of the Communist Youth, but her employer refused to give her a leave of absence. A man named Julio, who was a trade unionist as well as a Communist Party member, became the official leader of the delegation. By this point I was the only one from the MNR. Because I was one of the older delegates, and because there were so few to choose from, the coordinating committee elected me second-in-command.

The main festival was scheduled to start on July 27th and continue till the 11th of August 1978. But we met the other Central American delegations a week before to sail to Cuba together on a boat from Panama. Most of the Salvadoran delegates traveled to Panama on a bus, but that took five days and I couldn't get time off from my job at the television station, so I took a plane. I'll never forget walking off the plane in Panama: there on the tarmac was a crowd carrying insignias of the festival and a big banner that said, "Welcome to All Delegates of the Youth Festival." People were flying in from all over Central America and other parts of the world, and they were given this public welcome. After the constant tension of El Salvador, I was amazed that Panama was so open, and I was scared because it was so public.

That night the Salvadoran coordinating team and I met with two representatives of the Communist Youth of Cuba. They had come to do the preparation for the trip and accompany the Central American delegations on the boat to Havana. I was quite excited by the idea of meeting them, because like many young Latin Americans I had a heroic image of the Cubans. It didn't matter what party you belonged to: for the Latin American Left, Cuba was a symbol of freedom and of the possibility for all of Latin America to be free. These two Cubans took us to dinner, and we had a lovely conversation, just young people having a good time, nothing more. It was a surprise because I had thought that all we were going to talk about was politics.

After dinner we traveled to the harbor at Colón, where all the other delegates were assembling. At 2:00 in the morning we started walking onto our boat, a school boat called *El 20 Aniversário*. It was built to hold 300, with sundecks and classrooms and comfortable berths and staterooms. The Cuban merchant marine had lent it to the organizing committee of the festival to transport the Central American delegations; every single berth was taken. There was another boat called *El Vietnam Heroico* for the Venezuelan and Colombian delegations.

It didn't take long to get acquainted with the other delegations: the Sandinistas and a few others from Nicaragua, the Hondurans, and the Costa Ricans. In all there were about 350 of us. There were no Panamanians though—President Torrijos had sent them all in their own plane![2] And the Guatemalans had gone with the Mexicans by another route.

By far the largest contingent was from Costa Rica, with about 180 delegates, compared to about 120 from the rest of the isthmus. Costa Rica had diplomatic relations with Cuba at that time, and in any case it's a very democratic country, so it was not dangerous for them to go to Cuba. The Costa Rican communist party, Partido Vanguardia Popular, had not yet split into two and had far more popular support than it has now. More importantly, it was legal and could fundraise openly so it sent a lot of people to Cuba. A lot of other parties and organizations went too. The Costa Ricans had representation in all kinds of activities, from theater groups to a judo team. Among their delegation was the late Emilia Prieto, the teacher and folksinger who was the oldest participant in the Youth Festival. She was a small, white-haired lady, already in her 70s, but she fit right in with the spirit of occasion. There were also a few Chileans and Brazilians who lived in Costa Rica as refugees.

In fact, there were so many Costa Ricans that they just took over and gave the voyage a very cheery atmosphere. Once we got to Havana it was different because we were billeted in a school with 5,000 other Latin Americans and got lost among the larger delegations like those of the Chileans and the Mexicans. But on the boat, the accent was overwhelmingly "Tico," as we call the Costa Ricans in Spanish.

Because the groups from the other countries couldn't organize openly, our delegations were much smaller. We were also far more serious than the Ticos. They didn't care if they drank or not, or if they followed rules. For them it was a fiesta, while for us it was an assignment. Their attitude toward struggle was different, naturally, because they didn't have to struggle, at least not the way we understood the word. At times it seemed to the rest of us that Costa Rica had nothing to do with the rest of Central America. Those of us from El Salvador and Honduras had become very disciplined by necessity, while the Nicaraguans were right in the heat of their struggle against Somoza.[3]

Most of the Nicaraguan delegation was made up of guerrilla fighters, but it also included Nicaragua's most famous musicians, the Godoy brothers. At that time Carlos Mejia and Luis Enrique Godoy lived in exile in Costa Rica. Luis Enrique had a musical group called Tayacán, made up of musicians from Costa Rica, Venezuela, and Chile, and the whole group was on the boat. They practiced all day long in the billiards room, and it was like a party. But in general the Sandinistas were very intense, cheery but serious. They kept their security rules up even on the boat. All had pseudonyms. They were disciplined about getting up and going to bed, doing their homework and attending their meetings. For me they were quite impressive. They were the closest I had got to the guerrilla and I almost revered them. I knew they were fighting in the jungle, while I was a mere member of a political party.

The first night out of Colón, we got into rough seas and for about 24 hours everybody was sick. I've never seen or felt anything like it in my life. You would sit and tell yourself, *You're not going to get sick just because everybody else is getting sick... Don't get sick... I'm NOT going to get sick... No way!* And you'd end up getting sick. It happened to everyone. I went down to the infirmary and there were dozens of people there, all terribly sick. But at least there was always someone there saying, "Compañera, are you okay, can I give you a pill?"

Aside from that, the voyage was fantastic. Imagine 350 young people on a boat, not only concerned about what was happening in Central America and in Nicaragua and in the rest of the world, but at the same time full of life, full of fun, full of solidarity. It was just an incredible experience. Three days and three nights on this boat in that beautiful Caribbean ocean, singing, dancing, working, discussing, having meetings, sleeping, falling in love. At one point we passed the boat with the Venezuelans and Colombians, and it was a beautiful moment as 600 young people screamed greetings to each other from ship to ship.

I was amazed that the waitresses and the dishwashers in the galleys dressed like everybody else. It turned out that all the people working on the boat were members of the Communist Youth of Cuba, and they too were willing to have fun. Everyone was a *compañero* and everybody was equal. But one thing that surprised me: I had thought that machismo had been overcome in Cuba because of their revolution and 20 years of socialism. But the day I got on the boat, I realized that Cuban machismo was alive and well. It was my first lesson in demystification.

We finally steamed into Havana at about 9:00 on the morning of July 26th, the 20th anniversary of the Cuban Revolution. It was such an emotional moment, for a variety of reasons. I've already mentioned how important the Cuban Revolution was as a symbol to the Latin American Left. We were all proud that it had survived for 20 years. Secondly, we were struck by Havana's physical beauty. Its old Spanish architecture buildings had been painted especially for the festival in marvelous pastel shades of yellow and light blue and light green. Topping it off was the knowledge that we were joining 11,000 other young people from 141 countries, all of us calling for solidarity, human rights, and peace in the world.

All 350 of us were on the deck as our ship sailed into the harbor, and I remember tears running down my cheeks. I stood at the railing with a Salvadoran *compañero* who was a member of the PRTC, which was quite new at the time. He was killed in 1982 or 1983 when the Guardia Nacional surrounded his safe house and he died in the gun battle. We had become very good friends during the boat trip. I couldn't care less if I cry or not, but Salvadoran men are very macho and they can't let people see them cry. But he was gulping as he fought to keep back the tears. That's how emotional a moment it was.

Once we had docked, it took hours to get organized. Everybody was singing. There were children welcoming us, and people in the streets saying hello, waving little flags from all the countries. The organizers directed us onto a fleet of buses and off we went to the Lenin Vocational School, the high school for the best students from all over Cuba. It's an enormous boarding school in the even more enormous Lenin Park, one of the biggest in Havana. It had to be enormous, because there were 5,000 Latinos at the festival and we all were lodged there.

All the big delegations had one dorm for men and one for women. We Salvadoran women found ourselves sharing a dormitory with about a hundred women from places like the Dominican Republic and Puerto Rico, which had only managed to send small delegations. Our dormitory had 50 bunk beds and no locks on the lockers! At 27, I was one of the oldest women there.

For the Chileans, being together in their two dormitories had a special significance. There were about 200 Chilean delegates, and almost all of them were living in exile in countries like Italy, East and West Germany, Canada, and even the Soviet Union. Some had been in exile for up to seven years.[4]

The only country that refused to have separate dorms was Spain. Spain was coming out of the Franco era at that time, and there was an amazing energy to break with everything from the past. They broke all the rules that were supposed to keep order, from the way they dressed to the way they acted. I was impressed. There were 11,000 delegates and you had to keep them in order. I sometimes wonder how many pregnancies came out of that festival . . .

There were four other women from El Salvador—the rest of the 23-strong delegation was male—and we stuck together most of the time. One was a market woman, Doña Alicia Zelayandia,[5] who was a member of the Communist Party and COMADRES, the Committee of Mothers of the Disappeared, because she'd lost a son. She was close to 50, a typical Salvadoran market woman: strong and stocky, barrel-like, loud-mouthed. There was a second Alicia, who had also started her life as a market woman. But she was a young woman, only three or four years older than me at the time, and very good-looking. By the time of the festival, she had a store and she was closely involved with the Christian Democrats. The Christian Democrats had won the municipal elections in San Salvador a couple of times, and they did a lot of work with the market women, who are a very organized and political group. The third was Florencia Castellanos, who represented the Communist Party of El Salvador but lived in Costa Rica where her father was in exile. She was still in university then. Her brother would be killed around the same time as the FDR members in late 1980.[6]

The last of our little group was an artisan named María Magdalena Hen-ríquez, from the town of San Antonio de las Flores. She represented the women from the Christian Students' Movement, and she was enormous. Beautiful, but very fat; the Costa Ricans called her the "Venus de Kilo." I'd met her before when I was working in the Institute of Foreign Trade. Magdalena later became the press secretary of the Human Rights Commission in El Salvador, when she was still in her early 20s. In 1980 she was disappeared by the death squads.[7] When her body was finally found hidden in a tunnel near the house where she lived with her invalid father, it was clear that she had been brutally tortured. It was a terrible shock to all of us. She was a lovely woman.

By the time we were settled in the Lenin School and had lunch, it was about 1:00 in the afternoon. All of a sudden, there was Fidel's voice booming in our ears. Cuba has sound systems all over the place, and there were speakers in all of the school's rooms—every single room, bathroom, or whatever had little round speakers coming out of the ceilings. So there was Fidel, speaking from Santiago where he had made his famous "History Will Absolve Me" speech when he was sentenced at the Moncada.[8]

He talked for five hours. As everyone knows, Fidel talks and talks and talks. Of course I had heard his speeches before on Radio Havana, yet I remember being fascinated by this speech, and the fascination was general because everybody just walked around the halls and listened to his broadcast. Fidel is a wonderful orator in the Latin style, nothing to do with European or North American style. He can talk on coherently for hours with statistics and humorous examples.

Perhaps it was just the fact of being in Cuba on the 26th of July, in this beautiful modern school, with its enormous hallways that were open and airy and full of light. And sharing these halls with people like the Chilean singer Isobel Parra and Salvador Allende's wife Hortensia Bussi de Allende! Even the author Gabriel Garcia Marquez was there. Someone pointed him out to me, sitting on a little concrete bench and listening to Fidel like the rest of us.

That night the Latino delegates were taken to a concert in the Teatro Marx. All of the Left's musical heroes of the *nueva trova*—the new song movement that began in Cuba in the late 1960s—were there: Silvio Rodríguez, Pablo Milanés, Noel y Nicola, Felipe and Vicente Feliú, Sara González, all of these people. It was a special treat for the 5,000 Latinos in the audience.

Two days later, at the inauguration of the festival, Fidel made another speech, welcoming us. Among the people on the podium with him was the Yasser Arafat,[9] whose presence impressed most of us considerably. A nice moment came when Fidel saluted Emilia Prieto, the Costa Rican folklorist, as the festival's "youngest participant."

One evening a group of us went to the Malecón, the seawall running along Havana's seaside. There were people dancing and singing all over the place, and lots of kids asking for autographs—it seemed like every kid in Cuba had a little book for collecting autographs. All of a sudden a jeep stopped in front of us and who jumped out but Fidel! With his great big beard and his green uniform, he seemed enormous. The fact that he stopped was really overwhelming. He said hello to us and asked us all where we were from and chatted with us for a few minutes. Then he got back into the jeep and stopped again a bit further on, saying hello to everybody.

Everything was just perfect, and to the delegates it felt as if all of Havana gave its best effort for the festival. The program booklet was about 40 pages long, and each day there were at least a hundred activities you could choose from: swimming, music classes, political meetings, solidarity conferences, and workshops on everything from feminism to trade union rights. You could participate as an individual or as a delegation.

Through a fluke, I became the leader of the Salvadoran delegation. Julio, the *compañero* in charge, got appendicitis soon after we arrived in Cuba and had to be hospitalized. So, as second-in-command, I suddenly became the leader.

Life was taking me along at 150 miles an hour into totally new territory. I felt quite intimidated. I'd always worked in a reformist political line, but the political context in the festival was overwhelmingly revolutionary. It changed my way of thinking about El Salvador, particularly regarding the role of the mass organizations. Up till then, I had rather looked down on these mass organizations. I didn't like the way they acted, their techniques, their loudness. By upbringing and inclination, I was a bit more formal. But in Cuba, I got "massified" and I loved it.

As well as having a lot to think about, I had a lot to do. All of a sudden I had to represent the delegation in meetings and ceremonies. Invitations rolled in from the Soviets, from the Yugoslavs, and from the Jamaicans, all of whom had their own club buildings in Havana. There were about a thousand Russians at the festival, and they stayed at their place in Miramar, which had a pool and a ballroom.

I had never met anyone from Russia before. They were all big, blond, and "straight" in the way they dressed and acted. All during the festival they threw parties, major affairs with vodka and food and dancing. They even handed out hats and T-shirts. On one occasion all of the Central American delegations were invited to a party at the Russian compound, and something like 3,000 people showed up. There were folk dances, food, gifts, and speeches, and a lot of toasts in vodka. The contrast between the Central Americans and the Russians was wonderfully apparent at that party. Compared to them, we looked totally disorganized and informal, and we laughed about everything. We had our serious side, of course: except for the Costa Ricans, most of us came from pretty desperate situations—but when we came to a party, we partied.

No one slept during the 11 days we were there. I don't know how it was with the other places, but the Lenin School BOUNCED 24 hours each day.

On top of everything else, I got involved with a Chilean. It was almost unavoidable; I imagine almost every woman in the Latin American Left has a Chilean somewhere in her romantic past. To us, the Chileans in the late 1970s were tragic heroes. Partly it was the brutal facts of their history: the overthrow of Allende's democratically elected government in 1972 had been executed with the help of the CIA and the multinational corporations. The repression against the left that followed the coup d'état forced thousands of Chileans into exile, and they showed up all over the world. Everywhere they went they got into solidarity work. So if you had anything to do with the Latin Left, you soon met exiled Chileans. It's not too much of an exaggeration to say that in general they arrived in our political circles with several advantages: they were very good-looking and well educated, with organizational know-how from years of political work both in and out of power. They knew how to talk politically. Their cultural orientation has always been more European than other Latin American countries, and that gives them a certain sophistication. They believed they were the purest revolutionaries in Latin America. They always acted superior to the rest of us, and we adored them.

This privileged position in the Latin American Left only lasted until the Sandinista Revolution in 1979. Then it became a struggle within international solidarity circles, because by that time the Chileans had co-opted all the positions, and the other countries had to fight for space. The Chileans were very adept at organizational politics. In contrast, people like me from groups like the MNR were new at the world's international stage. We soon found the Chilean arrogance irritating, and it was a constant struggle to challenge their dominance of events and programs. We had the feeling that they looked down on us, as though in our countries we weren't suffering like they did, or that we didn't deserve solidarity.

But that was later. My Chilean lived in exile in Costa Rica and I met him on the boat—a beautiful man. We were dying to be alone together but the dorms were impossible. What can you do when you're surrounded by 11,000 people? There is no privacy in a dormitory, and there was not one unoccupied corner, not even a storeroom, plus the hallways were always full of light and full of people.

Each delegation had a few Cuban guides in charge, so I finally asked Lourdes, my delegation's guide, where we could go. She said, "Well, you could try the Havana hotels." We tried the hotels that night, and of course it was impossible because they were absolutely full of press people. So I went back to her and said, "Look, Lourdes, what should we *do*?" I was insistent. I liked this guy and I thought it was pretty normal for us to want to be together. From her side of it, I guess the Cubans weren't too enthusiastic about this kind of thing happening.

She told me there were a few motels we could try outside of Havana toward Santa María del Mar. So one night we took a taxi to a motel on the highway. When we got there, there was a line of about 50 couples waiting! They were mostly Cubans—I guess this sort of thing was pretty common there—and there's a whole sort of etiquette that goes with it. The first thing you do when you arrive is call out, "Último!" which is how you ask who is last in line. And that couple makes themselves known to you, and you do the same when the next couple arrives and says, "Último!"

The system is logical, but it was so embarrassing for two square Latin Americans. No matter how liberated we are, Latin American women are prudish, and Latin American men are just as bad, at least when it comes to a formal relationship. I was less shy than my friend—I think I was embarrassed because he felt embarrassed. But the Cubans are totally used to it. We waited around for half an hour and then gave up and took a bus back into Havana.

But when we got back to town, we found it was too late to get transportation out to the Lenin School, so we had to spend the whole night walking around. It didn't really matter; we had a great time. One of the things that struck us was that there was no advertising to be seen. There were billboards everywhere with salutations from the people of Cuba to the festival and the representatives of all the countries. But no Coca-Cola, no beer ads, no neon signs—just this clean, beautiful city welcoming us.

Eventually we did manage to get intimate together—there is always a way. The end of the festival was the end of the affair, but not of the friendship. On the boat back he confessed he was married. I didn't see him for years, until I was out of prison and went into exile in Costa Rica. The day after I got there, I saw a column in La Nación written by someone who was connected with that period. I wrote to the journalist and he immediately put me in touch with the Chilean. It was a very beautiful meeting. He really helped me get settled, and in fact he helped a lot of Salvadoran people in exile in Costa Rica. But that was a long time in the future.

As head of our delegation I had to participate in a lot of official events. Near the end of the festival was a reenactment of the arrival of the *Granma*, the boat that Fidel and Che Guevara[10] and the original *compañeros* sailed to Cuba to start the campaign that finally toppled the Batista regime. A replica of the *Granma* had sailed over from Mexico and was waiting off the coast. I was one of 21 delegates—the same number as the original *compañeros*, but from different parts of Latin America—who were taken out to the boat at about 1:00 or 2:00 in the morning to complete the trip.

I couldn't keep my eyes open. Just couldn't. I was exhausted from so many days of activities, not to mention my Chilean affair. But everybody else was playing the guitar and singing and having a good time. They kept saying to me, "Compañera, wake up!" and I could barely answer. Eventually we sailed into Havana, and of course there was a meeting and I had to stand with the sun on my head—I don't remember anything, just wanting to lie down and sleep and sleep and sleep.

"Compañera, what's the matter with you? Where's your enthusiasm?"

"What enthusiasm? I want to go to bed . . ."

And then it ended and we all returned to Panama on the boat. I arrived back in El Salvador feeling as though nothing was going to stop me in my political work or in my commitment to my country's struggle. I was ready to take up arms, and I knew that we could do it. I'd been given a huge feeling of solidarity in Cuba that was crucial to me as a Latin American. Despite the ups and downs, the deaths, the disillusionments, the struggles within the opposition, that feeling lasted until the deaths of FMLN *comandantes* Marcial and Ana María in 1983.

6

Repression Grows

Once back in El Salvador I started receiving invitations to speak or participate in overseas meetings. In Cuba I had met many people from international solidarity circles, particularly European ones, and Héctor Oquelí and Vera Matthias at the Socialist International in London really encouraged my work. So I began to travel a lot.

I was effective at international work. I could get solidarity for El Salvador just by describing how our people lived. I was comfortable in Spanish or English and could use either in an informal way. With youth groups of political parties or students, I could talk quite spontaneously and coherently about what was happening in El Salvador.

I usually traveled with two or three other Latin Americans in tours sponsored by the International Union of Socialist Youth, each of us with our story. Most of these meetings were organized by local solidarity groups in different countries who prepared for our visits. The audiences were very receptive because El Salvador was in the press quite a bit, and we used slides, movies, and books to back up what we said.

Much of our work involved fundraising. One problem with being offered help is figuring out how to receive it and where it should be used. Solidarity folks would say, "We want to do something for you—just present a project proposal with a budget!" So our fundraising had to be presented in the form of projects: educational projects, productive activities, support for trade unions, et cetera. At that time, the money I raised went to the MNR, but later there was one repository for international funding that was distributed around the country to all the organizations.

Unlike a lot of speakers, I didn't like to describe torture or the bloodier details of repression. I realized that in talking with American and European audiences, they did *not* want to hear the gory details. It's sad but too often true that when people who have undergone horrible experiences are sent to Europe to do solidarity work, they have little success in raising funds or support. Audiences often don't want to believe the details, because they're so explicit and so tragic. They just want to help.

But traveling on behalf of the MNR was not always fun. Conferences and meetings are actually a lot of work, and one of the most unpleasant aspects was the male majority in most of these events. When I went to the Socialist International Congress in Vancouver in November 1978, there were only about four women delegates, and the behavior of many male delegates toward me was unbearable. I was 27 and outgoing, and all a lot of them saw was a cute, *simpática* young woman from Central America. The men made a lot of passes—all ages, all nationalities, every man thought he had to try it on. Once I was sitting in my room and a famous political analyst from Yugoslavia wandered in. He was about 76, a charming man in that sophisticated Old World way. He knew every single political leader, and during the congress he had taken me under his wing to introduce me. But then he tried to get into bed with me.

I could handle a 76-year-old without too much problem except a bad case of disillusionment. But not long after that an important Central American leader cornered me in an elevator.[1] He was a powerful man in his party at home, influential in the Socialist International, and physically very big. It was horrible. He pushed me up against the elevator wall and tried to embrace and kiss me and be *cariñoso*—somewhere between fatherly love and sexual aggression. I pushed him away, silently, and tried to ignore it. He pretended nothing had happened—if I'd allowed anything, he might have pretended *everything* had happened. That sort of thing left me lonely and miserable in Vancouver.

On the other hand, I could recognize the practical importance of being female because it made it easier for me to get in touch with big political figures, or people in their delegations. I was able to make contacts for Ungo and set up meetings that he might otherwise not have gotten. For instance, we were invited to dinner with Willi Brandt, Clodomiro Almeyda from Chile, the Finnish prime minister Mauno Koivisto, Jaime Paz Zamora from Bolivia, and Ernesto Cardenal, who would soon become minister of culture of Nicaragua. I first saw Cardenal standing with Héctor in the hotel lobby wearing his trademark beret. He had arrived at the congress without a hotel reservation, so I stayed with Vera and he slept in my room until another arrangement could be made. Padre Cardenal is very sweet, quiet, and soft-spoken, and we became good friends. He's a poet and a priest and a saint—I'm not surprised he had such troubles at the Ministry of Culture.

There were a lot of social occasions, and a lot more passes made at me, but I refused to have anything to do with anyone. The Costa Rican politician Luis Alberto Monge used to call me *la sobrina de Ungo*—"Ungo's niece"—but I couldn't talk to Ungo about it. You're not there to give your *compañeros* problems; you are there to work, period. If I'd said anything, the answer would have been, "You can't come next time if we're going to have that type of trouble."

As 1978 came to an end I suddenly found myself working for the MNR full-time. As a result of the contacts I had made at the festival in Cuba, I was invited to go to Europe in September for two activities: a meeting of the International Union of Socialist Youth in Aricia, Italy, and a tour of Germany with the youth wing of the Social Democratic Party.

But since I had already gotten three other leaves that year from the television station, when I asked for permission to go to Europe they turned me down. Clearly, I had to choose between my job with TV and my international work with MNR. It was no contest. I quit TV and started rearranging my life to accommodate my political work and still make a living.

On the political side, I became a glorified administrative assistant for the MNR. One of my first tasks was to find a house that would serve as an office. The room downtown was just too small and depressing, and there wasn't much available after all the repression. Luckily, the German Social Democrats sent us money to do a training project with the trade unions. We bought a big concrete house quite near the original office, and that allowed us to hold trade union seminars, study sessions, and workshops of various sorts. So my first task was to set up the new headquarters, buy furniture, and so on. After that, I did everything needed to keep the office going: collected dues, kept the office maintained, looked after the library, even did the bookkeeping.

Figure 11. Ana Margarita with figures of the National Revolutionary Movement (Movimiento Nacional Revolucionario, MNR) (Courtesy of Elizabeth Fujimori)

For all this, the party paid me a stipend of about 80 dollars a month. That was not nearly enough to live on, so I got a job teaching English early in the morning at the national telephone company, ANTEL. I did four one-hour classes: one with international operators, one with administrative staff, one with executives, and one with the telegraph operators. I found the classes with the operators and the executives the most interesting, but I never talked politics—it was just too dangerous. ANTEL was controlled by the military, and while there was a very strong and aggressive union in the company, I had to be careful that I was not identified with it. The pay was 40 dollars a day, which was damn good for four hours' work in El Salvador. I also got my old job back at the cultural center, working occasionally as a substitute teacher of English.

Full-time work for the party brought all kinds of new responsibilities, and on a personal level it was interesting and exciting. But on a political level, I couldn't avoid the facts thrown in my face every day. Electoral politics was getting us nowhere. Even timid reforms by the government were sabotaged by the industrial and financial interests.

More immediately, the repression was growing. A few months after the fraudulent presidential election in February 1977, General Romero's government had enacted a public order decree. Its wording was tailor-made for the employers' association ANEP because it was aimed at containing the mass organizations and the trade unions. In practical terms, it was a license to kill for the police forces—Guardia Nacional, Policía Nacional, the Policía de Hacienda—and the army. They each had their specialties and they worked separately, with very little coordination. The big repressions were usually Guardia Nacional, and the big arrests were Policía Nacional. The worst tortures and disappearances were by Hacienda and the Guardia Nacional.

Nineteen seventy-nine was a confusing year, a terrible year for violence and a year of disillusionment for anyone hoping for a peaceful solution in El Salvador. For instance, in early May 1979 five leaders of the BPR were arrested and disappeared. All of a sudden they were gone. No one except the authorities knew where they were, or if they were alive or dead. Naturally, the BPR looked for ways to gain their release. The main tactic for trying to free disappeared people is to call maximum attention to it, both inside and outside the country if possible. So the BPR occupied three foreign embassies and the Metropolitan Cathedral. None of this was legal, obviously, but it called attention to a disgraceful act of repression in the most visible way possible. The occupations were peaceful, with no arms involved, but the government response was swift: on May 9, the army moved in and massacred 23 demonstrators on the steps of the cathedral.

Figure 12. Photos of disappeared persons in El Salvador (*Libro Amarillo*, 1987, https://unfinishedsentences.org/reports/yellow-book/, CC BY-NC-SA 4.0)

That was recorded by television cameras and on the news worldwide. But for every large-scale massacre at a demonstration, there were 10 individuals disappeared or assassinated, some well known and others from the most humble sectors of society. During those months I saw bodies in the street every day.

When foreigners talk about the current war in El Salvador, they usually refer to 1980 as the year it started. That is because in 1980 the forces on the left became clear and stable with the creation of the FDR on the political side and the FMLN on the military side.

As the months went by, the repression mounted. Each day we would hear of another student leader or a trade unionist who'd been arrested, and a few days later their bodies would be found mutilated and badly tortured. Whole directorates of trade unions were arrested and killed.

The contrast between the mass organizations and the MNR couldn't have been clearer. The BPR, the LP-28, and FAPU were made up of *campesinos* and factory workers who went into the streets to demand their rights. Their demands were simple and untheoretical: tortillas for coffee pickers, better wages. Not like us in the MNR. As intellectuals we loved to discuss things but would never demonstrate in the streets for everybody's rights. We were smug in our understanding of the current reality and the reasons for it, but we never took any action. We were even afraid to hold meetings.

Meanwhile the *campesinos* and workers in the mass organizations were risking their lives, occupying churches and government ministries and the streets for specific issues. They weren't afraid to die for others, to go out and scream for their needs and rights. So 1979 was full of demonstrations by the mass organizations, and strikes by the trade unions, which were met with murderous violence by the authorities.

It's hard to put this in perspective for a foreigner. The repression was massive and brutal, quite out of proportion to any "law and order" argument that might justify it. I'll never forget one morning when I left my house in Santa Tecla at 6:30 to drive to my job at the telephone company. I went under one of the underpasses and there was a body hanging from the bridge. It was a man in his shorts, with a cardboard placard saying, "Muerte a los traidores de la patria." Death to the traitors of the fatherland. It was signed by one of the death squads. Farther on, in the area of the American embassy and the Externado School, I saw another body. It was covered by a sheet with a drawing of what was supposed to be the flag of one of the popular organizations on it. And finally, on the sidewalk of the underpass by the Seguro Social building, there was a third body. The person had been tortured, and the bones were broken.

That was our daily routine. Terror followed us. Our friends, our people, were being killed. Earlier, I mentioned the murder of María Magdalena Henríquez, the "Venus de Kilo" whom I met in Cuba. In February 1980 the sociologist Roberto Castellanos and his Danish wife Anette Mathiessen were kidnapped and killed. The same month Mario Zamora, a Christian Democrat leader and brother of Rubén Zamora,[2] was assassinated in his home.

That is how the people of El Salvador were terrorized. Many of the killings were claimed by new organizations with bizarre names like the White Warriors Union and the Armed Forces of Anti-Communist Liberation–Wars of

Elimination (that one is hard to translate, but their acronym was FALANGE). It was hard to know where they ended and the government forces began. For instance, the White Warriors were linked to Major Roberto D'Aubuisson, who was head of the military's intelligence service.

So maybe it wasn't a war yet, if by "war" one means organized hostilities between two forces. But it could just as easily be said that for most of the 1970s, the Salvadoran Right had been waging war on anything that smelled progressive to it—which meant everyone from elderly Christian Democrats to Maoist students. A very one-sided war, with the authorities' well-organized and well-financed forces hitting repeatedly at a badly divided, underfinanced, and largely unarmed opposition. Statistics take the human element out of what they describe, and can always be challenged according to who's doing the counting, but the one-sidedness of the war can be seen in figures published by Italo López.[3] Between 1972 and 1979, the governments of Molina and Romero and their surrogates carried out 698 political assassinations or disappearances. That figure goes up to 704 if you include the priests killed by death squads. Those are the bald facts, and they pale in comparison with the thousands killed in the early 1980s. From January to September 30 of 1981, for instance, the same source has the government and death squads killing 10,714 people, almost half of them *campesinos*. These are probably conservative numbers, as a backdrop to the stage where the MNR was trying to push forward its legal political work.

Faced with such an unequal struggle, the Left made all kinds of attempts to find some kind of coordinated response to the repression. One was the creation of the Popular Forum alliance as a coalition of the progressive professional groups, like the association of technicians' trade unions, and the leadership of the University of Central America. Then another, an alliance called the Democratic Front, was established, representing all the opposition political parties, plus the BPR, the LP-28, the FAPU, and two or three more.

The situation was complicated by external factors, of course. After the fall of the Somoza government in Nicaragua, the enthusiasm in the Salvadoran Left was tremendous. *Si Nicaragua venció, El Salvador vencerá*—if Nicaragua triumphed, El Salvador will triumph. That set a lot of things in motion, including for me personally, and was when my father began his "campaign" to send me to Nicaragua. He would say sarcastically that if I wanted to play La Pasionaria in Nicaragua he would pay for the ticket. To tell the truth, I didn't even know who La Pasionaria was when he first mentioned it. I had to look her up, and I was proud when I learned that she was a hero of the Spanish Civil War. But I was insulted at the way he said it: little girl, if you want to play with fire, go set your fires somewhere else where you're not going to get hurt. He actually thought it would be safer for me there.

In 1979 I was chosen to go to Nicaragua with the Socialist International mission. It was August 2, only 15 days after the Sandinista Revolution. I went both as a delegate and as a translator, because some delegates didn't speak Spanish. We were with the Nicaraguan junta constantly during our 13-day visit. I got friendly with Violeta Chamorro. She was the only woman and the quietest one in the junta. She reminded me a lot of my mother, and I was amazed to find her in the new government (and later as president she would be the first elected female head of state in the Americas). I have no lasting impression of Daniel Ortega other than that I didn't warm to him at all. Tomás Borge, new interior minister, offered me a job as his personal secretary and translator because he liked the way I worked: I was a fast and sympathetic interpreter. But I have to confess that I didn't do a good job as a translator because I ended up doing more politics than translating.

The Sandinista victory left the United States scrambling for a policy to prevent the same thing from happening in the rest of Central America, but without sending American troops or too obviously abusing human rights. Typically, the US government was not prepared to support anyone left of the Christian Democrats, so from the beginning they were stuck in a contradiction: they wanted electoral democracy in El Salvador, but their policies couldn't recognize the legitimacy of most of the opposition groups. They couldn't face the fact that the oligarchy didn't like American policy any more than the Left did. It was the employers' association ANEP, after all, that sabotaged the American-backed agrarian transformation around this time.

Making things even worse, the economy was in terrible shape. Banks were failing, and the investing class was putting even less of its money into the country than usual. Instead there was a great deal of "capital flight," especially to Miami. As strikes increased, the multinational companies started to leave El Salvador.[4]

7

Civil War

The last chance for a political solution came October 15, 1979, with the coup d'état led by a few relatively progressive members of the military who called themselves the Juventud Militar, the Young Military.[1] In the end, the military always closes ranks to protect its interests, but these young officers had at least some political consciousness. After they deposed General Romero, they quickly asked the MNR and Christian Democrats to participate in a junta to be made up of both civilians and representatives of the military.

We had great hopes as people returned from exile to form the new government. As well as the MNR and Christian Democrats, it included the UDN, the universities, and a lot of trade unions. In fact, nearly every respected person in the country joined, the best of the best of academia and technocrats. It was the most progressive-looking government El Salvador had ever had.

Duarte was not invited into the government, and he was hurt.[2] I felt at the time that he was a clown and a megalomaniac. He was a big man and very expressive. I'm sure he had good intentions, and certainly he was charismatic and a populist. But he always talked emotionally about how his mother was a market woman and how she would swing him in a hammock made of flour sacks while she tried to sell a few vegetables to keep him alive, and about how his father was a poor carpenter—basically Jesus Christ and the Virgin Mary with their children. The truth is that his father was an engineer and his mother was a housewife. He went to a good Catholic school and he got a scholarship to the University of Notre Dame. When he showed his hand with missing fingers to imply that he'd been tortured, we knew that he'd actually lost those three fingers in a carpentry accident.

Many people knew he was lying, but he was a powerful figure who'd been mayor of San Salvador. Ungo, in contrast was a cold-blooded fish. Duarte exuded warmth and enthusiasm, and was all kisses and hugs, especially in his work on behalf of the market women. His return from abroad was greeted by an amazing reception. The streets filled with people who wanted to touch him. My father got stuck in the street and burned out the clutch in his car, and he was furious forever after toward Duarte, whom he'd easily seen through.

The junta declared its objectives: to restore rule of law and to redefine El Salvador's political and economic structure. It also proposed to dissolve OR-DEN and reestablish diplomatic relations with Honduras, broken since the war of 1969.

The coup was on my birthday and my mother never forgets that. She had organized a little party for me, but all people could talk about was this new government that was going to save the country. I told my parents I was going to work for the government, but didn't quite get the reaction I expected. For once I was on the right side, and they still thought I was crazy.

The MNR and Christian Democrats immediately declared their support for the new junta. But theirs was its only unequivocal support. The mass organizations were not invited to participate, and they all condemned it. And the guerrilla organizations did as well, on grounds that it was merely a trick foisted on El Salvador by the US government to prevent what had happened in Nicaragua. The ERP immediately called for an insurrection but found no popular support, so they declared a unilateral cease-fire. At the same time, the employers' association ANEP got busy condemning the junta from the right.

Nonetheless, things were quiet for a few days as everyone held their breath to see what the junta would do, and if it could rein in the police and army. There were no major actions by either the guerrillas or the mass organizations during that time. Major D'Aubuisson was dismissed from army intelligence, which seemed a positive step for human rights.[3]

That first junta lasted a little over two months. During those months I was working with the press, mostly setting up interviews for journalists and accompanying the leaders to them. Things were so busy that I didn't see much of my family during that time.

The government had a hard time making changes because of the obstacles thrown up by the military and from the left. The mass organizations had been negotiating with each other all through December of 1979, and the day after the new junta was declared, they announced the creation of the National Coordinator of the Masses, a strategy to strengthen the fragile government. But on October 29, the army killed 21 members of the LP-28, making it dramatically clear that the military was not going to respect the new government.

On December 23rd, the three civilian members of the junta resigned as a bloc, blaming the military's opposition to the immediate changes the junta thought essential: agrarian reform, educational reform, changes to banking. Their walkout was a form of pressure; they had counted on their resignations not being accepted.

But a very sad thing happened. In the first week of January, their resignations were accepted and Colonel Majano declared a second junta, this time with José Antonio Morales Ehrlich and Héctor Dada from the Christian Democrats taking over as the civilian element. In March, Duarte regained control of the Christian Democrats, splitting the party in two. He took over Héctor Dada's place on the junta and by the end of the year was its president. Duarte had been waiting for his moment. This man who talked about having been tortured by the military had been talking to them all along. He sold his soul. I have no shame in saying this. I think it's the truth.

Anyway, that was the end of the progressive government. It hurts me to think about it now, because there was so much enthusiasm in the country. It's part of Salvadoran history that not many people remember, but was crucial to what happened next.

On January 22nd, there was a huge demonstration to celebrate the creation of a coalition of left-wing groups and to commemorate the Matanza of 1932. Everyone was there: the teachers' union ANDES, student groups, trade unions, *campesino* organizations.

It was very well organized with lines of people stretching about 12 kilometers, each perfectly prepared with little bags of bicarbonate water for teargas, and banners and megaphones and songs. It gives me goose bumps still to think of these people, these Salvadoran people, demonstrating with joy. But the National Guard and the Treasury Police fired on the crowd, killing more than 40 people and wounding many more.

At this time I wasn't working directly with the MNR, but the party had asked me to be Héctor Oquelí's personal assistant in the Ministry of Foreign Affairs where he was vice-minister.

The junta limped on, under fire from both the left and the right. In February 1980, the attorney general, Mario Zamora, was assassinated in his home. Major Roberto D'Aubuisson had publicly denounced him as a member of the FPL. It was a ludicrous charge, because Zamora was a Christian Democrat of long standing. But coming from D'Aubuisson, the charge was Zamora's death warrant.

D'Aubuisson was a busy man. Even though he'd been fired from command of military intelligence, he spoke publicly on the radio and privately in barracks all over the country, all condemning the junta and its members. It was clear he was conspiring against it, and also that he had powerful friends.

Then on March 24, 1980, Archbishop Romero was shot just after saying Mass at the chapel in the Divina Providencia hospital. I heard the news while teaching English at the cultural center. Later on I went downtown with Enrique Barrera and a *compañero* named Ricardo. We made our way to the Palacio Nacional, the presidential building that faces the Metropolitan Cathedral, and found the square was so packed you could not move—tens of thousands of the common people of El Salvador, women, children, old, young.

Days later, in the same plaza on a hot and sunny morning, we attended Monseñor Romero's funeral procession. It started in the basilica and moved out into the square. At the same time, the popular organizations started an orderly demonstration, marching with banners. Everything was calm. Then all of a sudden there was an explosion, followed by the sound of shooting and bullets pinging off the pavement.

I can still see the crowd moving in slow motion, like a massive wave. I had time to register that some of the shooting was coming from the top of the Palacio behind us, sharpshooters whose heads and shoulders and rifle barrels were visible. Then the slow motion disappeared, and it was pure panic as people were running, screaming, falling, trying to find shelter from the crush of bodies and the confusion. All you could do was be taken up by the rush and carried along, trying desperately to stay on your feet.

Figure 13. Mural dedicated to Monseñor Romero, El Pueblo de Dios en Camino, San Salvador, 1998 (Courtesy of Rachel Heidenry)

The funeral procession turned around, trying to get back into the cathedral. There was smoke all over the place and bodies sprawled on the plaza stones. Women and children were in hysterics, and the screaming was deafening. People suffocated in the crush. Meanwhile the shooting continued, with teargas floating over us.

Enrique was somehow separated from us and I was worried, but Ricardo told me, "Forget about everybody else, you have to get out!" We held each other's hand and headed across the plaza and into the side streets. In my memory, it seems as though I was flying, that I never touched the ground. I was wearing sandals, and one slipped up to hang on my ankle as I ran, my skirt riding up to my waist. But I kept running. Later, we learned that over 30 people were killed and 200 wounded.

Early April, a final alliance came together of all the political and nonmilitary organizations in the Salvadoran Left. This became the Democratic Revolutionary Front (FDR). It included a new faction of Christian Democrats that had split off from the main party when Duarte came back. The FDR supported the armed struggle without itself being a military organization. At the same time, four of the five military organizations came together in a coordinated structure called the DRU (Dirección Revolucionaria Unificada).

Despite all this organizing, the threat to the government was still far stronger

Figure 14. Monseñor Romero funeral attack
(Courtesy of Museo de la Palabra y la Imagen)

from the right than from the left. D'Aubuisson's influence was growing, despite Duarte's going on record saying he was sure that D'Aubuisson had a hand in Monseñor Romero's murder. The newly arrived American ambassador, Robert White, also suspected D'Aubuisson and denied him a visa to the United States.

Yet D'Aubuisson still managed to show up in Washington in April to speak publicly to the American Legion and privately with a number of politicians. It took two days for the United States to expel him. Back in El Salvador he tried to organize a coup, and Majano had him arrested. But despite his implication in the death of Monseñor Romero, and the fact that he was caught with plans for his coup, D'Aubuisson had so much support in the military and on the right that he was released after only three days. He went to Guatemala for a time where the military government welcomed him with open arms. They were conducting their own genocide against the indigenous Maya population.[4]

Colonel Majano and the Juventud Militar lost more and more power. Eventually, in February of the following year, Majano too would be arrested by his fellow officers. Omar Torrijos of Panama intervened on his behalf and got him sent into exile. But whether Majano was in or out made little difference by then: politics had been upstaged by the fighting, as the mass organizations and the guerrilla groups were finally getting together.

The mass organizations continued their strategy of strikes and demonstrations. They also began to arm themselves, though not in the organized and intensive way of the guerrillas. Some momentum built as their demonstrations grew. The largest was organized in June by the Coordinadora Revolucionaria de Masas,[5] and it drew 300,000 people. Nothing had ever happened on that scale before, and it was amazing to see such popular support. The march started in Cuscatlán Park, and it went all the way up Calle 4, about three kilometers, to the Palacio Nacional and the Metropolitan Cathedral. As you go into the center of town the street narrows, so people were packed in tightly.

When the soldiers started shooting I was on the corner of the park, watching this amazing mass of people. Once again, shots rang from the roof of the Palacio. Imagine 300,000 people panicking. It was awful.

Outside El Salvador, the DRU and the FDR jointly created a political and diplomatic mission based in Mexico, which represented the opposition forces of El Salvador to the rest of the world. The mission included three representatives of the guerrillas and four from the major political parties, including Ungo and Rubén Zamora. At that time Dr. Ungo was clearly the most important member of the legal opposition, the one with the greatest clarity. He was also important to the diplomatic work because of his Socialist International connections. People outside El Salvador, shocked by the murder of Archbishop Romero, were receptive to the FDR-FMLN message.

With the creation of the political and diplomatic mission, the opposition could almost claim to have a government in exile. Predictably, in the United States the Carter administration ignored the FDR-FMLN policy initiatives, and Reagan's Central American policy promised to be even more Neanderthal. But the rest of the world seemed ready to listen, and to help. The Socialist International had already announced its support of the FDR in Oslo in June, and Mexico and France recognized the FDR as a representative political force of the Salvadoran people in 1981.

It was at this point that I came back into the MNR, which immediately put me to work as support to the FDR leadership. Most of that was necessarily in El Salvador, but in early November 1980 they sent me on one international trip, which was surely the strangest assignment I ever had. The event was the Socialist International Congress held in Madrid. Due to the diplomatic efforts of Dr. Ungo and Héctor, our struggle in El Salvador was to be a main theme of the congress, and they needed me to represent the MNR at the preceding Women's Conference.

For me, personally, security was more intense than any I'd known before. Officially, I didn't even participate—I was supposedly still in El Salvador! It was too dangerous for me to go as Ana Margarita Gasteazoro, so I traveled and spoke to the conference under another name: Mónica Pancho.

First I flew to Mexico City, where Vera had worked out the trip details, including my name. A Guatemalan Indian woman with the surname Pancho had been killed by the authorities. Vera was very affected by that so she chose Pancho in remembrance. We went out shopping in Mexico City for a suit and a coat, black pants, a few scarves, and black pumps, all very different from my usual clothes. While we were shopping, Vera informed me that Mónica Pancho from El Salvador would give the introductory speech at the Women's Conference.

When we got to Madrid, the security people from the Spanish Socialist Workers' Party (PSOE) took me in hand. Felipe González was not yet in power, and the party still took a lot of security measures because they too had lived underground for many years under the Franco regime.[6]

At the airport, the PSOE people whisked me into a car with darkened glass, and from there we went straight to my hotel. I was a VIP, so my passport and customs stuff was taken care of by someone else. On the way, they began to brief me: "Okay, the first item on the agenda is to change your looks. We're going to paint your hair blond and redo your features. When we're finished even your mother won't know you."

In Mexico, Vera had mentioned a proposal to change my looks and I remember thinking, *What the hell?* But I didn't say anything. Vera was my good friend and she was concerned for me. So in Madrid the PSOE people and Vera drove me to a beauty parlor to tint my hair. The woman at the beauty parlor took one look at my hair, which was down to my waist, and said, "Forget it. We can't dye her hair. It's so black and thick it would be far too much work. And it would probably wreck it." She paused and looked around the room. "Unless you want us to cut it?"

Everyone chorused, "No!"

So there was more discussion, and finally, Vera decided that the solution was to find a blond wig. Meanwhile, they took me back to the hotel and I tried to sleep a few hours. I was badly jetlagged and had various activities scheduled for the next day.

Early the next morning, a woman knocked on my hotel door and announced she was a makeup specialist from a local theater. So while I was still trying to wake up, she made me into someone different. First she applied a thick coating of base makeup. Then she changed my mouth, my nose, my eyelashes, and my eyebrows. Finally came the task of getting all my hair under that damned wig. She had to wrap my hair carefully around my head and pull a nylon stocking over it, and then arrange the wig just so. It was very hot and itched so much that when I finally got to take it off I was almost crazy with discomfort.

The new me was a horrible-looking blonde: Mónica Pancho. It was too weird, and I never got used to the new identity. I remember a reception a few days later, when I saw a very strange-looking woman staring at me and said to myself, *I wonder who that woman is.* It was me, reflected in the enormous mirrors of the reception room!

The subject of my speech was disarmament, the conference's main theme. It was definitely a good propaganda opportunity for someone from El Salvador to give this address, but after being so immersed in my own country's story, it was difficult for me to understand what disarmament even meant. Vera had already written the speech. She's an excellent speechwriter, but very British and journalistic in her style so I had to rewrite it to sound like me.

The night before I gave the speech, I got a lesson on disarmament from Vera and a woman I loved dearly, Irène Pétry. She was a prominent politician in Belgium and had been president of the Socialist International Women for many years. That was her last term, and in fact there had been almost a coup to oust her. So it was quite emotional, and we drank wine and cried a little as we told each other our troubles. But she briefed me, made me read the speech over and over—she understood Spanish—and helped me with intonation. I remember her so fondly: a beautiful woman, white hair and very elegant, who smoked like mad. I still have presents from her like an enormous suitcase she gave me when I was released from prison.

The next day, Felipe González opened the Women's Conference. Then they introduced me, "Mónica Pancho from El Salvador," and I walked up to the podium, feeling very strange and disoriented. I was dressed all in black, with glasses and a scarf around my neck and this ugly stiff blond wig down to my waist.

In front of me were over 500 people. I'm very touched by crowds. Their manifestations of joy or sorrow move me, and even a parade at Disney World can make me cry. Vera and Irène had given me a shot of whisky and a quarter Valium before I went up, because my voice tended to break and I had to be calm. After the first page I was okay. In the applause I could feel admiration for the Salvadoran struggle, and I was very moved that our struggle was at the top of the agenda. It was so different from when we used to struggle with the Chileans to make them see that the Nicaraguan and the Salvadoran struggles were also valid.

After I finished, Felipe González gave me a little hug and said some words about El Salvador and how heroic the struggle was. There was a coffee break and Héctor came over to say, "Puta mano, que fea te ves." How ugly you look. He was my friend so he could say that. In the next session, I saw Ungo come in and sit down at the end of the hall. I was sitting at the presidential table, and I came down to say hello. Congresses are very formal and have a lot of protocol and an agenda, but there is also a lot of movement. Behind the scenes, there's always lobbying in the hallways and in the bars and in the meeting rooms and pressrooms, so it was nothing strange to get up from the table to move around or take a call. Now, my relationship with Ungo was always one of great respect and recognition of his authority. I said, "Hello, Dr. Ungo," and he didn't recognize me at first, so when I went to kiss him he was already holding out his hand to shake. I don't think he was happy with what he saw, but at least he recognized me when he heard my voice.

At another reception, I was standing with a group of very important people, and up came the prime minister of Finland, Mauno Koivisto. I'd seen a lot of him in the Vancouver conference and wondered if he'd recognize me. When someone introduced us, he looked into my eyes and said, "You're Ana." He gave me a big hug and said, "With your eyes you'll *never* be able to hide yourself." Bad for security, good for the ego!

Every morning the makeup lady came to my room and turned me into the very white and very blonde Mónica, and for the rest of my time in Madrid,

Mónica Pancho went to her receptions and gave her speeches and participated in conferences like a good party worker. There are even newspaper photographs of her.

In fact, I didn't do all the things I normally would have done at this kind of event. Quite apart from security considerations, the wig restricted my movements because it was so uncomfortable and difficult to keep on. Madrid is very cold and windy, and if I went out, the wig would blow off. So once I'd taken it off for the day, I refused to leave my room. Whoever wanted to see me had to come to my hotel room. I couldn't do any lobbying, for fear of being recognized.

I wasn't only uncomfortable physically but also with my fake personality. In my international experience, I had learned that I could approach a person, look them straight in the eye, tell them who I was and where I came from, and immediately present my position or request for support. But that was me with my long hair and my eyes clear—Ana Margarita. Maybe an actress could have done it, but not I. They even gave me glasses! They had clear glass and no correction, but it was so different and so hard to look people straight in the eye or make people pay attention to me. I'm an extrovert, but it has to do with my whole person: my hair, my eyes, my Latin look. And here I was a horrible-looking, middle-aged, nunnish teacher. No one turned around to look at me. I had to punch people on the arm to get noticed by people who would normally say hello. There was even a former boyfriend who didn't recognize me. It hurt that he was ignoring me and instead was fascinated with a couple of female representatives from Venezuela.

It was all so uncomfortable that I asked to go home before the congress was over. There were four other MNR people there anyway, so I was given permission.

Back in El Salvador, I continued my work supporting the FDR leadership that remained in the country. Dr. Ungo and Héctor had gone into exile at the beginning of the year, so at this time the FDR was led by five men, the best of the country's opposition figures: Enrique Alvarez, the former minister of agriculture and livestock; my friend Enrique Barrera of the MNR; Juan Chacón of the BPR; Manuel Franco of the UDN; and the labor leader Doroteo Hernández. Between them they had about 50 years of experience in the struggle for change in El Salvador.

And then they were gone, all of them: arrested, tortured, and murdered on the same day, November 27, 1980, and their bodies dumped on the roadside 25 kilometers from San Salvador.

Imagine something like that in North America or most European countries. It's as if George Bush decided to send in the Green Berets to kill four of the top Democrats, plus the head of the United Auto Workers and John Kenneth Galbraith for good measure.

The FDR leaders met every week in different places for security. Each organization took turns finding a secure place for the weekly meeting. Since the political parties in the FDR did not have arms, it was up to organizations like the Bloque to look after them at meetings, but it was still a dangerous job getting the five of them together. The procedure was that the FDR leaders were picked up at different times the day of the meeting and spent the night at the meeting site so there would be no suspicious movements to catch the attention of the police. For example, Enrique could be picked up at 6:00, then two hours later a pickup of someone else, and another the next morning.

I know all this because I was in charge of security and organization for Enrique Barrera. He had been shot at several times already, once while in his car. But it wasn't just him or other leaders. The repression had reached new levels. It seems incredible to say, but almost a thousand members of the popular organizations were killed or disappeared in October 1980 alone. We didn't know the exact numbers at the time, but we knew it was bad, so bad that in a way death had become normal.

In the early evening of November 26th, I drove Enrique to his pickup place for the meeting. This time the *conecte* was on the street. We were always changing our security methods, and we had started doing "walking *conectes.*" That meant that you and your contact met after walking 100 yards from opposite directions. We always gave one another a 10- to 15-minute leeway, so I let Enrique off and after 15 minutes I drove around the block to check. He wasn't there, so I thought everything was okay.

I don't know why, but I decided to go around the block a few more times. As I was driving, I saw a van that looked familiar, and I had a feeling that something had gone wrong. So I waited a few more minutes and then went back to the same street where I had dropped Enrique. And he was there!

"Thank God you're here," he said as he jumped into my car.

"What happened?" I asked. "How were you going to get home?"

Enrique was furious. He'd made the connection and got into a waiting car and driven off, only to be told they hadn't been able to find a secure place to meet. So they dropped him off again, saying that the meeting would be held the next day at the Externado de San José, the Jesuit secondary school a few blocks from the US embassy.

He was absolutely right to be angry. In the first place, Enrique was a huge man with a full beard, and he was very visible and recognizable. Dropping him on the street without any way to get home was dangerous and irresponsible.

Someone like Enrique couldn't just take a taxi—most of the drivers were police informers. And to be told that the meeting would be at the Externado! The Externado had been used too many times and it posed a number of problems for security. In fact, it had been decided previously not to use the Externado again.

So I drove away with him ranting about the group responsible for this meeting's arrangements: "Why aren't they worrying more about security?" he said. "Security is not something that happens easily, it doesn't fall out of the sky!"

The next morning I called Enrique early, and he gave me the time and place to pick him up. So I took him to the Externado a little before 9:00. The meeting was to be held in the offices of the Socorro Jurídico, the legal aid office run by the Church. Another *compañero* was there, and we stopped in the parking lot and complained about the security.

That day I had to go to an MNR propaganda meeting at the University of Central America, but said that I would come back at noon to bring them pizza for lunch. I watched the *compañero* and Enrique walk into the school, but as I drove off down the Avenue of April 25th, I was struck by the number of military trucks in the street. It gave me an uneasy feeling. There was a union office around the corner from the Externado that had been searched and ransacked recently, and I thought maybe it had something to do with that. But I went on to the university, where the meeting was held in the office of Italo López. We kept the radio on very low in the background, and at around 11:15 a special news bulletin came on. It said the FDR leaders had been arrested having a meeting at the Externado de San José. Just that, no more, no less.

Such a blatant arrest by the government had always been a possibility and we knew exactly what had to be done. We immediately started writing press releases and calling all the newspapers and radio stations with statements and denunciations, demanding the leaders' immediate release. That was standard: the more fuss you made and the faster you made it, the better the chance of embarrassing the government into releasing detainees or allowing them to be visited. At that time the radio and TV were more open than the newspapers and gave more information about what was going on in the country. So we concentrated on them.

At first we treated it as a case of unjust arrest—an official action that would have to be acknowledged by the authorities. It never occurred to us that they had been kidnapped. We simply could not believe that the regime would do anything to them.

But as the afternoon wore on, we got more and more perplexed and worried. There were radio bulletins every five minutes, but without any new information. We called the minister of defense, the army, the Policía Nacional, the Guardia Nacional. No one admitted to having them.

Finally, that evening at 8:30 or 9:00, the radio reported that their bodies had been found, abandoned on a dirt road about 25 kilometers from San Salvador. Five bodies, all showing signs of torture. The announcement said they were found by the Guardia Nacional, and the bodies were taken to a funeral home, the one where all the bodies of the disappeared seemed to end up, especially those killed by the Guardia Nacional.

A couple of *compañeros* and I drove to the funeral home to identify the body of Enrique and take him away. The radio had said that all five had been tortured, but I was not prepared for what I saw. Enrique Barrera had been castrated and strangled with barbed wire. He was covered with bruises. The tall body of Enrique Alvarez was shapeless from the number of bones that had been broken. I had seen bodies that had been tortured before, but it was different to see someone who was close to me.

Next priority after identifying the body was to take care of his family. Enrique was married, with a four-year-old son. For their safety, his wife and son had to be taken out of the country right away. As this was a political murder, we then took over all the funeral arrangements.

And though it was a horrible shock to all of us, we had to get the story into the international press and get as much solidarity as possible from the international community. US ambassador Robert White condemned it. The funeral was held three days afterward in the Plaza de la Libertad, the scene of so many other bloodily repressed demonstrations, and everybody was terrified. The danger was huge and attendance very light.

In the following days the full story came out. The kidnappers were all dressed in military uniforms and had come to the Externado in two trucks. The Externado was on summer vacation, so the students were gone but the offices were open. People were in the teachers' rooms on the ground floor. The soldiers made everyone lie on the floor facedown and left a guard covering them before they moved on. They did this quickly and quietly room by room, floor by floor, putting people on the floor and leaving them guarded. Finally they found the meeting on the third floor. The FDR leaders were caught completely unaware. They hadn't heard a thing.

The military never took any responsibility. The government never took any responsibility. And the repression continued unabated. It was open season on opposition members. Lists were pasted on lampposts in the streets containing the names of people who were the next to be killed by the death squads.

Other lists were published in the newspapers saying things like, "The following hundred people will be killed by the Mano Blanco . . ."[7]

Ungo had immediately taken Enrique Barrera's place as the MNR's representative on the FDR. Within days his name appeared on a list, but he had already left El Salvador, going first to Nicaragua and then to Mexico where he set up the MNR's office in exile.

He wasn't the only one. Many people in the MNR came up on the lists and had to leave. It meant that other people had to take their place in the party operations in El Salvador, so there was quick movement up the echelons of the MNR. That's why I got so much responsibility so fast.

There were so many deaths, someone had to take over. Those of us who remained had to take the same security measures as the clandestine militants of the guerrillas. It meant living double lives, with assumed names and constantly changing movements to prevent allowing a death squad to choose the moment in which to assassinate you. We emerged as our public selves only at meetings and press conferences. I was public when I spoke to the foreign journalists as an MNR representative, but I was another person with another driver's license when I left the hotel.

But that was nothing new to me. Unknown to my *compañeros* in the MNR, I had already been living a double life for a year and a half.

8

~

Double Life

I never knew who Sebastián really was, not even his legal name, until we were arrested. By that time he had been sharing my house for a year, and my bed for eight months. To know so little about your lover may sound crazy, but being involved in armed struggle against a system like El Salvador's, it makes perfect sense. Compartmentalization—one of the absolute basics of clandestine security—means limiting to an absolute minimum your knowledge of one another's identities and activities. You only know what you need to know to carry out your task properly. The less you know, the safer you, your organization, and your *compañeros* will be. What you don't know you can't reveal if you're arrested.

When we met, Sebastián had been living the clandestine life for seven years. He comes from Aguilares, the town where Christian base communities originated and where Padre Grande worked and was killed. Sebastián had been his student in the seminary and was close to Padre Grande. He was typical of so many young men in Latin America who joined armed struggles during the 1960s and 1970s, whose first involvement was through church and student organizations.

Sebastián was recruited to the movement while studying at the University of El Salvador, where he became a member of a student organization, the AGEUS. Every corner of the campus was full of graffiti from the various groups, each faction with their particular acronym, each fighting for hegemony. That forest of acronyms was what Fidel Castro once called the "alphabet soup of El Salvador." You'd need to dedicate yourself full-time to keep track of all the organizations.

Sebastián qualified as a teacher and taught high school during most of the 1970s. He'd been a member of ANDES, the teacher's union, but by the time we met his covert work was full-time. He was married and had a daughter, but he and his wife had been separated for years and she lived in the United States.

But I didn't know any of this. Back in 1977, when I got involved with the MNR, I'd hoped it would be a democratic alternative like the social democratic parties of Europe. But even then the party was getting smaller and smaller. People were afraid to come to meetings and afraid to be seen with anybody who was a public figure. It was understandable—political activity was dangerous, not just with the MNR but all parties and organizations on the left. Even the Christian Democrats, the least threatening to the status quo, lost hundreds of members to the death squads. Not dozens—hundreds!

Maybe it was naive in the first place to hope that the legal route would work. If you looked at the previous 50 years of El Salvador's political history, it was filled with fraud and military dictatorship. El Salvador hadn't lived under rule of law for years; essentially, only the rich had rights.

So the MNR didn't have a popular base, and the party was neither large nor powerful. True, it was influential because among its members were leading intellectuals and professionals: university professors, trade union leaders, and a few students and people like me. What we mostly produced was paper: manifestos and analyses and other documents. We never connected with the *campesinos* or the urban workers except through their leaders.

What I came to question was the wisdom of the MNR's efforts. It was obvious to me that the only thing the government and the Right understood was force—I mean bullets. And the bullets had to be aimed accurately, and there had to be lots of them, and they had to be organized with an overall strategy.

By mid-1979 I just wanted to take up a gun and join the guerrillas. The step was very serious, and I had given it a lot of thought.

I was still taking a few courses part-time at the university, hanging around a couple of people who I thought had something to do with the political-military organizations. It wasn't that difficult because by this time various groups had become strong, although not operating openly, and you could easily find someone and say, "Hey, I'd like to collaborate with your organization."

I chose the FPL because of its discipline, secretiveness, and consistency. I knew what they did and why from the newspapers because all of their actions were followed by signed announcements. I didn't want to get involved with the Bloque street actions, even though I had a lot of friends trying to get me to work with them: classmates, artists, teachers, housemates. I didn't want to be part of the coalition of popular organizations, even though I understood the power they had. And I didn't like the Christian base communities either because of my distrust of Christianity.

Perhaps it was elitist or bourgeois of me, but I wanted the thing that was harder to get into. I made several attempts to join. At first no one paid attention to me, and I got quite frustrated waiting. Once or twice someone gave me some tasks and said they'd make the next *conecte*. I did the tasks—collected all the articles on agrarian reform, for example, or read the documents of the organization. I waited for follow-up contact at the appointed places, but no one ever showed. As I look back on it, I don't think it was because they were testing me. I didn't realize then that it's actually difficult for organizations to bring someone new in and start giving her work. There was so much to do, and so many of us trying to make *conectes*.

A *conecte* is a contact with someone you don't know and who doesn't know you. Usually it's a piece of paper where you have a *seña* and *contraseña*—sign and countersign. A typical *conecte* might have each of you holding a *National Geographic* magazine in your right hand. That's the *seña*. Then, if you are the one who has been called to the meeting, you speak first, using words that have been set beforehand: "Excuse me, could you tell me where I could change some German marks?" The reply might be: "We only use colones here, try the bank."[1] That's the *contraseña*. Classic security measures that have been around for as long as people have been conspiring against each other.

As the police discovered the methods we used, making *conectes* got very sophisticated and creative. There are funny stories, like the guy whose *seña* was "Gallito," a mint candy that's cheap and popular in El Salvador, and his place to meet his *conecte* was the bus stop in Apopa. But he took a live rooster—because *gallito* literally means "rooster." So his *conecte*, an urban fellow, had a little package of green- and white-striped mints in his hand and the other, from the country, a live rooster. Using *señas* and *contraseñas* became an everyday thing, and that's where creativity comes in. As *conectes* were burned, you constantly had to create new ones.

It took about a month before I finally met Sebastián. The *conecte* that led me to him came through a friend who later disappeared. He gave me a piece of paper with the date, time, place, and the *seña* and *contraseña*.

I went to an old cafeteria called Bruno Veri with fine Italian pastries that my grandmother always served. I stood at the entrance for a moment looking around, very nervous. Everything at that moment felt brand new. My underground life was beginning and I realized that I would be doing things that were totally illegal. Looking around, I noticed a man sitting at one of the tables and I immediately hoped it was him I'd be meeting. He was casually reading but his whole aura was staunch and serious. I stood a second more, noting that he was in his early 30s but very old-looking because of his seriousness. Almost totally bald, with glasses and a thick moustache. He looked like an intellectual, or perhaps a priest.

I took all this in before I noticed that he had the *seña* on the table, a *Time* magazine. My *contraseña* was the Mongol II yellow pencil in my hand. I walked over to his table and said, "Excuse me, did you bring the coffee for the party?"

"No, I didn't bring it, I was too busy." That was the reply as it had been written, word for word. It had to be exact; if not, the *conecte* was blown. And so I sat down.

Sebastián began with, "So you are interested in working with us." It was clear that he already knew a lot about me—that I worked with the MNR, spoke English well, and that I had been to Cuba for the Youth Festival. Not that it's so hard to get information about someone in a small country like El Salvador.

He explained certain regulations: the rules of compartmentalization, the need for security, my pseudonym, who I would answer to—my *responsable*. Finally he said, "Okay, you're going to have to demonstrate how much you want to give." I told him that it was a question of life and death, and I was willing to go all the way.

From that half hour with Sebastián, I knew I was part of something. He was exactly the sort of person I wanted to find: disciplined and serious, though dogmatic. With him, I felt that absolute strength and conviction about doing whatever needed to be done.

I almost immediately went underground full-time. My first tasks were largely logistical. I would be ordered to find a safe house for a meeting and to get people into the house at different hours so that no one would suspect that there was a group together. One way was to organize a party at someone's house, except the party was a meeting. It wasn't easy, but my enthusiasm, and my need to show that I wanted to be accepted, was enormous. I knew what I was doing, aware that I was risking everything, risking my life.

One time Sebastián called and said, "We need to take some people up to the mountains. Can you find a car?" I couldn't use my car because it was a Volvo, and we needed something that wouldn't be recognized. So I borrowed my sister-in-law Judy's car. She had a VW and it was perfect. The task was to take from 10:00 in the morning to 3:00 in the afternoon. Judy taught at the American School, so I would have her car back by 3:00, when she finished teaching. But it turned out that the trip wasn't that easy, and I came back at about 8:00 at night with the car muddy to the roof. I'd left my car in the American School parking lot, but she hadn't used it and had walked home.

My brother Javier was furious. He said it was the last time they would lend me anything. By then I realized that he had strong suspicions that I was "doing things that I shouldn't be doing."

I gave no explanation other than I went to a farm to drop off a friend—which wasn't a lie. But I'm sure he wondered, Why on a weekday when I should be working would I borrow a car when I have a car and bring it back like that? Judy's still angry about it and still believes that I was putting the whole family in danger.

After that there was no way. I had "burned" them and there was no further chance of cooperation. We call that "quemar colaboraciones."

But actually, with my family, there was something else that really did it—what I call the avocado story. It was Judy's birthday. She had the habit of serving dinner at 10:00 and I knew the party would go on and on. On that particular evening, I had to be home at that hour because of security and the danger involved in traveling alone to Santa Tecla.

Now, my brother and sister-in-law had an enormous avocado tree that produced a huge number of large avocados. As well, they shared a little farm with my mother that produced a lot of lemons and oranges and bananas. My sister-in-law's servants loved me dearly, and every time I visited the maid would collect a bag of fruit for me to take home. At that time I was hoarding food because there were so many people to be fed at my house, and at different safe houses. In the kitchen was an enormous basket with about a hundred avocados, and Doña Angela—she's now about 86 and getting tinier every day—said, "Niñita Ana hay fruta—¿le preparo una bolsa?" Ana, child, there's fruit, should I make up a bag for you? I got excited and said yes, and she prepared two big bags with lemons and avocados.

Eventually it was time for me to explain that I had to leave before eating.

I said that I had to get home, that it was dangerous to be on the road.

Judy said, "Come on, why are you leaving? You've always stayed here until 3:00 or 4:00 in the morning."

She followed me into the kitchen, where she saw the two bags that Doña Angela had prepared.

"What's this?"

She got really angry—threw everything on the floor or back into the big baskets. Then she handed me one avocado.

"This is for you," she said. "I am not feeding any of your communist friends."

She and I had been close until then, despite everything, but that was the breaking point. I felt really hurt and stopped talking to her. Looking back, of course, I understand her reasons. She was protecting her family.

We didn't talk for many months until just before my father died, a few days before I was arrested. We were both very moved, standing over him as he lay in his mechanical bed. He said he wanted us to be friends again. He told me he disliked the attention that I was causing by ignoring her so publicly, and he wanted us to make up. She apologized as well.

My close friends were becoming angry at me too, the ones who were not involved in anything political. They were resentful about what they saw as my rejection of them. That's the cost of a double life. But others were willing to help. With each task, you add to your network of people who are willing to do things, those who suspect but don't know and don't want to know, but are willing to help.

When I talk about support I'm talking about food, studios, cars, money. The logistics were so enormous that the movement could not have survived without the support of these people. I was just a tiny piece of a network that was endless.

I got training from other people, mostly around urban security—how to notice if someone is following you, how to check and recheck—all the basic security measures in urban guerrilla warfare. We had group lessons in different houses, when we usually used *capuchas*, hoods, so that we didn't see each other. There were also long seminars or study groups on the *línea*, the strategic line of the party. Logistically, it meant a lot of work to get people together who weren't supposed to look at each other or eat together. You had to get them into the house at different hours so that no one would suspect that there was a meeting. It wasn't easy.

I soon started working on propaganda. The task might be to write up a paper or make a radio communiqué out of a set of documents—not hard, as I already had three years' experience doing this for the MNR. But what *was* different was the greater plan these tasks fit into. For example, when we finished writing and recording a communiqué, other parts of the organization would take over radio stations! They'd burst in armed and masked, tie up the announcer and everyone else, put the recording on the air and leave immediately. The recording might be 10 minutes, repeated and repeated, but some of the communiqués could be long—messages from the guerrilla leaders, for example. Sometimes we'd have a 45-minute or hour-long tape, and if the police didn't come, it would go on and on.

When you're underground, you don't know anything about what others do, and you're not curious—at least not overtly. But of course you know something is going to happen. And when the radio began to transmit a *comunicado* you'd worked on, it was very exciting: "Oh man, they made it!"

We also recorded music from different groups to sell to friends and solidarity organizations. Some of the groups still exist, like Yolocambo Ita. For the actual recordings and the use of a studio, we depended on collaborators. A friend in a commercial radio station or a studio might give you a few hours in the middle of the night.

Figure 15. Radio Farabundo Martí (Courtesy of Museo de la Palabra y la Imagen)

My job was reproducing the cassettes, printing covers, and distributing them. The cassettes were very successful, but it was dangerous to sell them. I'd bring five of them to a collaborator and say, "Here's five, sell them." And they'd bring back the money. One cassette was called *El Pueblo Armado*, and we'd make about a hundred copies at one time, and then another hundred if we could recuperate the money.

I did a lot of work when we were setting up the clandestine radio station Radio Farabundo Martí. My part was writing scripts and helping make certain decisions. I knew that I was working for the radio, but I never knew where it was going to be transmitted. I just knew I had to produce—preparing scripts for radio programs, and organizing our announcer, Isabel, and getting her to the studio and picking her up. Or thinking up jingles or slogans like the famous Chilean one "El Pueblo Unido Jamás Será Vencido"—"The People, United, Will Never be Defeated." It was a lot of creative work. We did booklets and comic books that explained what was happening at the time and a lot of flyers for demonstrations. Once these leaflets were written, I didn't know where they were printed or how they were distributed.

Soon I became second to Sebastián in our cell. It wasn't that I wanted power; it had more to do with maturity and organizational capacity. I had a great facility for organizing things. I didn't know how everything happened, but if I heard the taking of a radio station, I would realize whose voice it was or hear a script I'd written. It would fill my heart with pride, which I had to forget immediately because it was *my* life, *my* secret, and I didn't have anyone to discuss it with.

I was soon so involved I dropped my courses at the university. The organization didn't pay me anything but I had to earn money, so I continued teaching English to international telephone operators. At the time I was making 10 dollars an hour, which was excellent money. I did three hours in the morning and perhaps another hour in the afternoon so the rest of the day was my own. Forty dollars a day was a lot. The activists in our organization who received a stipend got 125 colones a month—at that time about 50 dollars.

The organization paid the rent for the house, but everybody collaborated in getting anything they could get. For instance, they might pick up a pound of cheese and some tortillas for lunch. I'd stop by my mother's for lunch and go through her refrigerator. She bought meat once a month, and I'd put cuts of meat in a plastic bag while she was taking a nap. My nana would tremble, saying, "She's going to accuse me of taking it," and I'd say, "No, just tell her it was me."

With Sebastián, it was strictly work and security in the beginning. I wasn't particularly attracted to him and didn't think much about him in other ways.

He was my teacher in everything about underground survival. Safe houses were usually "clean" at that time, and if the police or Guardia Nacional came, we were not to put up resistance. But I did carry a .45 caliber pistol, and there was always a chance I might have to use it.

One day we were talking about urban self-defense, and Sebastián said, "If you are going to carry a gun, you have to be willing to use it." He went on to demonstrate. "Okay, this is the situation. We are in the street. You have a man at point-blank range with his hands up. You don't know yet what he's going to do but no matter what, do not let go of the gun. Keep your finger on the trigger. Because remember, you are going to use it if necessary."

He tried to take the gun away from me, just to show how easy it was. But I guess I wanted to show how dedicated I was to following orders. He'd said, "Don't let go," and I didn't let go, but held on very tense, very tight. He almost broke my finger because it stayed on the trigger, which cut my finger open all around the second knuckle. It was pretty ugly, and he felt so bad.

It was the first time he was sweet to me. He didn't know if we should go to the hospital, or get a doctor, and have it sewn up. Finally we just gave it first aid and it got better, but my index finger was useless for a week. And I still have that scar!

9
~

Making a Movie

One of my first tasks for the organization was to be assistant producer on a 16 mm feature film, *El Salvador: El Pueblo Vencerá*.

It was in 1979, while one of the biggest general strikes in the history of El Salvador was going on. I got a call from Sebastián telling me to meet him in a hotel downtown, and there he would give me a task. He didn't say exactly, only that I was going to take over responsibility for what he called a "character" from Costa Rica, for a task that had something to do with communications. I came to the Hotel Terraza in Colonia Escalón, wearing a Hindu skirt and blouse—pretty much what I wear now, sandals and jeans and so on. The Costa Rican turned out to be the actor and director Oscar Castillo. Sebastián told me that from then on I would work with Oscar, doing whatever he needed. We had a long meeting about where he was going to live and how long he was going to stay and the arrangements for the cameramen, Diego and Papo, who were coming. One of them, Diego de la Texera, is now a very famous Puerto Rican cinematographer and director. That meant there was a whole team to look after, so the logistics were going to be complicated. By the end of the meeting I knew I was going to be working on a movie, but not what type of movie.

When the meeting ended I took Oscar to the house where he was to stay. And on the way we talked a bit and made friends. Oscar is a very sophisticated man, a citizen of the world. I liked him and was very impressed with him almost instantly. And he was curious about me. He asked if I'd lived in Europe, because he noticed I didn't shave my underarms, and other little things like that. I was using my pseudonym and he used a pseudonym the whole time he was there—I don't think I ever called him Oscar the whole time he was in El Salvador. I called him Rubén.

The people providing the house were a family who were collaborating with the organization. Otherwise I didn't know anything about them. I took him in and introduced us, and the lady showed Oscar his room. Then Oscar called me over to a corner and said, "No, I refuse to stay here." It simply wasn't adequate, he said. Phoning would be difficult, getting in touch with me would be difficult. What would his cover story be, staying in this home with this family?

We had to get in touch with Sebastián, and the only way to do that was to go back to my house and wait for a call. On the way back Oscar said, "Let's stop and buy food for dinner." So we stopped by a gourmet shop and he bought a bottle of wine and some cheese and pâté and crackers. Typical Oscar. We had dinner and waited till Sebastián called, and in the meantime we told each other our life stories. He was an actor, divorced a year or two earlier, with three daughters between 6 and 14 whom he adored. He had worked with the Chilean filmmaker Miguel Littín and with the Sandinistas. He was open and didn't follow security rules—as a Costa Rican he believed he didn't have to. But he kept the details of the film close to his chest.

When Sebastián called, Oscar talked to him and then I got on the phone. Sebastián was embarrassed. Was it okay if Oscar stayed in my house? Could the organization ask this of me for two or three days while an alternative plan was made? Sure, I said.

Three days later, Sebastián asked if I would keep Oscar at my house during the whole project. It was a problem to find another place, but it was no problem for me—Oscar and I got on very well and are friends to this day.

In the end, the project took six weeks. Ninety minutes of finished film requires hours and hours to be shot. The film equipment had to be brought in from the United States, so we planned how to pick up the equipment from the airport, how to move it from place to place, how to get it through the army checkpoints to the guerrilla camps.

Oscar was the producer, not the cameraman. He didn't spend much time in the mountains, although sometimes I would drive him somewhere to be picked up in the morning and then fetch him at night. I was in charge of getting materials, which leads me to a story I've never told anyone before: I was the thief who stole the book *San Salvador at the Beginning of the Century* from the National Museum.

Oscar already knew a number of sources that he needed for the film. They included that book, old family movies, anything that could compare the lives of the people and the oligarchy. *San Salvador at the Beginning of the Century* was a precious book of photographs of San Salvador and its high society. Only 21 copies were ever published, and it was extremely important to the film to give a historical perspective. I had a friend at the library of the National Museum. When I visited the museum, they let me have the book for a half hour at a time before I had to hand it back. But we needed the book to reproduce some of the photographs.

I asked to borrow the book, but it was impossible. Finally, one day at noontime I was sitting at a table looking at the book. I turned around to check the room: everybody was at lunch. I closed the book, put it in my bag, and left.

About a week later my friend called me and said, "You stole the book."

"Which book?"

"You have to give it back. They're going to take it out of my salary."

It was an extremely expensive book. Unfortunately, by this time the book was in Costa Rica, because we were sending material there daily to Oscar's production team, in a studio run by Oscar's partner at the time.

I said, "No, I didn't do it."

She said, "But you did. You came in here on"—and she gave the exact date and time—"and the book disappeared right after you left."

I said, "It wasn't me. How can you prove that I stole it?"

It suddenly struck me just how big my commitment was. I felt very bad, because she was a very good friend and all she was thinking about at the time was to avoid problems. But I justified it by saying to myself that this was her contribution to the revolution. I couldn't tell her but I hoped she would understand, and it had to be done. That was it.

I saw her again but we never brought it up. I think she imagined what was going on. We had the same group of friends and by that time most of us were involved. She's in the States now, in San Francisco, I think. One of our best friends, the guy who introduced her to me, disappeared shortly after I was arrested.

And while I am confessing things, there is also the story of Señor Massi.

I knew of Señor Massi because I'd gone to school with his children at the American School. He came to El Salvador from Italy years earlier as a trainer for the air force. He was the one person in the country who had filmed the most important presidential inaugurations, weddings, *quinceañeras*, and so on, and we knew that we had to get these films. The plan was to try to get stuff from him voluntarily, so Oscar and I took on a front. He became a movie producer for Columbia Pictures, doing a movie on coffee production in Latin America.

Creating a front meant producing business cards, thinking up a whole story, training ourselves for what we'd say, how we'd look around the room, how we'd get in touch with him. My part was to get the appointment with him. And that's where my last name came in very handy because I could just call up—"Señor Massi, this is Ana Margarita Gasteazoro, daughter of José Gasteazoro." He knew who I was.

"Well sure, come right over," he said. So we went and watched movies for a whole day with him. He was charmed by me and wanted to show me his films. "Do you know so-and-so?" he'd ask, and out would come the Valdoque-Dueñas wedding, Poma family weddings, this and that inauguration. I'd sit being charming while Oscar was punching me under the table indicating "YES, I WANT THIS ONE!" and I'd be writing down secretly what we wanted and where it was.

He had rooms and rooms of 16 mm film, and we wanted footage for fill-in, to make parallels between the oligarchy and the people, and we tried to persuade him to let us borrow these movies. For days we went back to explain the project and beg him. But the answer was no. The collection was historical. He was happy to show it to us, but not to lend it.

After almost a week, we knew that the only way was to make a map of where everything was in his house and pass it on to another part of the organization. I don't know what happened after that, and I never asked. That's compartmentalization. Some of that material showed up in the film.

I never saw Señor Massi again, but he must have seen me in the newspaper when I was arrested and figured it out. It's why I'm a little nervous about going back to El Salvador. I don't know if he is alive or dead.

A lot of my work was simply getting the crew where they needed to be. But as I mentioned, we were right in the middle of a general strike. There were soldiers all over the place. One day our crew—the Puerto Rican, the Costa Rican, and the Salvadoran—was supposed to shoot the *tugurios*, the shanty towns, coming in along the railroad track into San Salvador. I was supposed to pick up the three guys in Soyopango, the last stop before the terminal station. They were carrying all kinds of professional film equipment—16 mm cameras, not video like you would have today.

The pickup had to be perfectly scheduled—we couldn't have them standing around with this equipment. My father had worked in that area years before, in a factory called Algodonera Salvadoreña that was in front of the station, so I didn't reconnoiter the area first. I was sure I knew it because I'd been there many times. So I just followed my instructions for the pickup and drove there in my red Volvo. As I reached the Algodonera and turned left to pick them up on the other side of the train tracks, I realized that the whole site had become a junkyard for the crashed cars that the National Police dragged away after accidents. In other words, it was not just a junkyard but the National Police's junkyard.

The only way to cross over the tracks to the train station was through the junkyard. *Well,* I said to myself, *here I go.* I opened the junkyard gate and drove along the narrow winding roads in between the piles of cars. Before long I could see in my mirror a man on a bicycle pedaling furiously behind me. A policeman. I parked beside the train tracks and he rode up and stopped.

"Hola," he said.

"Hola, how are you doing?" I replied, as *simpática* as I could be.

"What are you doing here?"

"Well, you know, I thought there was a road to the Soyopango train station."

"No," he said, "there's no access except through here. You did the right thing. But why did you come here?"

"Ah, well. I'm waiting for these three journalists that I think are on this train. But I'm not sure. You see, one of them is the boyfriend of a friend of mine and she asked me to pick them up."

"Well, this is the right place," he said, but then he started asking me where I lived and telling me that I was a very good-looking woman and reached out and touched my hand, which I allowed, and I kept up the chatter all the while thinking, *The train has got to get here—where is the damn train?* He was on his bicycle, leaning up against the car and I was stuck there waiting. We were flirting, and he asked me out, and I went along with it.

"You can't shake me off, you know," he said. "That car is distinctive, and I know your license plate."

"Don't worry about it," I said, "I'd never stand you up." And thinking, *Where is the damn train?*

The train came. The three guys jumped off the train and got into the car.

"See you," I said. I turned the car around so fast that I almost knocked him off his bicycle and rushed out of there. My adrenaline was running after all that tension, and when the guys asked, "Who was that man you were talking to?," I just snapped, "Shut up and let's get out of here." Away we went in my old Volvo.

Now that story should mean nothing, because the pickup was successful. But that same year, on the 15th of September I had a car accident. I knocked over a cyclist on the road to Santa Tecla, who turned out to be the brother of a policeman. And the man from the junkyard found me again.

It was a stupid accident. It was early in the morning, on a day when I had a lot to do. I'd had something at 5:30 but after that I could spend the whole day at home working. I was driving along the Santa Tecla road at about 90 kilometers an hour, and ahead I saw these two guys on bicycles. They were weaving back and forth along the road as cyclists do. It was a two-lane highway so I moved into the left lane to pass them and started braking, but it wasn't enough. The next thing I knew one of the bicycles was flying over the car.

I stopped. Several things worked out in my favor. First of all, the guy was 16 years old and he wasn't supposed to be on the road—I learned later that he was riding a stolen bicycle! A crowd gathered, and people were yelling, "Arrest her, take her keys."

But I reacted really fast. The guy I'd hit was stunned but he sat up, and I said, "Get in the car, I'm taking you to the hospital immediately." And that's what I did. I said very firmly, "Everybody MOVE! This man is going to the hospital."

When we got to the hospital, I was shaking. I'd never had a bad accident before. Eventually the guy I'd hit came out with a little bandage around his head. It turned out that he'd hurt his ear. But in the meantime, the guy riding the other bicycle had shown up and showed me his ID. He was a policeman from the paramilitary police, ORDEN, and he had called a friend from Santa Tecla to come to the hospital as well. It turned out to be the policeman from the junkyard.

"You stood me up," were his first words. But he saved me from problems with the boy's family. He said, "The kid is 16 years old and he's not hurt, so don't worry about it. First of all you have to get a paper signed by his family saying that they don't hold you responsible, otherwise they can accuse you and pursue you for money for two years. I would suggest you give them some cash." He went with me to take the boy home. Thank God he was underage and not supposed to be driving the bicycle in the street, because in El Salvador you need a license plate for the bike. It was a stolen bicycle, so the parents immediately signed the paper, and the policeman was my witness. He did all this for me that morning, even though I'd stood him up.

Later that day I went to my father and told him what had happened. I said, "Father, I need 300 colones, I have to pay it off or I could get in a lot of trouble." And he gave it to me right off, no suspicions. He knew what it could mean—I could lose the car and the license.

Unfortunately, my car was seriously "burnt," meaning it was too dangerous to use it anymore. And the policeman lived in Santa Tecla, and I'd run into him every once in a while and have to keep putting him off. Fortunately, I found out that he had a girlfriend, and the next time he stopped me I said, "Forget about you and me—I know you're committed to your girlfriend. Please, leave me alone. If you ever finish with her then maybe . . ." I can laugh about it now but at the time it was part of the tension of a double life.

In the middle of June, Oscar had to make some calls to the States and Costa Rica. The general strike was still on and we had strict orders to stay at home, but he had to make the calls so I drove him to the Telégrafo building. Afterward, instead of going straight home, we decided to take a short spin to see what was happening. It was 2:00 in the afternoon and there was not a soul in the streets, though there were tanks. The strike was a complete success.

Then, right in front of the Metropolitan Cathedral, we found Diego's car with both doors open and no one around. We thought that for sure Diego and Papo had been disappeared and spent the next 24 hours in absolute panic.

Finally Diego called the next morning. It had just happened that he was filming, he said, and he got a chance to ride in a helicopter. An army helicopter. The soldiers stopped his car and he gave them his story about reporting on the strike. Then he and Papo got out of the car and asked if they could go for a ride in the *tanqueta*, the city tank with rubber tires. And that went so well they were offered a ride in the helicopter. Hours later they went back to the hotel. They had just left the car at the cathedral because the strike was so complete and there was no one in the street. Some of the best takes of that movie came from that helicopter ride.

As the project reached completion, we had to send all of the equipment back to Costa Rica. It was complicated because at this time you were not allowed to carry a film camera in a car without a placard that said "Press" and a permit from COPREFA, the military's press agency. Oscar and I set out for the airport with a car full of valuable cameras and recording equipment that had no permission to be in El Salvador. And on the way, we were stopped by ORDEN.

The ORDEN guy started to ask me about the equipment, but I said, "Ay, Señor, I desperately have to find a place to pee!"

"Vayanse, Señora!" he said. Off you go, ma'am. That's all it took and we drove on. I don't know if this would work anymore, but I often used "feminine wiles" to get out of heavy situations. Nonetheless, Oscar and I were shaking, both of us. It could have landed us with very serious problems. We could have been disappeared immediately. By then, 10 people were disappearing a day.

Very soon after that we had to go to the airport again. The Guardia Nacional had occupied both the university and a high school that was right next door. We went to have a look, though we didn't have our regular equipment, just a video camera. Diego and Papo went in and started filming, just as a boy was coming down the steps, a high school student, maybe 16 or so. He was begging the Guardia not to kill him but the Guardia opened fire, and as they killed him they realized that someone was filming. It was only about 45 seconds that went on film, a horrible scene.

I was outside in the car waiting for them. Diego and Papo ran out and said, "Let's get out of here!" We got away, but now we had to get that film out of El Salvador as soon as possible to give it to the international press. It meant another anxious trip to the airport, and finding someone who would carry it out, but we managed it, and the killing of the boy came out in the news the next day.

That was when the heat started on us, especially the cameramen, as the government realized that we were up to something. They realized that Diego had taken the film, and that he was the same guy they'd taken up on the helicopter. The car we used had to be hidden for several months. But we were now at the end of the project, and Oscar and Diego got out in the next day or two.

The film took a long time to be edited, to decide what kind of movie to be—a film about just the organization or of the wider struggle. And even then there were problems. When they were processing the film, the interview with Marcial, the top commander of the FPL, turned out yellow. It was because the colors of the FPL are yellow and red and there were flags all over the place where they did the filming, and it affected the color balance. That was a terrible thing to happen because it had been such a feat to organize the interview. Marcial wore a *capucha*, a hood, because at that time he hadn't shown his face and no one knew what he looked like. That part had to be shot again.

The film finally came out and did very well. We managed to distribute video copies in El Salvador, and that is where I first saw it. In 1980 it won the main prize at the Havana Film Festival.

Diego now lives in New York and has done many other movies, but I haven't been in touch with him since *El Pueblo Vencerá*. Oscar and I renewed our friendship after I came to Costa Rica in 1983. Just recently he showed up in Puerto Viejo with his wife Maureen—I hadn't seen him since he left for Paris after his film *Eulalia* premiered in Costa Rica in 1987.

Figure 16. Poster for the film *El Salvador: El Pueblo Vencerá*, 1980

10

Domestic Notes from the Underground

Richard and I had broken up only a few months before Sebastián came to live with me in the little house in Las Delicias, and I knew the neighborhood was beginning to ask questions. Why was my friendly, bespectacled North American no longer around, and who was this new, more taciturn fellow? So, soon after Sebastián moved in, I walked down to the *tienda* near my house to spread a little misinformation.

A *tienda* is a neighborhood store and the most important place to give and get information. Often it's no more than the front room of someone's house, stacked from floor to ceiling with the basics. You order at the counter and the owner retrieves items one by one, marking the price down on a scrap of paper. It's terribly inefficient but obliges you to stop and talk with people. Everybody goes there.

So I joined the crowd at the local *tienda* waiting to buy bread and milk and soap and rice from the owner, Doña Bernarda. Shrewd and sharp-eyed, she knew me well from my three years in Las Delicias, and Richard from the two years we'd lived together—she was probably dying to know why she hadn't seen him recently. When my turn came to add up my purchases, I casually mentioned, "By the way, I got married last week to that guy Sebastián. You've seen him here a few times with me."

"Felicitaciones!" said Doña Bernarda, happy to have new gossip to trade with her other customers. And home I went, knowing that the next day the whole *colonía* would be telling the story: "La loquita de la esquina, se fue el Canadiense y ahora se casó con un Salvadoreño." The odd girl in the corner house—her Canadian left and now she's married a Salvadoran.

The truth was Sebastián moved in because of a security problem where he'd been living. Because of the strict compartmentalization that ruled our lives, he never told me what happened, and I never asked. My guess is that a *compañero* who knew the house had been arrested or disappeared, forcing Sebastián to abandon the place immediately. Whatever the circumstances, the fact was he needed a new place to stay and the Orga, as we called the organization, asked if he could live with me.

Our marriage was simply a *leyenda*, a cover story to satisfy the neighbors. That was absolutely essential in El Salvador. Dozens of people were denounced to the authorities by neighbors who had no evidence, but simply felt that something not normal was going on next door.

I already had a reputation in the neighborhood as a bit bohemian, which is why they called me *loquita*, crazy. It wasn't only because I didn't shave my legs or wear tight dresses and high heels like so many Salvadoran women my age. People knew my house had always been very open—atypical in El Salvador, where family ties are the strongest bonds, and largely govern who you spend time with. At my house, as the neighborhood was well aware, people were always coming and going, staying a while and then leaving. That was Richard's and my lifestyle. This changed when I went underground, and even more when Richard left and Sebastián showed up. Marriage was the most natural way to explain a more quiet life and a new man in my house.

But saying we were married wasn't enough. Sebastián and I had to set about creating and maintaining the patterns of a normal couple. It wasn't hard. The best *leyendas* are the simplest and involve the least amount of invention. We went to the store regularly to buy bread. We were friendly with the neighbors, stopping to chat in front of their small houses even if we were impatient to move on. We even left the house at regular times each morning, as if going to work. I'd normally leave by car at 7:00 and Sebastián in his van at 7:30. Leaving earlier or later required a ready excuse in case someone noticed and asked, no matter how casually. Airtight, simple excuses were vital.

Paradoxically, once the *leyenda* was established, its simplicity offered freedom. Many in the neighborhood already knew my unconventional ways, which gave the crazy girl in the corner house some latitude if she did something out of the ordinary occasionally—working late or disappearing for a few days.

After a few weeks the Orga sent another *compañero*, a young photographer named Tomás, to live with me. So I made another trip to the *tienda* to drop a little more misinformation.

"Doña Bernarda, guess what? Sebastián's brother has come to live with us. He's okay, but I hope he doesn't stay too long."

She clucked sympathetically, so I knew she accepted the story. There aren't enough houses for everyone in San Salvador, so it's quite common for relatives to move in.

But what a change it made to my life. All of a sudden my pretty little house became a security house. The moment three clandestine people come to live together complicated security measures are required.

Unless you've lived it, it's hard to imagine how much these measures change your life. So many details to track—you might easily spend an extra two hours each day just on security.

Sebastián had taught me to vary the routes I took every morning leaving our house in my orange Datsun. For the eyes of neighbors, I always drove off in the same direction, then a few blocks away I'd take new streets. Predictability can be the enemy of security or its friend. Adversaries looking for you know where to look if you are always in the same place at the same time. But if you vary your routine, people who *aren't* looking for you notice that something is out of place. So in some situations, predictability is what helps you become invisible.

It wasn't hard to vary my routes to my teaching jobs or to the MNR office or to my parents' house, but it stole time from my already busy, carefully planned days. If I was moving equipment or propaganda material across town, I spent extra minutes at each end casually checking to see if the street was clear before unloading. More time, say half an hour, I'd take to avoid a risk if I saw police or ORDEN roadblocks—there were many around San Salvador during those years.

A couple of times, when I was really in a hurry, I drove through roadblocks, smiling at the cop and acting normally, even though I was carrying something incriminating. My handbag had a secret pocket and my car a hidden compartment, but it is foolish to take risks if you don't have to. So rather than take chances going through a roadblock, I would take a longer alternative route—which frequently meant rescheduling my *conectes*. Minutes here, a half hour there . . . It added up.

Security governed how we ended the day as well. Without some reason to stay out later, we were all in the house by 7:00 each evening. That way, we'd know something had happened if one of us weren't back on time. The three of us ate together, and then returned to whatever task we'd brought home.

Sebastián remained controlled and business-like, but sharing a house with someone humanizes you. Whereas before he had been my *responsable*—my strongest link to the Orga—I began to see facets not apparent when he'd simply been giving me tasks. He was extremely contrite after nearly breaking my finger during weapons training. His sudden, unexpected sweetness was disarming, and I found myself trying to piece together who he was. He offered no personal information, but living so closely I couldn't help learning things, such as discovering in my propaganda work that he was a talented caricaturist. When I asked, he helped me with drawings for publications or posters. Once a *compañero* viewing a pamphlet I produced for the FDR said, grinning, "Oh, I know who did this!" El Salvador is that small.

After a few months we had to think of yet another *leyenda* because of the periodic visits of Isabel. She was 19, dark-haired and pretty, with a wonderful radio announcer's voice—too bad for her because her life's dream was to go to the mountains and be a *guerrillera*. That's why she'd joined the Orga. She wanted to be "in the war," to prowl around in the jungle and live with a gun in her hands. Instead, she lived with me half the week in Las Delicias and read communiqués on the guerrilla radio. It was a big disappointment for her.

The *leyenda* we chose was that she'd be Sebastián's cousin. That wasn't hard, but Isabel came with an extra security challenge: compartmentalization required that she and Tomás never saw or learned the identity of the other. So we worked out signals that they used while they were both home. If Isabel wanted to go to the bathroom she'd knock twice on her door and Tomás, who might be writing in the next room, would turn his face to the wall as she passed in the corridor. If I made lunch, I often took a plate for Tomás to eat upstairs while Isabel ate with Sebastián and me in the kitchen. It wasn't easy in my tiny house, and unfortunately Isabel proved a handful.

She was a nice girl with her heart in the right place, but she strongly resented orders that kept her out of the "real war." Sometimes she had temper tantrums and refused to leave the house, even refusing food for two days. I was responsible for making sure she kept to the radio's schedule, so she was my problem.

Even worse, the house was so small she had to sleep with me upstairs, while Sebastián and Tomás slept on cots downstairs. It's not much fun to share your bed with a 19-year-old who is furious with you. I tried to explain to Isabel that her contribution to the struggle as an announcer was essential, just as important as that of the person packing a rifle in the jungle. I never quite convinced her, and she got her wish after six months with us. The order came to send her to the mountains, and after that I never heard more about her.

Dealing with Isabel helped me fully understand and accept what I'd been telling her: that winning the war depended on each person doing whatever she was best at, not what her romantic fantasies told her. The myth of the woman guerrilla with a gun in her arms and child on her back is bullshit. Perhaps not total bullshit—a few such women do exist, though a child is no asset in a fire-fight. But what if everyone insisted on carrying a gun? What happens to the organizational tasks, the logistics, the political work a struggle requires?

I realized I was never going to be a *guerrillera*. No matter what organization I worked with, I would always remain a political activist because of my particular skills and qualities. The combat training I got was enough to satisfy the part of me that wanted to take up a gun. Once I realized I contributed most by following orders and doing what I did best, I felt most useful.

Now convinced of the impotence of the legal opposition, I no longer wanted to be part of the MNR. Not that I necessarily wanted it known publicly, but deciding to leave the MNR and turn to the armed struggle took a huge mental shift. But then the struggle sent me back there full-time.

This new assignment moved me to another part of the Orga, in which Sebastián was no longer my *responsable*. I was transferred to the *democráticos*, the part of the Orga in charge of strengthening (and infiltrating) all the democratic organizations of El Salvador, including the MNR.

I had liked having Sebastián as my *responsable*. He was strong and clear thinking, and I respected his knowledge and experience. But the Orga had sensible reasons for me to remain in the MNR. First (and later, crucial to my staying alive), membership in a legal, well-known party provided security for me and my work. It was good cover to be legal. Not that it was a guarantee. As the assassinations of Martín Espinosa and Enrique Barrera had proved, people in legal parties like the MNR risked as much those who were clandestine—maybe more.

Also, staying with the party kept me in touch with what was going on in the legal opposition. It allowed me to participate in decision making and continue working internationally.

Most important, there was a strategic consideration. Despite their differences in ideology and strategy, the Orga felt that as a strategic ally in the struggle, the MNR should be supported and strengthened. The party had to survive because its principles were based on socialism and it sided with the people. It had a solid reputation internationally, and excellent connections with the progressive governments of Europe through the Socialist International. Since I was now experienced politically, I had a lot to contribute.

I had never officially left the party, so returning to it was easy. As always, there was too much to do and too few people to do it. I doubt anyone suspected that I was double. They probably thought I'd simply gotten tired and decided to take it easy for a while. Dr. Ungo was his usual detached and acerbic self, but people like Enrique were glad to have me back in the office again. Perhaps Enrique was the happiest of all; there were lots of people in the office to discuss politics, but who else could talk with Enrique about cooking?

Looking back, I don't have any problems of conscience with this decision. The MNR needed to be strengthened because it was critical for the struggle, and that was what I was doing. There was no ugliness or double-dealing: I was there to work for the MNR, not against it.

I know many others were or are still in my position, leading double lives in both the legal and clandestine opposition. At that time the only guerrilla members whose identities were publicly known were the top *comandantes* like Marcial, Ana María, Joaquín Villalobos, and Fermán Cienfuegos.[1] Otherwise, the organizations allowed people to go public only for very specific propaganda reasons. One was the occasion I mentioned earlier, when José Antonio Morales Carbonell published the open letter to his father, the vice president. Another case was Salvador Samayoa, when he resigned as minister of education and said he was joining the FPL.

Knowing there were others in my position, even if unknown to me, helped me cope with the demands of my double life. And actually, I led triple lives: the semi-clandestine but legal one with the MNR, the totally clandestine one with the Orga, and the staid one of eating lunch with my family most days. Despite my training, maintaining security was mentally taxing, especially on top of unrelated administrative work. I had to concentrate to keep my stories straight and remember what I'd told to whom.

Besides my other duties for the Orga, I was put in charge of three security houses, including mine in Las Delicias. As well as creating and maintaining security procedures, I paid the rent, ensured the houses were stocked with food and furniture, and paid the *compañeros* their monthly stipends. Like me, these *compañeros* led double lives, some much higher in the Orga than I.

A cardinal rule was to abandon a security house immediately if someone didn't show up to a meeting or was arrested. You couldn't sleep there even another night; if the *compañero* was tortured and talked, you could all be arrested. Under torture a person might hold out for days or be broken immediately. However long it took, once it happened the authorities would surround your house within the hour. And they might easily start shooting before giving you a chance to surrender.

It happened to us about six months into living together in Las Delicias. Isabel had just left us and life was more relaxed with just Sebastián, Tomás, and me. Then one afternoon we got a message that Angel, who I'd worked with on a propaganda task, had disappeared. He also had been to my house so we had no alternative but to leave Las Delicias. Just like that, we had to pack up and leave, be gone in 45 minutes. I told my neighbor across the street that we'd decided on the spur of the moment to go to the beach but left it vague about when we'd return. It wasn't much of a story, but it was better than nothing and there was no time for anything else.

I was sorry to leave Las Delicias and my little house with its oddly curved design. It held happy memories: living with Richard, cooking with Enrique Barrera, the excitement of harboring Oscar Castillo during the filming. But I've never dwelt on the past, so I simply focused on getting reorganized quickly.

We quickly found another house in Santa Tecla, but I continued paying rent to keep the one in Las Delicias. Nothing happened, so after a few months the Orga arranged for other people to live there. It wasn't a risk if Angel hadn't known them. Luckily, Angel surfaced in prison, and the message was quickly relayed to the Orga. He was alive, and nothing had happened to us, so the house could still be used.

Sometimes after a security problem or when heavy police activity was nearby, we had to mount watches all night. Everyone did a couple of hours. We had a hammock in the living room of the Santa Tecla house, and you could lie in the hammock on watch or sit or walk around. But whatever you did, you had to be extremely quiet. Living under constant tension leaves you more exhausted at day's end than your actual tasks, so it wasn't easy staying awake. Often, I'd press the cold metal of the gun to my belly to shock myself into keeping awake. But after a while it would warm up and I'd have to pull it from under my shirt to cool off.

If clandestine life sounds grim, in many ways it was. But no matter how dangerously you're living, you can make time for fun. And you must if you want to stay human. There was no TV in the house, but sometimes if we had a few minutes to ourselves Sebastián and I would wrestle. This was not training, just having fun. I grew up with three brothers, so wrestling came naturally. I remembered the tricks that I'd used on my brothers, and they worked the same on Sebastián. For instance, if I let myself go limp, he would get furious and snap, "Come on, wrestle back!" just as they had.

That's how we got involved physically. I never wrestled with Tomás; he was a nice guy and we were like brother and sister. But with Sebastián it was different, and it worried me when I realized I liked him and we were living so closely. It got worse when Sebastián would come up early in the morning, get into bed, and start tickling me.

When Sebastián came into my life I knew he had a relationship, but I was familiar enough with his daily routine to know he barely saw her (much later I found out he was married). I was also aware of the rules of the Orga: no romantic involvement without permission, not even kissing. Very dogmatic, but in the interest of security, sensible. Sebastián knew the rules and stuck to them—in his own way. I guess his interpretation was: no kissing or making love, but you could wrestle and tickle in bed.

So we did, and it was all very platonic. Much of the time he just wanted to talk. He might lie there a few minutes, then get up and that would be it. The trouble was I wanted more. As a liberated, open woman I could admit to myself that it turned me on to wrestle or snuggle, leaving that awful feeling in the pit of my stomach that said I was falling in love.

So one Saturday afternoon I decided the situation was ridiculous. We were still in Las Delicias: Sebastián walked by me on his way out of the house, when I called to him. "Sebastián, I need to talk to you."

He stopped.

I said, "I'm falling in love with you."

His face went white. "It's impossible. I'm leaving this house. Tomorrow. I have other commitments."

"I don't know about your other commitments," I said. "But you like me, I know. We spend most of the time together. You get in bed with me, you're sweet with me, you wrestle with me, you play too rough sometimes, but you're constantly *with* me. In your off hours you don't go to see your woman. You stay because you want to be with me, so let's face it—you like me too." Very straight.

He was just as straight: "This is going to be reported to the Orga today, and tomorrow I'm out of here." And he left for his *conecte*.

The idea of Sebastián leaving the house could have killed me. This is where the contradictions of clandestine life, the reality as opposed to the rules, ambush you. The reality is that you're living together, sleeping in rooms next to each other, and you need love—holding someone and being held. But the rules of clandestine struggle say you must control yourself with the same discipline you bring to the rest of your work. They demand that you be an ascetic. And I'm not.

But I also didn't want to lose him. So when he returned hours later I spoke again.

"Look," I said, "if it's not possible, I'll respect your relationship with this woman, whoever she is. I know in the Orga you can't have two relationships at a time. So let's leave it." And I steeled myself to bear it.

Monday we traveled to La Libertad for work. It's a port town on the Pacific, with long wharfs, fishing boats, and small seafood restaurants. We finished our tasks early and decided to go for a swim in an estuary. I'm a good swimmer and I don't think it pleased him; men often don't like women to be better at sports than they. After a while in the water he started to play rough, tickling me and wrestling hard. I swallowed water, which made me angry, so I coughed and sputtered: "That's not fair!"

He took my face in his hands, saying, "You know, I love you too? And we can sleep together now—we have permission!" So romantic—I was coughing salt water! But such wonderful words to hear.

I remember clearly that first time we slept together . . . with permission. I could feel the tension leaving Sebastián. I suspect he'd felt guilty because he was dedicated to the discipline of the Orga. He'd also been educated in a seminary.

So Sebastián finally began spending the night with me. We even had a little honeymoon. But after we'd slept together several times the Orga ordered us to stop! It seems some step was missed in getting permission.

The Orga brought us in separately. A woman talked to me and a man talked to Sebastián. Both said this: because of my newness in the Orga—I was not yet a full member, not yet sworn in—and because of Sebastián's other unresolved relationship, we should not sleep together anymore.

I reacted badly and was inclined to question the decision, but Sebastián was disciplined and adamant: whatever the Orga said was law.

Soon my new *responsables* in the *democráticos* side of the Orga gave me permission, but Sebastián's *responsables* were not so sure. They thought he was unstable in his relationships and needed more self-control. Weeks passed as we awaited their decision.

We moved from Las Delicias during this period, and Tomás was assigned elsewhere. Sebastián and I now shared a house in Santa Tecla with Geraldo and Mama Mari. Again there were *leyendas* to create. Geraldo was a sweet-natured young *compañero* who also worked in propaganda. Naturally, he became a brother in Sebastián's *leyenda* family. And in Mama Mari, a 55-year-old *campesina*, I acquired a fictitious mother-in-law.

Mama Mari's entire family had been killed by the death squads—eight children and her husband. They had lived in a guerrilla-controlled zone, and all eight children had joined the Orga. One day they were betrayed, perhaps by a neighbor, perhaps by an informant—who knows? The children were hunted down and killed one by one, while her husband was murdered in their house before her eyes. Because of the family's sacrifice for the struggle, the Orga would take care of her and find work that would make her feel useful.

In many ways, Mama Mari was perfect for the role of Sebastián's mother. She was very white-skinned, like Sebastián, and both came from the country-side. Unlike him, however, she was an uneducated *campesina*, but this isn't uncommon in El Salvador. Many urban people are only a generation removed from their rural roots. Like a proper *campesina* mother she cooked and looked after the house, taking a weight off my shoulders.

In our new house, Sebastián slept on a small mattress that he put out every night. It was clearly uncomfortable, but every other room was occupied and the only extra space was my double mattress. I felt horrible seeing him on that little mattress, and I'd beg, "Come on, sleep in my bed—we won't do anything." Of course we always ended up making love. And then Sebastián had to go to "confession" with the Orga and confess that we'd "fallen." All the while we awaited permission to have a formal relationship.

Finally, we got permission to live together as a couple. But that brought its own problems. Sebastián and I had some serious conflicts—if we'd lived together normally, or if only Sebastián had worked underground, who knows if it might've worked.

In guerrilla organizations married men often maintain relationships apart from the family. No matter how hard the men try to compartmentalize their two lives, the families—and particularly the wives—are affected by the husband's double life. I remember a woman named María pouring out to me the frustrations and resentment she lived with for years. She was close to my age but had much less experience. Her husband was the only man she'd slept with. She told me, "I didn't know him very well. He was a lot older but I sort of liked him. So I married him." The husband was deeply involved in underground work, and he expected her to support that work without knowing the slightest detail about what was going on. A typical example: he'd come home and say, "Make food for six people this evening, and then lock yourself in the bedroom, turn on the radio, and don't come out." He was having a meeting in the house and didn't want her to know anything about it.

This division of a couple's life is cruel, but entirely logical and necessary from a security point of view. If the wife knows nothing, it protects both her and the Orga. And despite the hurt and resentment, María accepted it. She stuck with him all those years and never considered leaving him.

Because I was as much a participant as Sebastián, I didn't feel that resentment. But being in the struggle sometimes forced our personality conflicts into the open—our class backgrounds, our political formations, even our basic outlooks on life. And laughably, the *leyenda* of posing as a typical Salvadoran family with a live-in mother-in-law contributed to our problems.

Sebastián and I both put in long hours and did the same amount of work, but he always got preference in the household because he was a man. I wasn't about to let that go, so we got into arguments about machismo. For instance, why was it that Mama Mari would wash his clothes but not mine, leaving my dirty clothes to accumulate? Or at the dinner table, if Sebastián wanted more frijoles, Mama Mari, who had arthritis in both legs, would immediately get up to fetch it for him. And I'd say, "Please don't get up, he has both his feet." And then we'd be in a fierce argument.

Sebastián had definite views on proper behavior for a revolutionary, and I often didn't fit his definition. He didn't approve of the books I read or the magazines I brought home. Not even my hobbies escaped criticism, particularly the way I cut bits out of magazines to paste on the wall in collages. This was all evidence to Sebastián that I was decadent and would never rid myself of my bourgeois characteristics.

And to be sure, I contributed to the bickering. I was beginning to realize that deep down, despite the strong attraction and respect, we weren't really suited to each other. All our contradictions were showing, but there was no way for them to be resolved. I was not under his complete control anymore, and I had political responsibilities that he could not know about. All that secrecy and discipline made communication difficult. And Sebastián was never one to talk about his feelings.

But even if he had been the type to talk things through, we didn't have time to do so. When we formally received permission to be a couple, we were deeply involved in preparing for the Ofensiva Final—the Final Offensive—of January 1981.

11

The Not-So-Final Offensive

The Ofensiva Final is one of the saddest memories of my militancy. I look back on it with mixed feelings and misgivings. What I'm going to say may seem very critical of the FMLN, but I guess we have to be critical of such things.

The creation of the FMLN in September 1980 finally brought together all five guerrilla groups to coordinate military strategies. There had been other groupings of the guerrilla in the past but none that joined all five. The decisions were guided by democratic centralism, in which a majority vote determined the outcome. I know nothing about those discussions, but the very fact of the *ofensiva* meant that the ERP had prevailed. The ERP argued that the time was ripe—if an insurrection were declared and war spearheaded by the guerrilla, the people would rise up in the same way the Nicaraguans had in 1979. The FPL was opposed. In line with its *guerra popular prolongada*, prolonged popular war, it argued that far more work needed to be done among the peasants and workers before the conditions for revolutionary triumph would be present. But the majority of the groups agreed with the ERP, so the FPL had to join in the *ofensiva*.

In hindsight it's easy to see why people didn't take to the streets in a general uprising. They might have done so a year and a half before, when they'd flooded the streets in demonstrations of hundreds of thousands. But after a year of massacres, assassinations, torture, and disappearances, we couldn't get even 200 people out to the funeral of Enrique Barrera and the other murdered FDR leaders. That's how terrorized people were.

And yet, we who were working in the struggle thought that it might happen. We worked like dogs, as the *ofensiva* approached, encouraging each other to maintain our enthusiasm and excitement. The FMLN was recruiting massively for the military campaign ahead. People were slipping away to hidden camps in the mountains and attending crash military training courses at the university.

I can't say much more about the military plans because I wasn't part of them. My work, as always, was on the political side. And the *ofensiva* was clearly not just military; it was a political offensive too, with the FDR in charge. And that is where I came in. My major focus was the trade unions, which we hoped would support military action with a general strike larger than that of the year before. I talked with a lot of trade unionists, went to a lot of meetings, and wrote a lot of manifestos that we hoped would be used in the general strike.

When I say that the FDR led the political offensive, you have to remember it was a beheaded FDR. The murdered leaders had to be replaced, and so the FDR groups put up new representatives. Each representative had a support team, and at the time of the murders I had been part of the MNR team supporting Enrique. About 25 people were working in support teams, and as I look back, I believe the work was actually very well coordinated.

But now Enrique was dead. It turned out that the new MNR representative was Guido,[1] a man I love and trust who'd been a mentor when I'd joined the MNR. He'd been working in Mexico since 1979 and had been on his way back to El Salvador when the murders happened. Two days later, I made the five-hour drive to Guatemala City to pick him up, a job that fell to me because the *compañeros* who were going to do it had to leave suddenly for Nicaragua. That was the way things stood with the MNR then: the party, small at the best of times, had almost no one left in El Salvador. Guido, Italo López, and I were basically the only people left with any authority.

Guido and I talked a lot on that drive along the Pan-American Highway, some the catching up of two good friends and some of it deadly serious. The danger he was in was obvious, so at my suggestion we discussed changing his appearance. Before long he agreed to let me disguise him. Funnily enough, though the MNR never knew it, the idea of protecting Guido came from the Orga. Worried about his safety and doubting the MNR had the security knowledge to look after him, the Orga advised me to suggest the disguise to Guido.

We decided to make his hair white, have him grow a beard, and give him glasses. That didn't sound too difficult, but I came to grief over his hair. I've never used hair products and I was absolutely the worst person for this type of thing. But I finally chose a pharmacy in Santa Tecla and bought hair coloring. The instructions on the box weren't clear, and I couldn't find anyone who could tell me how to use it. Time was short, so, hoping for the best, I sat Guido down in his kitchen, put the stuff on his hair and told him to wait 20 minutes as instructed.

It turned his hair red.

"Look Guido, it's not working. I think we should wash it out."

"Leave it on," he said. "Maybe it needs more time."

So we left it on an hour and a half, and when we started to wash it off, bunches of his hair fell out. I didn't know that I had to strip the natural color out of his hair first. Poor Guido—he had nice thick hair before he got that assignment. Now it's much thinner and stringier.

Guido and I were very good friends and had always been straight with each other even though there was a side of my life I couldn't tell him about. It was a joy to be working with him again, and in the midst of the excitement and work leading up to the *ofensiva*, in the rare quiet moments alone, we would look at each other and agree, "This is not going to work."

Though we took it on faith that the military commanders and *compañeros* in the mountains had their situation in hand, there seemed to us little chance that the *ofensiva* would work in the city, that people would rise up in a popular insurrection. But we could only share these doubts with each other and continue writing press releases, going to meetings, working the calls to insurrection, contacting the unions.

The trade unions were not ready, and in fact most of them opposed a general strike. El Salvador has hundreds of trade unions, some of them small and regional. Many had been virtually beheaded by the murders of their leaders and strongest militants. That left no actual organization in half of them, seriously disrupting communication from the officials to the base. As a result, much of our organizing proved fruitless. A strike must emerge not just from the leadership but also from the workers themselves, and many union locals never got the message.

It was the same with student and peasant groups, the Christian base communities, even the market women. The insurrection strategy depended on all joining in when the *ofensiva* was declared. The Sandinistas could not have taken Nicaragua by military force alone in 1979; a broad front of people from all walks of life rose up to throw out Somoza. But in El Salvador, not only were the organizations terrorized and beheaded, but in such an atmosphere it was terrifically difficult to arrange meetings or even to distribute *comunicados*. You had to call around endlessly to set anything up and frequently start over when plans fell through. We never had the time to properly talk to even half the groups we should have reached. I'm not excusing us, but those were the conditions we were working under.

Two months before the *ofensiva*, the Orga restructured and moved most people into the military branch. Of the 80 people doing democratic propaganda in October, only 10 of us were left by the time of the *ofensiva*. The rest had gone to the mountains or were waiting to join the insurrection when it began in the city.

The movement to the mountains also worked by *conecte*, but there were so many people to move that *conectes* had to be made in batches. I remember one evening when I dropped by a security house. A small group of *compañeros* was working around a table, producing *conectes* on big pages of paper folded into 16 exact pieces. Each piece had its essential information: place, date, hour, *seña*, *contraseña*, and the two pseudonyms. Dozens of pieces of paper.

All these pseudonyms, all those people they represented. At such moments my unease sometimes became overwhelming. I'd see all this activity and think, *What the hell are we doing?* Even now I hate thinking back to those desperate moments, suddenly seeing nothing but disorganization when you'd thought plans were going perfectly. And nothing to do about it.

Despite compartmentalization, I knew many *compañeros* on Sebastián's military side of the Orga. Some were close friends. They were all saying, "Goodbye, we'll see you at the *toma*"—literally, the taking of power—"when we enter San Salvador." Though some hid it better than others, they couldn't hide a certain attitude: "Oh I'm sorry, you're on the political side—you'll miss all the excitement."

I envied their enthusiasm and confidence, and yet held terrible doubt that things would work out. I could only express my doubts to Guido, not to Sebastián. If I started to talk about it, Sebastián always cut me short. This was partly because of compartmentalization and partly, I think, because he would not or could not entertain the thought that anything might go wrong.

Our respective jobs were now totally compartmentalized. We lived in the same house but had nothing to do with each other's work. He no longer had authority over me and always had a sort of sneer about what I was doing—after all, I was working with the *democráticos*. His dismissiveness had started months before when we asked our respective *responsables* for permission to sleep together. Even though I was working on orders from higher up in the same organization, he always projected an attitude that his was the real, pure line and I was in the liberal crowd.

In a small and tentative way, I was beginning to realize that the organization wasn't as united as I'd imagined. I didn't quite grasp where the line was between the *democráticos* and the purists, but I daresay now that it was between the Christians and the hardline Marxists. It made me uneasy, but there was no time to think deeply about it. In any case I didn't trust my analysis, which was more of a gut or intuitive feeling that something was wrong, something smelled off. So with the *ofensiva* approaching, I said nothing to anyone. I just worked.

The planned date of the *ofensiva* was January 11, 1981. I remember December 1980 as a blur of 18-hour days, some doing the semi-open work of the

MNR, some entirely underground with the Orga, and the rest immersed in time-consuming domestic and security activities. A typical day would begin at 7:00 in the morning when I taught my first English class at ANTEL, the national telephone company. When I finished I went to see my parents and stayed for lunch. At 2:00 in the afternoon I might be found in the MNR office writing a pamphlet that denounced the flight of capital from the national economy; three hours later I'd be in a meeting with trade union officials, discussing their participation in the general strike. In between those various tasks and appointments I might be getting water, lamps, candles, and food together for one of the Orga's security houses, anticipating difficulties in getting supplies when the general strike took place.

Before I knew it, Christmas had arrived. With so much going on there was no way I could spend much time with family. They would have been hurt to know I was in the city but not with them, so I told them I'd be away for Christmas with my "boyfriend."

A few days before Christmas, I went home to say goodbye and drop off presents. As usual I went into the kitchen, where I saw a huge stack of tamales my nana had prepared for my mother to give to friends. Tamales are a traditional part of Christmas in El Salvador. My nana's tamales are terrific, and she had made over 200 to give away. When I saw all those tamales I immediately thought of my four security houses. I had to make things look normal, which is to say Christmasy, and I also had to feed the *compañeros*. So I gathered up 60 tamales while my mother napped.

My nana moaned, "Ay no, Ana Margarita, please don't!"

"Don't worry," I said. "Tell Mother I took them."

"But she's going to be so *angry* when she sees they're gone."

"Just tell her I took them to give to my friends before I go away. It will be all right."

It wasn't all right, as I learned later, but at least everyone in the security houses got a tamale for Christmas. That was good for morale, but there was no forgetting, even during the holidays, what was going on in the country.

Just before New Year's Eve, I received horrible news that I had to give to Pedro, a *compañero* in one of my security houses. His wife, a doctor working in the mountains in Chalatenango, had been killed. That's all the information I had. As the person in charge of the house, I had to tell Pedro. We'd organized a New Year's party so the house would look normal to the rest of the neighborhood, but the news made celebration impossible. We spent New Year's Eve mourning her death.

Later, I heard the full story. Her whole camp had been in a *guinda*, a tactical retreat undertaken when you're told the army is advancing. Somehow medical equipment was left behind, and Pedro's wife and a nurse went back for it. They were captured by an ORDEN patrol, who did their patriotic duty by raping, mutilating, and finally killing them.

Soon after New Year's, I went to Mexico to consult with the leadership of the FDR. When I returned, I went to Father's gas station to ask for some gas. When he saw me drive up in my orange Datsun, Father called me into his office. It wasn't a typical gas station office; it had a drawing table in the middle and the walls were filled with beautiful paintings.

As I walked in, he was waiting for me at the drawing table. He took off his glasses, put them on the table, and stuck his fingers in his thick, silvery hair. It was long and heavy, always well-combed and kept in place with Brylcreem. Then he laid his head on the table. "Ana Margarita, why did you have to steal the tamales?"

There was a certain desperation in his voice. Not anger, just desperation. "Why do you have to do that sort of thing?"

And I actually said, "Which tamales?" It wasn't sarcasm or evasiveness: I'd already forgotten. So many things had happened since then, and the *ofensiva* was eight days away.

In a tired, desperate voice, he again offered to pay for me to leave El Salvador and go to Nicaragua.

"Please do it for me," he said. "Your mother is going to kill me. She didn't leave me alone for one second during Christmas vacation because of the tamales. She thinks you are involved in some very serious things, and she's making my life impossible because of you. Why don't you just go play in Nicaragua?"

I confessed to taking the tamales. He begged me not to take things from the house again, and then sent me on my way with the gas.

As I drove away, I suddenly realized that he was very worried about me. Unlike Mother, he had some idea what I was up to. Not the Orga, of course, but I had told him when I joined the MNR and when I went to Cuba. I always confused him, I think, and he was never quite able to understand why I did what I did. Deep down he was proud of me—I know that because friends of his have told me so—but always worried that I would do something crazy or that something would happen to me.

In the final few days, we received orders to clean the security houses out. Not one weapon, not one scrap of paper was to be left in the houses.

And then the *ofensiva* began. On the morning of January 10 the FPL's Co-mandante Marcial issued the call to revolution over Radio Farabundo Martí in the name of the FMLN General Command: "Todos a la lucha!" Everyone to the struggle!

In the capital nothing happened. A few bombs went off here and there, and there was sporadic shooting. But it was nothing like the hoped-for popular insurrection.

Outside San Salvador it was different. We had some impressive victories in the first few days. Despite the number of people who knew what was coming, the armed forces' intelligence was lousy and the guerrilla caught the army off guard in some well-planned and executed operations. The Santa Ana barracks near Ciudad Arce in the western part of the country were taken over, and several uprisings occurred in Mejicano and other places. In fact, Ciudad Arce experienced a complete popular uprising. But this was one city out of the whole country.

Quite simply, the FMLN General Command was wrong about the moment being ripe. The great mass of Salvadorans didn't join in the uprising, and severe organizational problems prevented the guerrilla from maintaining the *ofensiva* and holding the few positions they captured. Almost immediately the United States freed up $10 million to provide military equipment and instructors for the government forces.

Though the *ofensiva* lasted a few days, by 9:00 a.m. of day 1, it was clear it wasn't going to work. Unlike the year before, when the general strike shut down San Salvador, now fewer than 10 of the 150 or so trade unions went out. Only 2 of the approximately 100 bus lines stopped running. The life of the city went on as usual.

For us it was devastating. We had fooled ourselves with our enthusiasm and our mystique. We had acted like circus seals, applauding everything and ignoring personal doubt as we awaited the triumphant takeover of San Salvador.

Having said that, the *ofensiva* was not a failure—the terrible strategic mistake was to call it "final." The military achievements were real, but the word "final" had been announced so many times that we were laughingstocks, and the benefits were largely lost. Even if there's no comparison militarily with the *ofensiva* of 1989, the later one couldn't have happened without the earlier. All through the 1980s we continued advancing and learning. In fact, I think that if the US hadn't pumped in enormous amounts of money to the military, we would have taken San Salvador in two or three years.

Anyway, it didn't happen like that. The *ofensiva* was followed by pure chaos, a moment of absolute uncertainty that took months to recover from. Compartmentalization had become so necessary that even MNR members and trade unionists used it, not just those on the military side. So now, with everything disrupted, no one knew how to get in touch with one another. We "lost" some important people because we didn't know where to find them. On the propaganda side, I had some bad moments because I couldn't find the graphic artist who designed our leaflets and newspapers.

On a larger scale, hundreds of people were left stranded by organizational inadequacies. While many had successfully made it to the camps in the mountains, many others in the city were left waiting for their gun and their *conecte*—and nothing happened; no one contacted them. Many had quit their jobs and were now "burned" as we say in Spanish, their covers blown. Others had guns in their house, and no way to get rid of them. Many left during those days as refugees to Costa Rica or Canada. Many Salvadorans still remain in Costa Rica who were stranded by the *ofensiva*, something I didn't know until I ended up here myself three years later.

For a few weeks it looked like I too would be leaving the country because the MNR appointed me its representative in Austria. I have some German as well as English and had international experience, so I was a perfect fit. Even the Orga was in favor of my going, because it considered Austria strategically important. The European countries were key to international solidarity. But I didn't want to leave my country and kept putting it off, arguing with Héctor and Vera who were making the arrangements.

In any case, the death squads relieved me of the need for further argument. Soon after the *ofensiva*, the newspapers published a list of 121 names threatened with execution. All were members of the legal opposition, and half were out of the country already, including Dr. Ungo, Héctor Oquelí, Héctor Silva, Rubén Zamora, and Jorge Sol. But Guido's name was also there, high up on the list. Disguise or no disguise, he had to leave immediately.

And who did that leave next in line as MNR representative on the FDR? Me.

12

~

Woman in a Man's World

Guido had been responsible for the FDR's propaganda, so automatically I took on his tasks. It was like climbing a mountain, especially since we had to start creating our network again. We had grown to about 60 people who did press releases, little newspapers, international broadcasts, and a lot of activities with foreign journalists.

All of a sudden I was responsible for payments to 60 people, ensuring that everyone got their 125 colones a month. It was nothing much in terms of money, but it was literally what they needed to survive. And then there were tasks like buying huge amounts of paper and ink and getting them delivered to an underground press. I didn't do the delivery personally, but I had to make sure it happened. There was a network and so I had assistance from people who knew a lot more—but at the weekly meeting of the FDR's executive committee, I was the one who was responsible for the entire propaganda effort.

It felt both overwhelming and surreal—I kept thinking, *What am I doing here?* I had no formal experience in journalism except what I had gathered in a small way over the years. Thank God for those around me who knew what they were doing and helped me. It is the collaborators who make it all possible. The presses, the layout artists, the people who manage to steal paper from the national printing office and get it to us. Without them we couldn't have done the things we did. And especially my new *responsable* from the Orga, the one who had replaced Sebastián. I'll call him Samuel here. He was the one who got me organized, who taught me how to make a calendar for my week, prioritize tasks, establish objectives, and not become totally confused and go crazy with all the tasks. At a time when we were both running incredible risks to our personal security, he was teaching me things I'd never known were necessary to survive in the business world.

The president of the committee was Eduardo Calles. Besides me, the others were Max, Cantarito, Mariano of the BPR, and the representatives of the MIP-TES, the MPSC, and FAPU. Of the seven two are dead: Cantarito and Max. Cantarito's name comes from the word *cántaro*, those round ceramic clay pots with two little ears and a small opening which is kept for cooling water. He was strangled with barbed wire and killed while I was in prison. Max was in the Commission of Human Rights. He and his wife and child were taken from their house and disappeared, all three of them. Eduardo Calles is still in Nicaragua in the FDR-FMLN, and the guy from the MPSC is still in the MPSC. Mariano was arrested while I was in prison, and his wife was arrested too. He was a teacher, and now he's a teacher again in El Salvador, trying to find his life again and participating in the teachers' struggle.

It was always a strain to be the only woman on the committee, and I had to be more aggressive to hold my own. At the same time I felt very insecure because most of my *compañeros* were very political and very sophisticated, or at least their discourse was, whereas mine was very weak and new. I'd come from the underground where things are called by their names and you don't learn political discourse. My training was totally empirical and theirs was totally intellectual. Although I had taken courses in philosophy and sociology, my experience had been in women's organizations and youth organizations, where the language is very forthright and radical. In contrast, the committee had to use very selective, diplomatic language. The only way I could defend myself was showing work and results. This is what Samuel taught me: if you are going to chair a meeting, start it by asking for everyone's reports, give your report, *give your results*—this many things were distributed, this much money was spent, be exact. I remember his words so well, and they helped me by demanding respect from my *compañeros*. There may have been distrust but also a lot of respect because *here it was*: I was supposed to write something and *here it was*. I remember him saying, "Just do what you have to do, finish your task and turn it in. What you say doesn't really matter, it's your work, what you produce that matters, not what comes out of your mouth."

I was very quiet at the meetings and I only talked when I had to talk. When there were political discussions of strategy and line, I pretty much kept to myself and listened. It was afterward that I consulted Samuel about what my position should be.

My insecurity was mostly in my mind, and I generally felt the respect of the other members of the committee. But they usually monopolized the discussion, and it was very hard for me at those moments when I had to articulate the position of the MNR. It made me sweat and shake and gave me hives—in fact it was horrible, and I didn't like this responsibility I'd had to assume. And they didn't reach out a sympathetic hand. On the contrary, when they felt I wasn't making sense, they would interrupt me: my three minutes were up. I usually make sense, so I don't even know if it was true. Men don't like women being more intelligent than they are. But all along, Samuel said take it easy, do your job and present the results of your job and stick to that. As it turned out, there weren't that many meetings because I was arrested soon after, thank God.

I particularly resented being separated from my underground work where I felt very productive and very sure of myself. I think it affected my relationship with Sebastián, and maybe was why I was removed from his control. My life had been easy with him when I was under his responsibility. I needed his absolute straightness. Now that I had so many responsibilities of my own and couldn't talk with him about them, that was more difficult. My discussions with Samuel and Guido and other friends were much more intellectual, and it was easier to discuss existential problems with them. While my *democrático* friends were full of doubts, Sebastián didn't seem to have any existential problems. And when I expressed one, he immediately dismissed it as a bourgeois deviation.

My propaganda group received material from all the trade unions and groups like the Mothers Committee and published a lot of it in different forms. So it was logical that when the political prisoners started to smuggle information out from the prisons, they'd send it to us, and for the Committee of Political Prisoners of El Salvador (COPPES) to become an important part of my work.

COPPES was created at Santa Tecla prison in November of 1980, and it was largely the initiative of José Antonio "Tono" Morales Carbonell, along with Héctor Recinos. Tono was the son of José Antonio Morales Ehrlich, a well-known Christian Democrat who was one of the members of the second junta. In fact, his father is mayor of San Salvador at the moment. But Tono had joined the FPL, and it was big news when he was arrested. Héctor was a trade unionist, one of the leaders of the state electricity workers' union. When they went out on a big strike in August 1980, he'd been arrested along with the whole leadership of the union (his wife and daughter were disappeared while he was still in prison, and nothing was ever heard from them again). He and Tono were imprisoned at Santa Tecla and began to organize COPPES there.

Prior to 1980, there were actually very few political prisoners, and they suffered horribly. But international outrage about the disappearances and massacres had some effect, and the authorities' policy changed. People started to get arrested and not simply disappeared, and more and more were ending up in prisons. As well, prisoners were often the last to see some of the disappeared. Sometimes it happened that people were arrested together, but only one would surface again in prison. So not only did COPPES denounce the situation of the political prisoners but it also publicized the disappearances.

I had never met Tono or Héctor, though I certainly knew of them even before they were arrested. I have still not met Tono although we became very close because we wrote to each other weekly. Their work was important to the FDR not just for the propaganda value, although that was considerable, but because they represented our own people, our *compañeros* in jail.

COPPES got its information out of prison in the time-honored fashion of prisoners everywhere, using their ingenuity to hide letters in the most banal or unexpected places. The Salvadoran word for it is *embutido*—"a sausage."

Most of my work was now in El Salvador, with very little travel. There was one MNR meeting I attended in Mexico, a short three-day seminar where our position in the alliance and our line in the revolutionary process were ratified, and our statutes revised. I gave my report about what we were doing, and I saw Vera and Héctor Oquelí and everybody, and that was it.

It was around the 8th of April that I returned to El Salvador and my underground home life with Sebastián. I came back to find that my father was very sick with asthmatic emphysema. He was 62, had been a heavy smoker all his life, and was very careless with his health. This was the third time it had happened, but he'd previously had long periods of convalescence when he had been in good health. He'd been in hospital about a year before, but this time he refused to go into hospital. A friend of ours had lent him one of these modern electric beds that moves and gives massage, and he had a nurse in the house. However, his oxygen intake was very diminished, with not enough to keep the body going all the time, and even taking a step was exhausting. So my father had to use oxygen all the time. My mother thought we had to prepare ourselves for Father becoming an invalid, that he'd be in a wheelchair like many emphysema cases in the last two or three years of their lives.

At the same time, I had another source of stress to cope with: Samuel was no longer my *responsable*.

Right before Samuel told me he wasn't going to be my *responsable*, we drove to Guatemala for a meeting. Those trips were always full of discussions of existential problems. And I realized that I had made a serious mistake to get together with Sebastián. A few days before the trip to Guatemala, I'd had an argument with him about a little radio I owned. It was mine, but someone was leaving for the mountains and needed one, and he decided to give it to this person. I said, "No, it's my radio," and we had a serious ideological argument about property. If I'd known about the difference between social property and personal property (in Cuba they call it *propiedad personal*—clothes and so on), and if I'd had enough ideological clarity, I could have handled that discussion better. But the fact that he felt he had the right to take my radio was a breaking point in our relationship. And he did take it, accusing me of being deviationist and selfish, and much else.

On the four-hour drive to Guatemala with Samuel, I poured out my unhappiness and my anguish about being with this man. It had been okay when he was my *responsable*. Samuel understood it and tried to solve it. He said, "Okay, when we have time we'll try to move you from that house. You have to understand that he's not of your culture. You have very different class backgrounds and education." I still didn't know his name, but Samuel and Guido and Mariano all knew who Sebastián really was and knew him personally.

But soon after we came back from Guatemala, Samuel told me he was not going to be my *responsable* anymore. Instead, it was going to be Mariano. Samuel couldn't even tell me where he was going. I had depended so much on him that this news was like death to me. Mariano was good, but he was having some personal problems at the time and I didn't know how it would be to work with him.

To make things worse, we had an immediate, serious problem to solve. The organization had given us a pile of communications equipment to look after. There were amplifiers, recording equipment, and a lot of other things I didn't know about. They were supposed to have been taken to a camp but that hadn't happened yet. Then someone I didn't know, who worked in Sebastián's part of the organization, was arrested. All of a sudden Sebastián, Geraldo, Mama Mari, and I had to move, and do it immediately in one day. The first thing was to put Mama Mari and Geraldo in safe places, and we did that. But then there was the question of whether we could leave things in the house. Sometimes people left furniture and so on when it was time to run, but we couldn't because of the equipment. (By this time most of my dangerous stuff was at my parents' house, under beds. My mother never knew about it . . .) A friend offered us a house we could put the equipment into. It was secure, and I said to Sebastián, "Let's just put a mattress in the room, and take out the kitchen and then we'll be in a house of our own." So we moved there.

All of our stuff was piled up in the front room, and we lived in the last room out in back. The rest of the house was empty. It was supposed to be temporary, just until we found a more secure house. But time started passing . . .

My father died on April 23. The last time I saw him was on the 22nd in the evening. I took along this little dog that I had adopted, and he sat on Father's bed. (I should add that Sebastián hated this dog. On top of everything, not having a house of our own, living the way we were living, I had taken in this little dog.) Father was in wonderful spirits, and that was when he made my sister-in-law and me talk. He said, "Come on you two, you better start talking to each other. This is sickening and I can't handle it. I'm sick and you're making my life impossible." We spent a couple of good hours and I left saying that I'd see him the next day.

The next day was so busy that I didn't even call in the morning to see how he was. Among the activities I had programmed for that day, I had a call saying that there were serious relational problems in the Santa Tecla house, which was still my responsibility. There were about five kids, young militants, living there, a cell. Things were deteriorating there very heavily so I had to deal with that and see who I could pull out of there. Remember, these are a bunch of people who don't know each other. No matter how strong the discipline, it's difficult. Anyway, I found a solution, but it meant I would have to go to Santa Tecla that evening. So I decided to drop in to see my father after that, because my brother Tono was coming in from his university in the United States. My brother Chico, the priest, had already come from Guatemala because my mother had intuitively called us all to be together, although the doctor had said Father would be okay. But at 3:00 I had an appointment at the UCA that brought me near to my parents' house, and as I was driving by I saw all these cars in front of the house and I knew my father was dead. My mother came to the door sobbing and said, "We've been trying to reach you all day. The way you live, you make us suffer so much. We never know where you are, we couldn't even phone you to tell you that your father was dead!" Ten minutes later my brother Tono arrived.

Father had had two heart attacks, from the strain on his heart. It had started the night before, but they couldn't call me because they didn't have my phone number. I assume responsibility for this. It was part of my life at the time. But I did feel bad. He was laid out on the bed with his hands crossed over his chest. I touched his hands and kissed him. He had grown a little beard. I suddenly thought that I hadn't really touched my father since I was nine years old. I cried a little bit, then my mother pulled me away and sent me home to change into black clothes.

When I got to the house I found out how hard an organization can be. How hard fanaticism can be. I said to Sebastián, "My father died a few hours ago."

And he said, "So? Did you go to Santa Tecla?" He knew the people were in his area of the organization, although I controlled the house.

I said, "No."

"You should have gone."

I said, "Sebastián, my father just died today."

And as I got dressed, he said, "Where do you think you're going?"

"Back to my mother's."

He didn't want me to go back for security reasons, but in the end he let me.

When I got home late that evening I wanted to cry. But Sebastián said, "No crying. Remember you're a revolutionary. You can't cry about this."

And I didn't. I never cried for my father until years later when I did psychotherapy. Now I cry for my father all the time. But at that time I obeyed. I went to sleep, and the next day I went to my father's funeral, which was very beautiful. My brother Chico conducted the ceremony and the Mass. Some of his friends that I knew but that my mother and brothers didn't know were there. A lot of people came up to me to give me the *pésame*, condolences, and many of them said, "Your father was so proud of you," and things like that. I'm glad that it happened then and not after I was arrested. I can't imagine what it would have been like if it had happened after I was arrested.

I went to all the masses on all of the nine days. Then Tito went back to Honduras, Chico went back to Guatemala, and I went back to my work. The revolution didn't stop just for his death. Funnily enough, a lot of people blame me for his death. I think he died because he wanted to, because he couldn't bear the thought of being an invalid.

The day before the arrest, a Monday, there was a meeting at the house where Sebastián and I were staying. One of our leaders said, "What if the police come? What are you going to say about all the junk you have here—the communications equipment?" But we just laughed. We were sure that our cover was sufficient to protect us. Besides, that same afternoon we had rented a secure house where we were going to move.

13

~

Disappeared

"Nobody Knows, Nobody Cares"

The night before we got arrested Sebastián and I had a fight. I'd been looking forward to coming home to our new security house, because for the first time in months we were going to spend an evening together, alone and with nothing else to do. But when I got home Sebastián told me he had to bring a *compañero* home to work later, and for security reasons the guy and I couldn't see each other. That was disappointing enough, but then when he asked if I would feed them, I got upset. I said there were only sardines and soup because there had been a meeting at noon and everything had been eaten. The pot of beans I made every two days was finished. And Sebastián raised hell because there was no food in the house. Typical Salvadoran—if there's no rice and beans, there's no food. Sardines is not enough. Soup is not enough. Rice and beans are basic.

So we had a fight. But the next morning when I woke up I turned to Sebastián and said, "I'm sorry about last night." It was still dark outside, before dawn. He had to leave very early and we both had busy days planned. There was no time to talk things through, so we just cuddled for a little while and loved each other. Then he got up to go to the bathroom and the knock came at the door. Every time I thought about it afterward, I was glad that at least there were no bad feelings between us.

As I had got more involved in clandestine work, I became increasingly conscious of the dangers of our life and of how much we were risking. There were so many disappearances at that time, so many corpses appearing on the streets, many of them mutilated and showing the signs of torture. You never knew what was going to happen that day, if you were going to die.

As a result, I'd made the decision that my relationship with Sebastián had to be in good shape every morning when I left my house. I'm a complicated person; I fight a lot, and I can be bitchy and horrible. But I became set on that objective: no matter how nasty an argument we might have had, before leaving the house we had to be okay, say goodbye nicely, and leave with a happy memory.

Then came the knock at the door. As with most houses in El Salvador, the front door of our house was made of heavy iron, with plastic panes to let in light. It makes a lot of noise when you knock on it normally, but that morning, the moment I heard the banging of a fist, I knew what was about to happen. Sebastián came out of the bathroom and we didn't say anything. We had lived with the possibility for too long to be overly surprised.

Both of us kept our papers in a small envelope next to the bedside table, just in case anything like this happened. In a second we decided that he was going to run for it with those papers and I was going to open the door. He put on his shorts, grabbed the papers, and ran out the back part of the house we used for hanging laundry.

I gave him a few seconds and walked toward the front door. The other *compañero* that Sebastián had brought home the night before was awake and standing half-dressed in the hall. He had slept in the dining room and we had never seen each other before, but there was no time to say anything.

Another few seconds passed before I unlocked and opened the door. Immediately, a squad of men—30? 40? it seemed like an entire regiment—burst in. As they started ransacking the house, I demanded to know who had given them orders to search my house. They said they didn't need any orders and continued opening everything and smashing whatever they couldn't open.

They were dressed in green uniforms and military boots and carried M16 rifles. The uniforms had no identification, no shoulder flashes or insignia that would tell me which force they belonged to. They all looked like typical Guardia Nacional: short, broad men with crew cuts. Gorillas. With my adrenaline running and the terror I felt, it was impossible to try to remember faces.

The other *compañero* didn't move or say anything, just tried to look as normal as possible under the circumstances. I moved toward the phone in the dining room, thinking that the first thing was to call someone to let them know what's happening—my brother Javier would be best. I got as far as unhooking the receiver before one of the men tore the phone off the wall and snarled that I couldn't call anybody.

Then I heard a commotion out back. I found out afterward that the *militares* had surrounded not just the house but the entire block. They'd caught Sebastián almost as soon as he'd gone up to the roof. Now they were kicking him down the metal stairs and beating him with the butts of their rifles.

Once they brought him back in the house, we were pushed into our bedroom and ordered to dress. I was wearing a long nightgown with long sleeves. They watched as Sebastián and I put on clothes. Then they separated us, taking Sebastián to the dining room while they marched me to the front room. Occasionally I could see through the hallway into the dining room and get glimpses of what was happening. They tied up the other *compañero* and put him in a corner in the garage, but they didn't tie me up until later. Instead, they started to interrogate me.

The lack of insignia on their uniforms was scary. It was important to know which security force they came from, because some are worse than others. I kept asking who they were and they wouldn't tell me, so I steadily refused to answer their questions or tell them anything. It was a standoff. Meanwhile, the men doing the search were destroying the house. They opened the cushions and mattresses with knives, smashed open the ceilings, and strewed books across the floor. When they finished with the first floor, they went upstairs and tore that apart too, even though the rooms were empty.

All this time I kept trying to see what was happening to Sebastián. There were between 6 and 10 men in the dining room with him. First they blindfolded him and turned him facedown on the couch. Then they tied his hands behind his back with the security forces' favorite knot. It's very simple, just a single piece of string that ties the thumbs together, but extremely painful because it stops the circulation and keeps the blood in your hands. Once he was tied, one of the soldiers took out two large wires and stuck them into the wall socket. Taking up the other ends, the soldier started giving Sebastián electric shocks in the feet. I couldn't see much but I could hear Sebastián moaning. It was horrible, and there was no way to stop it.

Or maybe there was. I decided to tell them I was a member of the MNR. That excited them and they focused their attention on me. It was the first piece of information they had received since the *operativo* began, and they thought they had something important. But since they weren't hurting me, I refused to tell them anything more. I just repeated that I was a member of a legal political party and that it was common knowledge.

Since they were getting nowhere with me, they sent for a superior officer, a captain. When he came into the room, I immediately saw the insignia of the Guardia Nacional on his collar. That meant it was really a bad situation. The Guardia Nacional was perfectly capable of killing us, as they'd done with so many people. So I said to the captain, "Look, I've been a militant of the MNR for the past six years. I'm the only one involved in anything political. Sebastián doesn't know anything about me or what I do." It would have been much worse if they'd known we were from the Orga. With all the international work I had done, I calculated that it would be a big deal as soon as the MNR realized that I had been arrested. I was a known social democrat, so I thought I risked the least if I used the MNR at that moment to protect the three of us.

It was daylight by the time they took us away, maybe 7:00. First they blindfolded me with one of my kitchen towels and tied my hands behind my back with one of Sebastián's ties. Then they marched us out of the house. I couldn't see or hear what was happening with Sebastián and the *compañero*, but the Guardias threw me in the trunk of my car and started it up. I was scared that we were being taken to different places but occupied my mind with trying to figure out from the sounds and the turns the route the car was taking. The house was on a main street, and I said to myself, *Okay, we're turning onto an avenue, that was a left turn,* and so on. The ride was mostly straight, though I think they did a few extra turns to confuse us. After about 30 minutes, I guessed that we had got to the place where both the Policía de Hacienda and the Guardia Nacional buildings face each other, and I could feel us going over those bumps we call "sleeping policemen," which I knew were in front of both barracks. Then we stopped.

Again I started to worry about whether Sebastián had been taken somewhere else. It was a terrible feeling. But then I heard the *ting-ting-ting* sound that Sebastián's van made when it backed up, so I knew that we were in the same place, and that he'd been brought there in his own vehicle. That was a great relief, but I had lots of other things to worry about. I didn't know anything about the other guy in the house, not even his name, and we didn't have a story about what he was doing there. In fact, our security was so complete that I knew almost nothing about Sebastián. I didn't know what he did, and by that time he didn't know what I did. Obviously, we each had some idea about the general areas we worked in, but no details. We were lovers, but we had been very strict about compartmentalization.

After pulling me out of the car, they marched me up some stairs. When they asked, "Name?" I screamed out my name so the other *compañero* would hear if he was nearby. It was the only thing I could think of to give him a bit more information. The Guardia escorting me told me I didn't have to yell.

After that, they sat me on the floor and handcuffed my arms to a chair. I was still blindfolded, but I felt it was a big room and that there were more people, although it was quiet. I could only hear murmurs and steps as people moved around. Out of nervousness I had to pee every few minutes. It meant calling a guard, who had to come and undo the handcuffs, put one handcuff on his own wrist, and then lead me to the bathroom. I was still blindfolded, and I only had one hand free to undo my pants and find the toilet seat. Some of them were such jerks. As they walked me to the bathroom, they'd say, "Turn," and I would turn and walk straight into a wall.

At the same time one or two of them were decent to me. Again, out of nervousness my mouth kept going dry and I was constantly thirsty. So I kept asking for water. One of the guards was nice and he kept asking, "Señora, estás bien?" Ma'am, are you alright? At one point he took the handcuffs from my wrists and sat me on a slatted wooden chair. It felt wonderful to get off the floor and onto this chair, and this time he only cuffed one hand to one of its arms.

It was a long day, a horrible day. We had been taken at 4:00 in the morning, and I was in that big room for about 14 hours. There was nothing to do but sit there with the blindfold on and try to hear what was going on. At some point a television was turned on, which added to the noise of people coming and going. But there was also the muffled sound of torture from another room. I could hear people screaming, distant but unmistakable. Perhaps it was intentional on the part of the Guardia Nacional to have it that way, to terrorize the people who had to wait in the room by making them listen and wonder when it would be their turn.

With my blindfold on and the general confusion of sounds, I couldn't be sure of the time. At around 9:00 in the evening, the decent guard came by and said, "Here's some food." He gave me a tortilla and some beans, but I told him I wasn't hungry, just thirsty. He replied, "You have to eat, you'll need all your strength to bear this." I could feel a certain humanity in him so I took a chance and said, "Señor, my husband is bald and has a beard, and was brought in here with me this morning. Can you sit him next to me so I can be near him?"

And the next thing I knew, they had sat someone on the floor beside me and were tying him to my chair. It was Sebastián. With my free hand I touched his head and shoulder. Through his shirt I could feel that he was sweaty. I found out much later that he had been tortured again and that his toes were badly hurt from the electric shots. But when I asked him, "How are you?" he simply replied, "Good, how are you?" And that was all we said to each other because at that moment a man yelled, "Who put those two together?" and there was a big fuss while they pulled us apart and untied him from the chair. But it had been a wonderful moment; I had been able to touch him and I knew for sure that he was there, that they hadn't simply taken him out and killed him. I didn't see him again for another year.

Two minutes after Sebastián was taken away, some guards arrived and pulled me out of the chair, tightened the blindfold, and tied my thumbs behind my back. They marched me out of the room and down the steps to the first floor, then out of the building. There were two of them, and they were very rough with me. As they pushed me and shoved me along, they called me "mujer con cerebro de hombre"—woman with the brain of a man—over and over. I should never have got involved in men's activities, they told me angrily. "Are you sick?" they asked me, and said to each other with disgust, "This woman is not a woman, she's a man."

It was raining. I don't know how long we walked, but they kept hitting and shoving me and I fell frequently. Then they pulled me up and kept me moving, holding me by the arms. We went across a field, and I could feel the grass through my sandals. That was followed by some rougher terrain until we finally got to another building. I was still blindfolded and it was dark, but I could feel the concrete under my feet and could tell that we had come into the light.

We entered through what seemed to be a garage, and after a short walk came into another room where I could hear an air conditioner. I thought to myself, *This is it, they're going to torture me. This is the torture chamber.*

A voice said, "Take the blindfold and handcuffs off her and sit her down." They took off the blindfold and I saw that we were in an office, a luxurious one with maps of El Salvador on the walls. Part of the room was full of office equipment. It took me a second to recognize that the equipment was from the MNR office. They'd obviously broken in there and taken everything.

Behind the desk was the captain who'd been called to my house in the morning. He said, "All this equipment is yours, from the office you control." I said, "No," and he said, "Yes, it is," and began questioning me. His voice was controlled and educated, a pleasant contrast to the gorillas. He had my handbag on his desk and began to take out things one by one: my checkbook, my wallet, my agenda book. With each object he asked, "Is this yours?" and I said no to everything. Actually, I was ready to throw up, I was so scared, so convinced that the torture would soon begin. Perhaps he saw that I was in a state of shock because he switched to a different sort of questioning. Why did I have so much money in the bank? Who was I supposed to be meeting that morning? Opening my agenda, he said, "On the 8th you have written this code word, 'park.' What did you do in the park? Who did you see? Whose number is this?"

Now it's true that everything in the agenda was coded, but he was only guessing. I kept denying everything, so he changed tack again and asked me questions about the MNR and about the guerrilla. Where were the arms hidden? Where were the safe houses located? As the interrogation progressed, he became very loud and aggressive. It followed a rhythm: a series of aggressive questions followed by a sort of break when he'd ask, "Would you like something to drink?" I accepted a Coke the first time. Then he offered me a cigarette.

I hadn't smoked in about eight years but I took his cigarette. He never touched me, not that evening or in any of the subsequent interrogations.

By then it was very late at night. After about two hours, he got up and said several times that if I didn't cooperate, I was inviting a lot of trouble for myself. I kept insisting that I was a member of a legal party and had a right as a citizen to do political work in El Salvador. That it was a free and democratic country. He gave up after a while and called for the two guards to take me away.

As I stood up he said, "Okay, you know what you are into. I'm just going to tell you for the last time, if you don't cooperate you are in for a lot of trouble." It's funny, but despite my fear at the beginning of the interrogation and the screams of torture I'd heard during the day, I didn't believe him. Perhaps it was because of the shock and fatigue of the day, or maybe I was reassured because of his correct manners and lack of violence toward me. It took me a long time to figure out that it was deliberate and that he was setting me up for what followed.

The guards blindfolded and handcuffed me tightly, and as soon as we were out of the room, they started shoving me and hitting me with their rifle butts. It was the same routine of a few hours before. I fell down frequently, and they'd pull me up by the arm yelling, "You clumsy bitch, why don't you get up!" Out we went from the building, over the grass once again until we got to the edge of a precipice. Perhaps it wasn't very high, but with my eyes blindfolded, the only information I had was from my feet and I could feel that the ground dropped away. They stopped me and said they were going to kill me. So I stood waiting for them to put a bullet through my head. But then they threw me back down on the grass, kicked and hit me again with the rifle butts. They did this three times, the precipice, the threat, and the beating. Pure cat-and-mouse, spread out over a half hour or so.

Finally they took me back to the original building, which I found out later was the Guardia Nacional headquarters. I climbed the stairs again, thinking I was going back to the big room. But instead of turning right, we kept on through some corridors. They took me through a doorway into a room and told me to undress and give them my bra and underpants. When I asked why, they replied, "Because we don't want you to kill yourself. You have to be alive." They let me put on the rest of my clothes before they threw me down on a cot without a mattress. After tying my arms roughly to the cot, they left without saying another word.

I lay there for a few minutes, terribly scared. They had left me blindfolded but the light remained on, and after a while I managed to work the blindfold off my eyes and take a look at the room. It was a little cell about five by eight feet. There was space for a cot and a hole in one corner that stank badly and was full of excrement. The cell had once been a bathroom, judging from the mosaic tiles going up about a meter high. Next to the hole was a sink, a godsend I immediately thought, because there would be water. On the floor were rags strewn about among the filth and the cockroaches. Looking around, I could see three walls, the ones on my left, my right, and in front of me. All had words scratched into them, such as "God, please help me get out of here." It was terrible. The ceiling was plywood and filled with holes—96 of them. I know because I counted them dozens of times in English, Spanish, French, German. I even invented languages as time went on.

After a while I began to feel nauseous. I was so scared and the cigarette the captain gave me earlier made me sick. So I threw up on myself, but since I was tied down to the cot I had to lay there in the vomit. They kept me tied there for three days and didn't allow me to go to the bathroom. Which meant doing it in my pants, first that night and then during the next two days and nights. They wouldn't let me sleep either. The door to the cell was made of metal, with a little door in it that opened toward the outside. Every few minutes a guard would stop by and open the little door, and if he saw me dozing off, he would pound on the door and shout, "Wake up!"

At least I could see. At first, they would come in and tighten up the blindfold, but I would push it down again every time. Finally they gave up and didn't tie it up again. Soon after that I saw a nail lying on the floor near the wall. I was overjoyed to discover that nail. I kept thinking that if I could get my hands on it I could kill myself.

When they took away my bra and panties, the guards had discovered that I had my period, and they called me ugly names, a dirty woman. But I suspect that having my period and being "dirty" saved me from being raped.

After a while I heard footsteps coming down the hall, then the jangle of keys and the sound of the door being unlocked. A man came in and shut the door. He was tall and dark and wore a black T-shirt, a beret, and mirrored glasses. His face was acne-marked and he had muscular arms. He bent over me and took my face in his hands. I couldn't move, and in any case I was paralyzed with terror. He pressed my cheeks with his strong fingers, forced my mouth open and tried to make me scream with pain. He took my breast and squeezed as hard as he could, then opened my pants and touched me and called me filthy names. But mostly he said nothing.

I was so full of hate that I began to think about spitting in his face. He actually had a job, which was to bring my food. He came in about once an hour, and each time it was the same. He entered with the plate of food, undid one of the handcuffs and said, "Come, eat!"

I kept saying, "I want to go to the bathroom, I want to clean myself," and he simply replied, "No, you come and eat!" over and over again. And I kept replying, "I only want water," but he wouldn't give it to me. And then he'd handcuff my free hand to the cot and leave.

So I finally did spit in his face, and then he slapped me around badly. All the guards carried sets of handcuffs, and he took his out, put one around my breast and pressed it tight. It hurt like hell and left a ring. But again, having my period probably saved me from rape. Maybe not. He might have had instructions not to rape me, just to abuse me as much as he could.

The rest of the time I was alone in the cell. Little by little, I started to get a sense of my surroundings. Listening hard to the sounds, I realized that there were six or seven men in the cells near mine. They had a daily routine. In the morning they were taken out to exercise, and in the evening they watched television. They were fooling around a lot of the time, smoking and laughing like good friends. I could hear murmurs but I couldn't understand very much.

But eventually I figured it out. They were the soldiers who had killed the three American nuns and a lay sister about a year before. The killings had caused an international incident, and the US State Department put pressure on the Salvadoran government to prosecute the murderers. I knew through the newspapers that they had been arrested a few weeks before I was taken. The more I listened, the surer I became that these were the men.

As time went on, I started to recognize when it was daytime and when it was night by the noises. Early morning I could hear the guards marching and running outside, singing and puffing as they did their drills. The six men in the neighboring cells were also taken out for exercise.

But not me. On the second night of my detention, they still hadn't let me sleep. The man with the mirrored glasses had been in and out numerous times, and I was both exhausted and furious. Lying on that cot, the pain in my back and the pain from the handcuffs were driving me crazy. I started pounding with my handcuffs on the cot, pounding and pounding with both hands. At first I was making noise just to hear myself, to affirm that I was alive. But little by little, I got more desperate and banged harder and harder until I drew blood from my wrists. But I wouldn't stop. Then the guards began to scream, "Vieja puta, ¡cállate!" Shut up, you old whore! There was one guard walking up and down the hall doing his rounds, and every time he looked in, I would call to him, "Señor Guardia, Señor Guardia!" but he wouldn't answer me. I don't know how long I kept it up or when I stopped.

During those days that I was tied down, I would hear the screaming of people being tortured for hours without end. It was always men; I never heard a woman's voice. The screams of a tortured person are more painful than suffering pain yourself. It tears you up.

The guard with the mirrored glasses was the only person who came into my cell. He never said much and I never found out who he was. Every time he came in, I looked hard at him, trying to see through the mirrored glasses, and saying to myself, *I have to remember this face.*

By the third day, I knew that I couldn't take it any longer. I didn't know what I was going to do or what my breaking down would mean. I couldn't take the pain in my back, the guard's abuse, the beatings, the lack of sleep, not knowing where I was, not having any reference to the outside world. I was totally alone and thought I would be there forever. I also fantasized about killing myself with the nail. All I could do was look up at the ceiling and count and recount the holes. I occasionally tried pushing against the cot to relieve my back, but that hurt too. Everything was pain. My body felt every single sensation: the springs of the cot, the handcuffs, my butt, my head, my tangled, filthy hair, the excrement and urine and vomit.

Just when I thought that I was about to go mad, the little window in the door opened, and I heard the captain's voice asking, "Are you ready to talk?"

I said, "I don't have anything to say."

He replied with resignation in his voice, "This can get worse. I'm asking you, are you ready to talk?"

And I said again, "I don't have anything to say."

"Okay, it's up to you," he said. "We can keep you here forever. No one knows where you are, no one cares about you, no one has asked for you. You know we can keep you here forever. And things will get worse." Then he shut the door, and I heard his footsteps recede.

I thought, *Shit, this will go on.* But listening to him and talking to him, just those few words spoken in a reasonable tone, gave me strength. While no one talked to me, when I had no contact with the outside world, I felt myself weakening and unable to bear it. But his asking if I was going to cooperate gave me strength. And I started all over again—counting the holes, thinking about the nail, planning what I was going to do as soon as I got hold of it. Thinking back, I still am not sure why that nail was so important to me. It represented escape, I suppose, or the idea that I still controlled my life even if it just meant having the power to end it. It was just a small nail, maybe an inch long, but I thought that if I could reach it, I could cut my wrists. I clung to that thought, staring at the nail and then looking away because I was scared they'd see me looking at it, and if they took it away, I would be totally in their hands. When I heard a noise from outside the cell, I would worry that they were coming to take it away.

The nail and the holes were all I had during those hours. Sometimes I would go back to reading the walls and the messages written by people who barely knew how to write. I wondered who was alive and who wasn't, who had been tortured. I felt that I had to survive somehow and be strong. But I also felt that if it was my turn to die then I wasn't going to open my mouth about anything or anybody.

At the end of the third day I heard some new sounds that didn't fit with the routine. In a situation like mine you become attuned to the smallest details, so I immediately knew it was something new. I listened hard: it wasn't the guards next door and it wasn't the man with the food. My cell was the last at the end of a corridor. Except for the man with the mirrored glasses, whose step I knew all too well, the sounds of footsteps and keys always stopped before they got to my cell. But this time I heard the clanking of keys and the steps of two men approaching my cell.

It was two guards I hadn't seen before. They unlocked my handcuffs, saying nothing to me but remarking to each other how much I stank. I was so weak that they had to take me by the arms to stand me. They put the blindfold back in place, tied my hands behind my back and took me out of the cell for my second interrogation with the captain. It felt strange to walk again, to feel my wet pants, to be so aware of the filth. It was totally humiliating, and even now, eight years later, the memory can push me into a pit of depression.

But it was the end of being handcuffed to the cot. I had survived the first stage of my detention.

14

~

"I've Brought You My Dog Princess"

After the familiar walk down the stairs, out of the building, and across the grass, I could tell that we had come once again to a lighted area. We stopped, and I heard the voice of the captain. "I'm going to give instructions to them to take off the handcuffs and the blindfold," he said. "You are going to sit down. You're not going to look left or right, you're just going to look straight at me."

So they sat me down, took off the handcuffs, untied my thumbs, and finally took off the blindfold. The first thing I saw was the face of the captain. He was dressed in olive green and sat on the other side of a round table. It was a cabana table with a striped umbrella; we were in the officers' club, at least that's what I assumed. So there I was, filthy and stinking after three days tied down, and there he was, looking immaculate on the other side of this silly white table, with a machine gun in between. Around us were five enormous German shepherds. It was about midnight.

The captain had a steno pad on his knee and he started asking me questions. They were the same as before, and once again I denied everything. Eventually he made a proposal. In exchange for collaborating for 10 or 15 days, he said, he could get me a passport with another name. I could go to any country I wanted and would be given enough money to tide me over the first few months. Sebastián was included in the offer. The captain called him *tu imbécil de marido*, "your imbecile of a husband." When he was finished with the offer, I just sat in my chair. I wouldn't reply, so he carried on.

He started asking about my family—a lot about my younger brother, José Francisco. When was the last time I'd seen him? What had I taken him? In those days all priests were suspect, especially those who had been in the Externado as a schoolboy, where Padre Grande had taught. But there wasn't much for the captain to learn. Chico (my brother's nickname) was in the ultraconservative

Opus Dei, and in any case he was in Guatemala. Nothing was ever asked about Javier. Just about Chico.

The captain's manner by this time was kind and friendly, as though we were having a little social conversation. Which was a bit silly, given the machine gun on the table between us. The captain was always correct with me, even kind. It was part of the technique of a well-trained interrogator. He never touched me—that was the job of the gorillas, the Guardias who took me back and forth. They were the ones who hit me and insulted me. This sweet-and-sour technique is typical of security forces all over the world. Good cop/bad cop: its purpose to keep you off-balance by varying your treatment. The trick is to make you look for allies from among your captors, when in fact there is no division among them.

I cut the "conversation" short and complained about the way I was being treated, about being tied down to a bed and not being permitted to wash. About the food and the lights being on all the time. I said to him sarcastically, "You say you don't torture but I can hear torture going on all the time!" He brushed that aside, saying I was imagining things. Then I complained about the man with the mirror glasses, who had been abusing me. The captain said that the man would be called to attention, and it's true because he never again abused me.

Then he called the guards and they took me back to the cell—but not before they'd done the bad cop number on me, pushing me around and threatening to kill me. That always happened, no matter how much I complained to the captain.

Back in the cell, the lights were still on. But after they took off the blindfold and untied my thumbs, they told me they weren't going to tie me down. That was great news, so I pushed my luck and told them I wanted some Pine-Sol to clean the cell. They brought a cleaner, carbolic I think, whose smell I'll forever associate with prison. So I started cleaning that cell with the rags and the papers that were lying around.

After the place was cleaner, I took off my clothes and started washing them in the sink. It was disgusting, but eventually I had them clean and the sink too. Then the hole in the floor. And finally I washed myself. I didn't have a comb so I braided my hair. The worst was my hair, which was thick and down to my waist. By now it was all tangles. I'd had nothing to comb it with and nothing to hold it, and washing it properly was impossible with just the one tiny faucet in the cell.

A little later they brought me a filthy mop and a cotton mattress, but never any other clothes. The next morning they gave me a piece of soap.

Time was broken into days and nights again, and I began to have a more "normal" life in my cell and a better idea of what surrounded it. Most days I hardly saw any guards, but there was a lot of noise, most of it from the sergeants yelling and the troops marching outside the prison walls. Then there was the noise of people moving around in the corridors and occasionally the sound of torture in other cells farther away. But I actually saw very few people.

In the mornings, two young boys who lived in the Guardia Nacional building pushed breakfast through the little door of my cell. You'll find kids like them in all the jails and barracks in El Salvador. They grow up to be little monsters, totally immune to pain because they've been abused so much by the soldiers and the Guardias. Manlio Argueta mentions this in his book, *Un día en la vida* (*One Day in the Life*).[1] The boys' hair was cut in a military style: a little bit up top and the rest shaved off. Otherwise they were two normal, healthy-looking kids, humble Salvadorans, dark-skinned, with Indian features. I never knew their names and they would never respond to me, though I tried very hard. Communication is established first with the eyes; you say something nice and eventually the other person responds. But not with them. Beyond the insults, there was no communication whatsoever. Sickening, when I think back on it.

I tried not to think about myself. At first I thought a lot about what life had been like with Sebastián and about my family. Even about my little dog. All that made me really upset and depressed, so I thought up activities for myself. I washed everything in the sink—each piece of clothing, wringing it and drying it, trying to stretch every activity out as long as possible to take up the time. That included walking up and down the cell, doing some exercise, sit-ups or push-ups, drawing on the walls of the cell with the nail—anything. You have the time; in fact that's all you have in jail. I had absolutely nothing else, no paper or books, only this tiny space to move around in.

Part of the time, I spent listening to the guards in the cells next to me, the ones who had been arrested for murdering the four American churchwomen. They were there the whole time I was in the Guardia Nacional building. I listened hard and tried to remember what they said, what their names were.

I also thought about the women's prison and all the activities that I would get into once I was there. That occupied me for hours, lying on the cot and thinking carefully about all of the organizing I could do and other things like sewing and embroidery.

For some reason I was sure I was going to prison. Perhaps it was that I couldn't think that they were going to kill me. In fact it amazed me sometimes how optimistic I felt. Certainly, I was very excited about COPPES and continuing my political work. *Cada momento, cada situación es tu trinchera.* Every moment, every situation is your trench. That was part of the *mística*, or belief, that kept us going in those days, the idea that wherever you were you would keep fighting for the Salvadoran revolution. And it kept me entertained while I waited for the guards to come and take me to the interrogations. Actually it was more like *not* waiting for them to take me, if you can picture that as an activity. The activity was to think up activities so as not to simply wait.

They interrogated me every two days or so, but I could never predict exactly when. It might be three days in a row and then nothing for the next two days. Again, this is part of the technique of keeping you off-balance. I would hear keys or walking in the corridor and I'd get a rush of adrenaline. I never knew if it was to get me, or beat me, or bring food. But when the time came, it always followed the same pattern. First I'd hear the guards coming down the hall, always two of them. Then the door would open, and they'd come in. Then the blindfold and handcuffs before taking me from the cell. The interrogations were long, drawn-out things that lasted four or five hours. Always the same questions, over and over and over. There was always a sergeant present, taking everything down on a big black Underwood typewriter that went *clack clack clack*.

Sometimes following a session with the captain, after he left, the gorillas got to ask questions. They never beat me up when he was around. One was called Américo, and he would repeat the questions that the captain had asked me earlier, over and over and over to see if I would change my story. The gorillas had the bad cop role to play, and they gave me the worst beatings I ever suffered. They were careful not to mark my face—it was my chest and my back, my buttocks, my legs. A lot of it was just kicking me around. They'd kick my stomach if I did not say what they wanted me to say or if they were not happy with my answer.

I didn't understand the good cop/bad cop thing at the time. It was confusing. I never knew where I stood. In the 11 days that I was in the Guardia Nacional I must have seen the captain four times. And funnily enough, although I didn't trust his motives, I trusted that he wouldn't hurt me. So I would complain at the next interrogation that the gorillas had beaten me, and he would always say he'd do something about it. I thought I could at least protest to him and he might help, but that's exactly what he was trying to do, to establish a kind of trust on my part. It was all part of the technique of breaking down my resistance and making me feel powerless.

Back in my cell, there were ways that I could get on the guards' nerves. One night I screamed over and over for them to turn off the light. "Apágueme la luz, por favor!" Turn off the light, will you! Over and over. It was a very rudimentary form of protest, but I felt that since I was under their control, I had to bug them somehow, just to give myself a little power. I wasn't going to let them kick me around and take it quietly. I was not afraid that the abuse would be increased, though I ran that danger. It was a self-defense or survival technique. Being able to react to them gave me strength. And they finally gave in on the lights. They started to switch them off at night.

They never took me back to the officers' club though. Many of the interrogations took place in a room that had three bunk beds on one side and a table, two chairs, a light bulb. A place that was obviously for interrogations.

On the other hand, I began to understand that I was not entirely without status. I realized this when they changed the food I received. It wasn't good but it wasn't just beans and tortillas—they were giving me officer's food. They obviously thought they had a very important person on their hands, or someone who knew a lot. Even if it wasn't true, I started to feel more sure of myself.

As time went on I tried to make eye contact with the guards and communicate with them. I didn't have any training in this, but I felt that human contact led to trusting and that was what I was trying to do. If I could look them in the eyes, I would be able to see if there was any understanding, kindness, gentleness. This is what was so scary about the guy with the mirror glasses, because I couldn't see his eyes.

It got to the point that I could be jokingly rude with the two gorillas, within limits. "What do you want now?" Or, "Fuck you. Are you coming to pick me up again?" As if they were clumsily trying to take me out on a date. I would complain about the food, the kids, them lying to me.

In the beginning, they would always treat me roughly, with the same routine when they arrived to take me from my cell. They would say, "Let's go!" and they would tie me up and tie my thumbs. But after a while I would sit up and put my thumbs together for them to tie up, and say, "Okay, let's go," because it meant that we had a routine. It was deliberate on my part, just posing no resistance, demonstrating this communication that exists among human beings. Jacobo Timerman talks about this in his book *Prisoner without a Name, Cell without a Number*.[2]

Other than the captain, the guards who took me to the interrogations, and the boys who brought my food, I only saw two officers, who came separately, and only once each. One night the little window in the door opened and there was a lieutenant standing there. He said in a very well-mannered way, "Señora, I've brought you my dog Princess." And he held up this little black-and-white bitch for me to touch. I stuck my hand out the window and stroked her, and it was amazing. Princess squirmed and enjoyed the touch of my hand.

I looked at the lieutenant and tried to place him, thinking that I knew him from somewhere. He told me that he had been in the *operativo* that had arrested me, and that he felt really bad because he knew I was a teacher and his mother was also a teacher. It turned out that she was a member of the teacher's union, ANDES. He knew that I too was a member because something had been written about my arrest in the newspapers and ANDES had demanded that the government guarantee my life and freedom. I sensed that I reminded him of his mother, and even though he was Guardia Nacional and had arrested me, he had some feelings of sympathy for me. He said that he was not supposed to do this, but he'd thought that I would feel better if he brought me his dog. Then he closed the door and was gone. He never came back.

On another morning the window opened up, there stood another officer. He handed me a toothbrush, a tiny tube of toothpaste, and an olive green T-shirt. I was still wearing the clothes I'd been arrested in, and I was filthy. The military T-shirt was his, he said, and it smelled freshly laundered and beautifully clean. It's funny, but I treasured that shirt for a long time. I wore it all through the years in prison, even after another woman said I'd sold myself to the enemy for it. I used to wear it with a pair of white pajama pants that were a present from my sister-in-law. It looked funny, I guess, because my prison mates used to call me *la loca de las pajamas*—"the crazy girl with the pajamas." They also called me *la loca de la bolsa*—"the crazy girl with the handbag"—but we'll get to that.

Anyway, those two small acts of kindness were very special, especially having Princess brought to me. They made me feel I could love humanity no matter what my circumstance was. I felt full of life, and maybe a little more secure.

In fact, after 30 or 40 hours of intense interrogation and all those days in jail, I began to feel as if I knew my space and even controlled it to a degree. Then one day the gorillas told me I was leaving. They cleaned my cell and brought me a towel and a little bar of soap and one of those five-cent plastic combs, the type men keep in their pockets. They said I was going to have a shower—one of the happiest moments of my life when I heard that!

So once again I was blindfolded and handcuffed and taken out of my cell. But they only took me a few steps down the corridor to another cell. They undid the blindfold and the handcuffs and locked me in. This room had the same wall tiles as my cell, but it was L-shaped. There were three open showers, no stalls. There was also a cot full of newspapers. Someone had obviously been sleeping there recently and using the newspapers as a mattress. I started to read a paper from the 10th or 11th of May, the time of my arrest. On the front page was the picture of a woman who had been arrested and sent to the women's prison on the afternoon before they'd come for Sebastián and me. I realized that they must have had her in those cells close to me, but I had never heard her. I met her later on in prison.

I only paused to read for a moment. Then I took off my clothes and had the most wonderful shower of my life. I spent a long time under the stream of cold water, and then a long time untangling my hair with that little comb. I stretched out untangling my hair the same way as I'd stretched out all my other activities in those days. Wonderfully satisfying.

Then I was given some clean clothes. As I started to put them on, I realized that someone outside must know about me because I recognized the clothes. They belonged to my sister-in-law, and I guessed that my mother had sent them. As I put on a skirt and a baby blue T-shirt, I felt a great happiness because it meant that what had been said to me all along—that no one knew what had happened and no one was trying to find me—was untrue. So that gave me a lot of strength, and it felt terrific to be nice and clean again and have my hair untangled.

When the guards came back, they went through the same routine with the blindfold and the handcuffs and took me down the steps of the building. But this time they left me in a long, narrow, and dark room, which I soon realized was a real darkroom, with a photographic enlarger and pictures all over the walls. I sat and waited. Then the door opened, a dim light came on, and in walked my mother and my brother Javier. Amazing!

Mother broke down and started crying. She embraced me and gave me a rosary she was carrying.

Javier kissed me before he started right in: "Why didn't you accept the offer to leave the country? You're stupid! You should have accepted. I never thought you'd be so stupid! Who do you think you are? You're pretending to be from the people, *pero sos una burguesa*—you're a bourgeois! You'll always be a bourgeois and everybody will hate you, the bourgeoisie and the poor people of our country." He got really excited. And Mother just cried and cried.

I didn't argue with Javier. I kept my mouth shut. I just said something like, "It's impossible." He wanted to know why, and I said, "Don't even ask me." I felt like I knew what I was doing. For me there was nothing to talk about, nothing to say.

Then Javier said, "Don't worry, they won't kill you. We've already seen you, so they can't."

And Mother said, "Be strong, pray, believe in God," her usual discourse, but she couldn't help crying. She kept touching me. And she never used to touch me when I was a kid, or when I was in my teens. I just sat with her, holding her arm tightly.

We were together about five minutes, and then someone came and took them away. I put the rosary over my head, and in the newspaper photographs that were taken later on, you can see the beads hanging out of my T-shirt.

I've never heard of anyone else being allowed to see their families under those conditions, and they never told me exactly how they came to be in the Guardia Nacional building. All I know is that Vides Casanova, the current minister of defense, was a friend of Javier's and at that time director of the Guardia. So I assume that he'd told Javier that I'd rejected the offer to leave the country. Which is why he was so furious and called me stupid—because it was too late to reconsider the offer and no way to avoid going to prison.

It was weird, but seeing Mother and Javier gave me strength. So when I was marched back to my cell and left there, I felt happy and clean and strong. I paced back and forth, feeling more confident with each moment.

Once again the guards came for me, put on the blindfold and handcuffs, and marched me to yet another room that I'd never been in before. The walls were a dark pastel blue, and there were a couple of tables there. Altogether there were four men in the room, including the typist and the two sergeants who normally took me back and forth from my cell. The two little boys were there too. The typist gave me a piece of paper and said I had to sign it. I started to read. The document was my "extrajudicial declaration," and it began: "I, Ana Margarita Gasteazoro Escolán, confess that I am a communist . . ."

I read only a paragraph and threw it on the table. I felt very sure of myself at that moment. I said, "That's a bunch of lies, and I never said any of it." They said, "But you have to sign it," and I replied, "I'm not signing this, it's all lies and I want to see the captain!"

They showed me another declaration signed by Sebastián. "You must have tortured him to sign it," I told them. "I'm not signing anything. I want to see the captain!"

They took me back to my cell, and after a moment the captain came in and sat down beside me. "Is there anything wrong?" he asked. I said, "I'm not signing anything!" And he said that no one was obliged to sign anything in our country, that it was a free country, and that I could sign or not sign anything I wanted. It was my constitutional right, and not to worry about it.

"They're never going to force me to sign anything!" I declared again. Now I can laugh about it, how sure I was. I felt so strong and sure of myself—I was going to dominate the whole damn Guardia Nacional!

The captain again said that no one would make me sign anything. He said he admired me, that he really respected me because I'd stayed true to myself and not accepted the money or the offer to leave the country. But I had to realize that I was a subversive and that I would be sent to prison the next day or so. We were getting along so well I even asked him what he would have done in my place, and he said he would have done exactly the same thing for his ideals. Then he shook my hand and said, "Don't worry, no one's going to kill you. I'll never see you again but I wish you the best of luck." He left, and I sat there on the cot feeling happy.

Then *WHAM!* The door burst open and the gorillas rushed in. They tied me up hard and put on the blindfold and kicked me around, then dragged me back to the room with the tables. "You bitch," they yelled, "so you think you aren't going to sign this confession?" And the beating began in earnest, with me trying to say, "But the captain said I didn't have to sign it!" It was horrible because it was so calculated, and I finally realized how badly I'd been fooled. I'd thought I knew everything, and now I had to face that I didn't know shit. I was nothing but somebody's football to kick around. They even had the little boys there to watch and laugh and call out at me, "La vieja puta! La vieja puta!"

After a while they brought out a paper for me to sign, but they wouldn't let me read. I kept repeating what captain had said, and the reply I got was, "You old whore"—punch—"you think you don't have to sign it? Well"—kick—"WE give the orders here!" And the kicking was redoubled. So I started to sign the paper and its three copies, but hoping to fool them, I tried to sign with a different name and handwriting. That was foiled by one of the little boys leaning over the table watching all this. He had my *cédula*, my identity card, in his hand, and he yelled, "Sergeant, sergeant, that's not her signature, she's not signing it the same!" So they hit me again, and said, "Sign it right, you bitch!" And I signed.

When they took me back to my cell, I broke down. It wasn't the worst beating I'd endured, but it was the worst moment of the whole thing. I hadn't broken down once since I was arrested, but now I sat crying and crying and crying, certain that I had let everybody down by signing that confession and that I'd signed my death sentence. It was like I finally understood how cruel the world could be. It was so wrenching and powerful a desolation that I felt sick and tried to throw up, all the while sobbing a river of tears. I think it was hours before I was able to calm myself.

Finally the sergeants came again, handcuffed and blindfolded me, and took me down the stairs and out of the building to a waiting car. It was a big car, with a driver and someone else sitting beside me. We had driven only two blocks when they took off my blindfold and I could see that we were inside the Guardia Nacional complex, next to their sports stadium. We stopped at a little building, and they marched me through a door and left me in a little room with another door other than the one we entered through. And there I waited until the sergeants came back in. They stood me up and took me through the other door without saying where we were going.

And all of a sudden—*FLASH!* There were camera lights and flashbulbs going off. When I could focus, I saw three chairs in front of a round table and facing that a crowd of people. To the side was another round table full of papers and pictures. I walked straight over to the second table and started looking through the papers, seeing my name and various charges against me. Finally it registered: this was a press conference and it was expected that I would make a *declaración*, or admission of guilt. The papers said I had killed the head of the national lottery, who'd been murdered a couple of months before. Why me? I don't know. They also said I'd been caught with radio equipment and even weapons. I started to laugh and said, "This isn't true, I never had this stuff."

Immediately the guards pulled me back and sat me down by force on one of the chairs. When no one sat down beside me I said, "Are we waiting for anyone?" I looked around wondering if the chairs might be for Sebastián and the other *compañero*. There in the audience was the captain and the officer who had given me the T-shirt. The captain said, "No, no one else is coming." As I looked across the audience I spotted an ex-boyfriend that I had met in university, who was now a photographer for Agence France-Presse. He was wearing an Egyptian scarab I had once given him as a present. It gave me strength to see him there, wearing my present, and instead of waiting any longer, I started the press conference myself by talking straight to him.

It was funny. The Guardia Nacional had made all these efforts to break me, and they'd succeeded, but then they had undone all their work by putting me in this press conference, because now I was on my territory. I knew all about television and press conferences, and I was not at all intimidated by the cameras. I looked directly at them and sat up straight as the questions came at me.

The journalists were very aggressive—they had been carefully chosen and given a *comunicado* about me—but I was aggressive back.

"Have you, as charged, been attempting to recruit foreign journalists, to brainwash them and to feed them untrue information?" asked one reporter.

"There is no need to recruit or brainwash journalists in El Salvador," I replied. "They can see the reality, the poverty and the violence."

And what about my role in the MNR?

"I have always been a member of the Movimiento Nacional Revolucionario. My membership has been public. There is nothing to hide. My arrest is unjust because I have done nothing illegal."

More questions: Was it true that I had put bombs in such and such a place?

Was it true that we had killed the chief of the national lottery? I answered easily, sometimes sarcastically, refuting the charges. I was only careful when they asked how I had been treated in jail and whether I'd been tortured, saying only that I didn't want to make any comment. I was still in the Guardia Nacional's hands and scared of the consequences if I denounced their treatment of me.

Finally I asked if there were any more questions. There weren't, so I summed up by referring to the stuff on the table and saying that the authorities had planted all these things on me. Later on I read that some of the journalists

Figure 17. Ana Margarita's press conference confession, May 1981 (Courtesy of Iván Montecinos)

had been shown "evidence" that included radio equipment and even a few weapons mixed in with stuff they'd taken from the MNR office.

With the press conference over, the sergeants took me back to my cell. I expected that I would be taken to prison later that day because that had been the pattern with other political prisoners. I still felt bad about signing the confession, but I was recovering my confidence so I demanded that I be taken to prison that same afternoon. It didn't do any good; I spent another night in my cell.

Figure 18. Close-up of Ana Margarita's press conference confession (Courtesy of Iván Montecinos)

The next morning I finally left the Guardia Nacional building in a car with two escort cars, all with machine guns sticking out the windows. The cars were unmarked civilian vehicles, but with all those guns, it was totally obvious to anyone who saw us what we were.

At about 7:30 in the morning, and as we drove to Ilopango, I said to the sergeant who had done the typing, "Stop and get me the morning newspapers."

"With whose money?" he asked.

"You buy them for me," I said. And they did it! There was my face on the front page of all those newspapers. We drove until we stopped outside the prison. The sergeant shook my hand and said goodbye.

Part III

A Nice Prison like Ilopango

15

~

First Day in Prison

There's only one way in or out of Section A of Ilopango Prison for Women. That's the big iron door leading from the main prison compound. The other two sections in Ilopango are for common prisoners. Section B is for young women between the ages of 16 and 25, while Section C is for mature women 26 and older. Each section had a big iron door, which was kept open during the day and closed at night after everyone had been locked into their cells. The wall was concrete that had been painted blue.

The door to Section A was already open when I walked up to it for the first time, accompanied by a *celadora*.[1] I didn't know what or who I would find behind the door, but I was keyed up for getting involved, for doing something, for becoming a friend and *compañera* to anyone who shared my status of political prisoner. *Cada momento, cada situación es tu trinchera.* Unfortunately the first prisoner I saw from Section A, a young woman who was standing in the doorway, didn't return my smile. That was a bit of a letdown. Here I was, ready to make the prison another battleground in the revolutionary struggle, and this woman just turned her back on me and went back into the section. She was my introduction to one of the hard facts of political detention in El Salvador—a lot of people arrested as political prisoners haven't got a political bone in their bodies.

This woman Magdalena was a good example. She was a prostitute from the port of La Libertad, a tough-looking girl accused of killing a man from ORDEN. But she didn't kill him because of his death squad activities, or the torture and murders he'd been involved in. It had been a "crime of passion"; he'd been her lover and for one reason or another she killed him. But the authorities decided to call it a political crime. Of the 11 women in Section A when I got there, only 7 were really politicals. It suited the government to inflate the number of political prisoners so they could say that they weren't just killing everybody as they'd done before.

Figure 19. Ilopango Prison for Women (Courtesy of Museo de la Palabra y la Imagen)

Luckily I didn't have time to be disappointed by Magdalena, because there were 7 other women waiting to meet me. They knew who I was because they had heard from the women of the prison kitchen, who had read about my press conference in the newspapers that morning. Word gets around fast in a prison, and in the time it had taken to do the entrance procedures, the women of Section A had heard that they had a new *compañera* called Ana Margarita Gasteazoro. Some of them had heard of me before because of my MNR work.

I knew who most of them were too, though I'd never met any of them before. The first person to greet me was a woman whose face I had seen in the newspapers recently.

"My name is Esperanza," she said. Well, I knew better than that. Her name was actually Ana Mercedes Letona, but she was far better known as Comandante Clelia, one of the most important leaders of the ERP. I remembered her arrest in February and being amazed that she had not simply been killed by the Guardia Nacional. The police had caught her with a small group of ERP members in a security house. There had been no shootout because safe houses were usually "clean" at that time. All of the people arrested were sent to prison.

Her pseudonym had been Ana Esperanza and she had been arrested under that name. So during the next two years, I and everyone else in Ilopango knew her as Esperanza. She introduced Marta, and the two sisters, Paquita and Ana. I knew their faces too, because they had all been arrested in the same raid. The other was Vida Cuadra. She was director of a news agency that ran a weekly magazine called *Información Centroamericana*, and she also had a column in

El Salvador's most progressive newspaper, *La Crónica*. The last thing she published before she was arrested was Ungo's statement about why he had left the first junta. They'd arrested her in January, along with her colleague Lupe.

Everybody was dying to know what had happened to me, but at first they were discreet—perhaps delicate is a better word—about asking what I'd gone through. That gentleness was standard with us whenever someone new came into Section A. Many of the new arrivals came in immediately after torture by the police, so we made sure that a woman's first contact with us wasn't another interrogation. We tried to give her a feeling that she was among other women now, she wasn't alone, she was safe. You could almost touch the solidarity in those moments.

Esperanza, Paquita, and Ana started to show me around. Most of our section was a three-story building, but it also had a little dirt plaza created when the section had been walled off from the rest of the prison. Up on the walls surrounding the plaza were three turrets with guards looking down on us.

I should have been depressed by it, but I wasn't. In fact, there was even one beautiful feature: the trees we had in our plaza. The prison had once been farmland. That first morning I discovered we had a mango tree, an almond tree, a lemon tree, an avocado tree, and a guava tree. And from outside the walls, the sweet yellow fruit of a nance tree fell in. It made things very different to see greenery instead of just concrete and iron bars, to see that things could grow even there.

The layout was the same on all three floors: a big room in the center and three rooms of different sizes on each side. An iron door on the left led into a dark, dingy room with two toilets and three showers. At the time I arrived we all slept in one big cell on the first floor. Our dining room was the enormous room in the center. It had scruffy Formica tables and chairs like in a greasy spoon. On the next floor there was another enormous empty room, and a "workshop" with a single sewing machine in it. Esperanza snickered as she pointed out the sewing machine: "That's how we're supposed to rehabilitate ourselves and make a living while we're in prison."

Most of the rooms were locked, but within a year so many new prisoners arrived that other rooms were turned into cells. At our most crowded, there would be less than three feet between beds, with two tile squares marking the space between each cot.

Paquita asked if I wanted to take a shower. "You can, but you'll just have to use a bucket in the shower stalls." There was water in the early morning only, and they had to collect water in whatever containers they had before it shut off. And some days there was no water at all.

The four of us decided to talk about COPPES. The section had a little hot plate, so we made coffee and took some chairs up to the second floor. My credentials from the MNR and FDR were enough to include me immediately. It felt great.

Five *compañeras* had already done their first activity as COPPES two weeks before, on Mother's Day. That was May 10, shortly before I was arrested. At that time the political prisoners received their family visits during the same hours as the commons. So they decided to do something that would have a little impact on the commons' families. And that was to sing a Mother's Day song.

Paquita said, "We had it all planned, with a banner and slogans. The *celadoras* didn't know what to do. No one was going to stop us singing a song, but it was clearly an activity of COPPES, a sort of introduction: Hello, we're the Committee of Political Prisoners."

I was wondering why Vida Cuadra and Lupe hadn't joined in the meeting, but it soon became clear. Creating a COPPES chapter in Ilopango was going to be complicated politically. All of the women involved were from the same organization, the ERP. Vida and Lupe, the other bona fide politicals, were against the idea. They thought organizing would result in longer sentences and make us more vulnerable to pressure by the authorities. According to their analysis, the longer we stayed in prison, the less effective we'd be in the struggle, so the major objective was to gain our release as soon as possible.

I suppose the tension might have been expected, since groups thrown together like that are never homogenous. But we who were in favor of organizing were already the majority, and we worked very hard to stay that way. Though Vida and Lupe stayed out for almost a year, eventually they came into COPPES.

We talked about how COPPES could continue the struggle from within the prison. We agreed that the same discipline we had kept outside had to be applied here. All that was different was the work itself and that we had much more time to do it in. Some *compañeros* on the outside were fighting a war with bullets, others with propaganda; we political prisoners had to keep fighting too. That determination was very strong as we talked.

The four of us started with a short list of very practical objectives. We were all experienced enough to know that it's no good attacking every problem in sight. You waste energy and you open up a new possibility for argument with each new issue. So we kept it simple in those first weeks.

The first objective was improving our food. I had already been introduced to the water problem, but food was even more pressing. Lunch was badly overcooked spaghetti in a watery sauce, with the basic prison ration of frijoles and tortillas.

Frijoles and tortillas were handed out three times a day. The beans came in a small pile on a plastic plate, with two tortillas leaning on it like a little roof on a house. And that's what it is called throughout the Salvadoran prisons—the *rancho*. Once a week we got an egg, and occasionally some cheese or whatever vegetable happened to be cheap and plentiful. Very occasionally there was a beef or chicken stew.

Your family or friends can bring you food or things to make your life easier like an electric cooker. The authorities didn't mind; it made it easier for them to keep the prison budget very low—50 centavos per prisoner per day. And that included food, gas, and electricity. The prison budget had been cut so much that we didn't even have uniforms. (Which was fine by me!) In any case, it didn't matter what the food was: it always tasted horrible because it was cooked by prisoners from the commons sections.

Paquita explained that they were already sharing whatever their relatives brought them. There might only be a bit of cheese or a plantain for each person, but it made a difference. And we decided we had to do better.

A second objective was to maintain a small pool of money to buy basic necessities from the outside like toothpaste, sanitary napkins, and so on. The prison system had no money budgeted for that sort of thing, and it could be very tough on women without resources. I had a family to bring me things but some of the girls didn't even have families. So after talking it over, we established the Common Fund. It wasn't complicated: if a relative brought one of us three or four dollars, we would put it in the Common Fund and see how far it went.

A third issue was work. We knew that if we made things for sale outside the prison, we could improve our life inside with the proceeds. It was also clear that women who were occupied would have better morale than women with nothing to do.

And of course, we decided to do political work. At this early stage it simply meant finding ways to propagandize the work of the FMLN and the FDR. We knew we'd have to start small. To that end, Esperanza and her *compañeras* had just requested a blackboard from the Red Cross. While they had justified it as an educational tool, in reality they intended to make it into a bulletin board, the first small step in propaganda.

It was all very exciting for me. I had spent hours in the Guardia Nacional thinking about what I would do when I got to prison, and now I had these experienced, practical *compañeras* to work with. I felt wonderful: I had been there only two hours but I could see clearly the work ahead. I felt we were capable of organizing the whole damn prison. It was a very constructive, dynamic meeting. I don't want to be chauvinistic, but it's typical of Salvadorans to get together like that, women and men. Wherever you find them they're ready to work together, to take care of each other.

After lunch I went out in the plaza for my first work session as a prisoner. The task was tying together short lengths of wool and rolling them into balls of wool to knit with. It wasn't so bad. There was no foreman to push us along and we could talk all we wanted. The pieces of wool were waste cuttings from a glove factory in the nearby free trade zone that the prison got for free. A number of factories there did piecework or assembly work on products that were then reexported to the United States. It's typical of industrial development in Central America in this century. It only works because very little money is paid to the workers, and the conditions are not good.

But we made beautiful things out of those pieces of wool, each one about a hand's width in length and in a multitude of colors. I'm very much my mother's daughter in my appreciation of colors, and I was enchanted by cuttings from woolen mittens made in the earth colors. Once you had tied and rolled a few balls you could knit, and I think I made a cap that day.

In the evening at 8:00 we were locked in the cell. The lights were turned off at 10:00 at the order of the *celadora*, who had her own small room with a little door that opened out so she could look at us, very much like a Catholic boarding school. In fact, the prison was created by nuns from the order of the Buen Pastor (Good Shepherd). They guard woman prisoners all over Latin America as part of their vocation. By the time I got there, however, they had left El Salvador in protest over Monseñor Romero's death. So all of the *celadoras* were civilians.

It may sound funny, but standards at the prison went down sharply when the nuns left. It was probably good for COPPES because they were tougher on discipline than our *celadoras*. The nuns allowed much less freedom of movement and might have made our activities a lot more difficult. I was told that the sisters used to make the prisoners get up at 4:00 and kept everyone working constantly. The floors had to be kept as shiny as mirrors, and that wasn't easy, especially when it rained and dirt got tracked in from the plaza. We politicals kept the floors clean but not like mirrors—six passes with the mop and that was it.

That first night, after the lights were turned out I lay in bed looking up through the iron bars of the ventilation space in the wall. It was about a foot wide, and open because it's never very cold in El Salvador. Through it I could see a couple of stars. I know it doesn't sound like much, but after 11 days in the Guardia Nacional that tiny bit of the sky above my head was beautiful. There was life out there beyond the wall, and even if I was locked in this room at least I was in the company of other women. And even if some of them were criminals, there was this chance of communication, maybe of building something together. I was here, I was alive, and *cada situación es tu trinchera*. I lay back and listened to them talking. The talking gradually diminished till all I could hear was the breathing of the women in the closest beds. We were here, we were alive. Eventually I dropped off too.

16

~

Organizing Inside

We had our first hunger strike in August, three months after I arrived. It lasted just over two weeks and was carefully planned by COPPES in co-ordination with the men in Santa Tecla. We knew what we wanted and which of our demands had a chance of winning agreement from the authorities. As it turned out, our calculations were pretty realistic. But becoming able to or-ganize a hunger strike, or coordinating publicity for it and getting the support of a majority of the politicals—that was a long and difficult process. COPPES was not built in a day.

Two weeks after I arrived, there were about 18 of us in Section A. A whole lot of people started coming. Of course, they weren't all bona fide politicals. In fact, the ratio was probably three non-politicals for each person who'd actually been in the struggle.

Many were there as the result of telephone numbers the police had posted all over the country to encourage people to report on their neighbors. A few people were arrested for nothing more than a neighbor's grudge—no con-nection to the struggle, no evidence, just a phone call and before you know it you're being interrogated by the Guardia Nacional. More had some tenuous connection, usually a relative or friend who was in the struggle. It's true that relatives are often "recruitable," but most had nothing to do with anything; they were simply arrested under guilt by association. Still others had the mis-fortune of someone else hiding things at their house, with or without their knowledge.

For instance, a woman I'll call Doña Emilia arrived a few weeks after I did. She was a *bruja*, a traditional midwife. She had a boyfriend in one of the guerrilla organizations who had hidden some homemade bombs at her house. And there were prostitutes and common criminals. Bona fide or not, we had all been arrested under Decree 507 and dumped in Section A to inflate the official numbers of political prisoners.[1] It made us a very disparate group and not easy to organize.

COPPES at Ilopango started as a political initiative with political objectives, but it would never have got off the ground if it hadn't also been an organization of survival. It only took a person a few hours on the first day to understand the basic problems at Ilopango.

Nonetheless, in those early days it sometimes seemed doubtful that COPPES would actually get going. Besides the sheer number of non-politicals, we had to contend with the opposition of Vida Cuadra and her friends. The women coming into Section A had to choose between two factions: COPPES and non-COPPES. Even though Vida's group was against formal organization and didn't have a name, the fact that they were against something made them into a sort of organization despite themselves. And since something had to be done about the horrible food, they were forced into working together like the COPPES women, recooking or adding to their prison rations. Vida had a small hot plate, and she did her food on that until she finally came into COPPES. But that took almost a year.

I have a clear picture of Vida in those early days, sitting by a little aluminum table in a corner of the corridor. The table had a few ragged chairs held together by plastic strings that were full of knots because you had to tie them together when they started tearing. She ate breakfast by herself and then sat there, all day long, knitting.

Now Vida was a progressive woman and a very respected journalist. I knew her work from *La Crónica*, the most progressive paper in the country.

Figure 20. Committee of Political Prisoners of El Salvador
(COPPES) (Courtesy of Museo de la Palabra y la Imagen)

(How progressive could be seen by the fact that it was bombed and burnt down shortly after she was arrested!) Her friend Lupita was a social worker and activist who'd been arrested shortly before I was.

In the whole two years I spent in Ilopango I never got friendly with Vida, in the sense that we never spent time together. Most friendships in Section A were established by sharing some activity that lasted hours—sewing, cooking, crafts—and chatting. Your friends were the people you killed time with, but Vida kept her distance. We were coolish but well-mannered to each other, as befit our upbringing.

"Good morning, Vida."

"Good morning, Ana Margarita."

And that was that. Perhaps we were too similar.

I was aware that people looked at me strangely from the day I arrived, at least during the first weeks. Part of it was a class thing, because except for Vida I was still the only upper-middle-class woman in our section. So they watched what I did. For instance, I made my bed differently. I usually had two sheets: a bottom sheet and a top sheet, and a blanket on top of the top sheet. Most of the girls had a bottom sheet and then put the blanket on top and that was all. It was a class difference: I grew up with more linen. I kept a routine of reading for an hour after lunch and then taking a 20-minute nap. I got a small water plant and put it next to my bed.

I decided early on that I was going to dress comfortably in prison—who was there to dress up for? It's probably an attitude I picked up at the American School; Central American women generally find it harder to dress down. So I started to wear rough cotton pajama pants and loose T-shirts, and that immediately set me apart. I also carried around a big plastic shopping bag. Mother and Javier had brought me a ballpoint pen and paper, and lots of other little things during their visits, and I needed something to carry them in. So I asked Mother for one of those transparent plastic bags that we use in El Salvador to go to the farmer's market, big enough to put all your fruit and vegetables in. Mother was always very efficient, and on her next visit she brought my nana's market bag.

It was very convenient; I carried my book and my knitting and any other junk I might need during the day. But it caused a stir with the *compañeras*. Up till then, the only other person who carried a shopping bag was Guillermina, who was mentally ill. So behind my back the others started calling me *la loca de la bolsa*, "the crazy girl with the shopping bag." They called me that for a long time, but finally everyone carried a shopping bag. The aesthetics of it weren't wonderful, but it made sense to carry your stuff with you. And as they got used to my ways and saw that some of my projects worked, I got more respected.

Actually, I came in with automatic respect simply because my position in the MNR gave me immediate status with the newly formed COPPES. Within days of my arrival we created a *directiva*, a steering committee, which was Esperanza, Ana, Marta, and me. At first we were pretty much self-appointed. It depended on your willingness to work, but also on your position outside and how much you knew about the political situation. I was an experienced member of the MNR, I knew about organizing, and I supported the aims of COPPES, so I immediately became a member of the collective. Later on membership in the *directiva* was representative of the political organizations outside the prison. There was no general vote, but each group elected its own representative.

The *directiva* met three times a week. It wasn't hard to find space in the beginning. We had this enormous building all to ourselves and we lived in one cell. The other cells were locked but we managed to get some of them open and chose a room on the second floor to meet in. When we were in a meeting no one would bother us. There was a lot of respect. So when we got the tortillas and whatever else the prison gave us, we thought about how to make it a little better with what we got from our families, and we convinced everyone else to share too. That was the first objective, and it made sense to everyone and improved everyone's diet.

The Common Fund I mentioned earlier allowed us to buy things from the outside. We could get the prison to order it for us, or we'd give money to family members when they visited and they'd bring everything during the next visit. We got support from trade unions, from professional associations like the teachers, and from the Committee of Mothers of Political Prisoners and Disappeared. Sometimes they collected donations and we would tell them what we needed, like sheets or underpants or rubber thongs for our feet. But it wasn't enough, especially as our numbers were growing fast. So there was a clear need, and it seemed totally easy for everyone to agree on. Someone had to look after the money of course, so we elected Carolina as treasurer.

Carolina was the daughter of a market woman, tall and solid with curly hair and dark skin. She was pregnant when she arrived in prison and had her baby about five months later. I think she had some African ancestry, which is unusual for El Salvador. She stood a whole head taller than me, yet she was baby-faced and always had a sweet expression. She was the perfect person to be the treasurer because of her pleasant personality and her market background. One of her duties was to carry about four dollars petty cash, and if anyone wanted something—a soft drink, say, or cigarettes—they asked Carolina. Or if you wanted to buy some bouillon cubes to give more taste to the beans we were cooking, you asked Carolina and she ordered it from one of the relatives during *visitas* on Thursday or Sunday. She also was in charge of ordering toilet paper, sanitary napkins, toothbrushes and toothpaste, and so on, which she distributed every Sunday night after the relatives had gone. Everybody got a roll of toilet paper and a bar of soap for the week. We shared toothpaste, and groups of us kept our toothbrushes in a glass.

In those first meetings, Esperanza, Marta, Ana, and I agreed on four basic objectives, but deciding something doesn't mean it'll come out that way. The food objective was no problem. Everyone had to eat and so everyone saw the wisdom in sharing the food that relatives brought in. But the Common Fund didn't work so well in those first weeks. Eight or ten of us put all our money in that fund, but some non-political women contributed nothing.

And then there was always the group that didn't want COPPES. Vida and Lupe were the only two bona fide politicals in the anti-COPPES faction, but for a while they attracted some of the new arrivals. And that was a complication because at least Vida and Lupe knew what the rules of the political game were. One of the people who hung around with them in the early days was a 14-year-old kid named Sonia, who over most of my time in prison was alternately a joy and a sorrow to me. My first and last dealings with her were physical confrontations. She arrived a few days after I did, and Vida's group had been kind to her. One afternoon, a week after my arrival, I found her blocking my way, denying me entry to the cell we used as a storeroom.

That may not sound like much, being challenged by a 14-year-old girl. But Sonia was a big-boned tomboy who always wore jeans or dungarees and a T-shirt or plaid shirt. We used to call her by her surname, because she looked and walked like a boy. In fact, at first glance it was hard to tell if she was a boy or a girl, with her short hair cut in bangs down almost to her eyebrows, like the early Beatles. She looked quite tough and had got that way by hanging out with street gangs.

She was with her gang the day she got arrested, hanging out in San Jacinto Park. I think they gave a hard time to the policeman on duty. That isn't a good idea anywhere, but it's a terrible idea in El Salvador. More police arrived and, Sonia being Sonia, she went too far and got arrested. At the police station she was so insolent that they hit her, and that just made it worse. She was very proud of how tough she was, and in response to their abuse, she accepted all the standard accusations they made at her. Yes, she'd been involved in politics. Yes, she'd been a guerrilla. Yes, she'd placed bombs and killed people, and if they didn't like it they could shove it! So they beat her up even worse. When she arrived in Ilopango she had been detained for six weeks by the Guardia Nacional, a ridiculous thing for a 14-year-old apolitical kid.

Vida and her friends took Sonia under their wing when she first arrived, and they often spent time in one of the empty cells on the second floor when it was raining. It was also where the leftover wool from the glove factory was kept, and one day I went up there to get some wool. There was no one in the room, but a number of women were sitting in the hallway, including Sonia. She had decided this room was like a clubhouse for the anti-COPPES group, so when she saw me she sprang up to intercept me. I found myself nose-to-nose with her.

"Where do you think you're going!"

I said I was going to get some wool.

"You can't go in there!" she said, pushing up against me.

Jesus, this kid! My heart was pounding but I kept my voice even. All the women were watching.

"Sonia," I said, "I can go wherever I want."

"No! You have the sewing room for your group."

I pushed past her and got my wool and left. She didn't dare do anything about it, and nothing more was said. Funnily enough, she was the only person who joined me in my first major project.

As far as the other women were concerned, my vegetable garden was another one of Ana Margarita's crazy ideas. But to me it seemed perfectly logical. We needed to supplement our diet, and the section had a little patch of earth that I thought I could grow things in. One of my cousins owns an enormous fertilizer company, so through my mother I asked him for help. He sent me all kinds of seeds and a book on how to keep a garden. When Sonia understood that I wanted help, she got very excited. It was the first time in her life she'd had a chance to do any gardening, and she plunged into it with enthusiasm that equaled and even surpassed mine. That's why I say that Sonia was both a joy and a sorrow. I saw both those sides of her as we worked on the garden.

It turned out to be a heartbreaker. To begin with, the soil was largely beaten-down clay, and we had only one tool to work with, a hoe that the prison provided. But that was okay; we were both enthusiastic and we had all the time in the world. But after we started our various crops, all the possible gardeners' nightmares happened, one after another.

First there were slugs. We had about 50 corn plants started, all about three inches high. Then one morning we came out and they were all on their sides, broken at the bottom by the damned slugs. We put in an order through a family member to buy slug poison, but we had to wait for the next visiting day to receive it. And the poison had to be left at the entrance and checked before it was approved, which took even more time. So the slugs ate everything, but at least we had the poison in case they came back. So we replanted.

Then came the birds. These were city birds, not crows but black and quite aggressive. They swooped in at every opportunity and scratched and pecked up the seeds.

Undaunted, we decided to put up a scarecrow. Sonia created a funny, gorgeous scarecrow with blue shorts and an orange jacket made of artificial velvet. The colors were electric, like a hallucinatory Pepsi ad. Most of the clothes belonged to Guillermina, who by then had been sent back to the insane asylum.

Guillermina was a sad story. It's said that if you want to tell the economic state of a country you should look at its mental hospitals and prisons. El Salvador's insane asylum is totally inadequate, so the most dangerous insane women were sent to prison and kept in the solitary cells. Guillermina was classified as criminally insane, and so that was what had been done with her. She slept in solitary's horrible cells, but during the day she was free to wander the main compound and often came to the political section. We were more tolerant of her than the commons, and even found ways for her to participate. When we worked with materials from the glove factory, Guillermina would sit with us and tie pieces of wool together. She was so spaced out that she couldn't knit the bags and sweaters and tam-o'-shanters that we made for sale—she couldn't even handle rolling the wool into balls. But she was quite happy to sit and tie knots.

I don't mean to say that it was easy to have her around. First of all, she was physically a little intimidating, being strong and heavyset, though actually quite good-looking. We had to be careful not to leave knives around because she might pick one up and chase someone with it. And even when she was being good, she was disconcerting. She had a habit of standing very close to you, or sitting at your feet, watching fascinated at whatever you were doing. Usually she'd sit quietly, rocking and smoking cigarette after cigarette. It was usually okay, especially because we were careful to give her cigarettes.

But the strangest thing Guillermina did was to climb the section's trees and take off her clothes. Up she'd go, off would come the clothes, and there she'd sit for hours, stark naked. It didn't really matter, so we paid her no mind. When she was taken back to the asylum, she left a lot of clothes hanging in the branches of the trees. And since Sonia was adept at climbing too, she would collect the clothes that poor Guillermina left behind.

So that's what Sonia made the scarecrow from. She stole some wood for arms and legs, dressed it in these odd clothes and stuffed it with straw. It worked very well, and stood for almost a year, deteriorating slowly from the rain and wind and sunshine.

But after the birds there were the ants. They ate everything, even our little corn seedlings from the second planting. Big, black, horrible ants. Once again we ordered a pesticide, and helplessly watched the ants destroy our crop while we waited for the pesticide to arrive and pass the prison approval.

The only vegetables that looked hopeful were the cucumbers. By mid-August we had about 150 of them, and their flowers began to bloom. The other *compañeras* began to take the garden seriously, after months of scoffing at our efforts.

We had our first hunger strike just at the time the cucumbers were ripening. I was in the hunger strike and so Sonia was left in charge of the garden. She worked very conscientiously. One day she came up to the cell where we hunger strikers stayed. She was all fired up; the cucumbers were beautiful she said, and I had to come and see them. During a hunger strike, strikers spend most of their time conserving their energy, but I got up and asked permission to see the garden. Sure enough, they were beautiful. She and I discussed what we would do with the ripe cucumbers: pickles and cucumber salad and so on. I went back to the strike, and didn't think anything of it when she came a few days later and asked for the gardening book my cousin had sent me.

Cucumbers grow on vines and are usually cultivated on the ground. But Sonia read that cucumber plants should be raised on trellises, so she stole some wood and made a very pretty little trellis for them. Then she picked up the vines and hung them on the trellis. In fact, there are two ways of growing them, but you can't switch from one to the other in the middle of growing. The ones that grow on trellises send secondary shoots into the ground, and in pulling the vines off the ground Sonia pulled out all the secondary shoots. About three hours later all the little cucumbers fell off the plants. Though some women snickered and said I told you so, everyone in the hunger strike mourned the cucumbers—we'd all been looking forward to eating them. Sonia was devastated. She felt terribly guilty and was upset for days. We never tried gardening again.

By that time the pro-COPPES group was strongly in the majority and Vida's group was very much the outsiders. There were almost 40 women in Section A by then, and most had joined us. We had opened a second room to sleep in. But the very numbers forced COPPES to make important changes. The original arrangements had worked until July, when our number had risen to about 30. At a meeting of the *directiva* we talked about the fact that we were being taken advantage of by the women that did not agree. Some had nothing to contribute and no relatives to help them, but others were simply taking from the Common Fund.

However, we realized that the problem was more complicated than that. There were five or six women that were taking advantage of the situation—that was one issue. But a lot of women, even some who were politically aware, weren't keeping themselves occupied and were getting very depressed. Some of us worked all day long, and in a way it kept us entertained. In my case, for instance, COPPES itself kept me very busy with meetings and planning and so on. But the rest of the time I would sew and knit and read and work on my vegetable garden. And that was the case with all of us in the *directiva*, because we were all busy and in reasonably good spirits. But other women were just lying around all day and getting very depressed and sad and being unproductive. They felt no need to worry about work or where they got their income. The Common Fund and the prison gave them everything they needed, at least the basics.

So some of the women were taking advantage of the situation, and others were stagnating. The discussion went around the table, and each *compañera* spoke. We agreed that our communal organization wasn't working, but that whatever solution we proposed should be as close to a commune as possible. After thinking hard, we decided to try organizing work as a cooperative and to start a store on cooperative lines as well. No one had any direct experience of cooperatives or retail, but we understood the principles: everyone works, everyone participates. The cooperative can only function and command respect if it provides goods on the one hand and work on the other hand so that people can buy the goods. Everybody in the political section would have access to some kind of work and make money so they could buy stuff at the store. The Common Fund would continue and would be financed by dues of 50 centavos a week.

We started work on the store immediately. First, we made a list of basic items we would sell like toilet paper, sanitary napkins, bath soap, and toothpaste. We decided to make between 10 and 15 percent on every article, because we knew that usually store owners made 20 percent, at least the small general stores in the barrios. We felt we should make less because, after all, we didn't have to pay rent or electricity.

The store was in a little room on the first floor. It had a lock, and I think we had two keys, one for me and one for whoever was actually running the store. The store was the responsibility of one of our committees, and I'm not sure why but I was always in it and I always had a key. I knew only a little about basic accounting and had never owned a store, but it turned out to be easy.

A business needs working capital, so we collected among us about 200 colones, at that time about 80 dollars. Our first orders went out with family members who bought wherever they normally shopped. But later on we worked directly with wholesalers, who would truck the order out to the prison. When I left, our inventory was worth about 3,000 colones.

The prison searched through our orders once in a while, but they needn't have bothered because we never tried to smuggle anything in that way.

Between the Common Fund and the store, we had money available when it was needed. For instance, it allowed us to become self-sufficient in medicine. The International Red Cross gave us a lot of first-aid items that you need like aspirin and bandages. But many *compañeras* or their children needed special medicine.

One example was Mercedes. Not only had she been terribly tortured after she was arrested, she was epileptic and had attacks constantly. She needed medicines that were far more specialized than what the Red Cross gave us. By the time she arrived, our finances were pretty stable, so we could order what she needed pretty quickly, provided it was during office hours. But if it was the weekend, the office was closed. In an emergency you had to go to the guards at the door or in one of the turrets and tell them, and they would go all the way to the front gate and call the Red Cross from there. It was the International Red Cross we'd call in emergencies like when a pregnant *compañera* had to go to hospital. They gave us a lot of help.

One Saturday Mercedes had an attack about 8:00 in the morning. She was by the sinks, and when she fell down, she hit her head and cut open her tongue. There were no *celadoras* or administrators, and the guards in the observation posts wouldn't do anything. They said they needed a signature. At noon Mercedes started having attacks again almost exactly on the hour, every hour, and there was no way to get her out until the next morning. All we could do was stay with her, doing whatever we could. The next morning the first person who came to visit called the International Red Cross, but even then all that could be done was to sew up Mercedes's tongue.

By August there were around 40 women in the section. One of them was Beatriz, my best friend in Ilopango. I think just about everyone had a best friend there, because friendship—sisterhood—is fundamental in a situation like that. When I see people who say, "I don't need anybody else," I feel it's close to neurosis. Nobody is that tough. Everybody needs the sharing. In my case, friendship is based on intuition. I usually "feel" people. Sometimes you meet people with lots of things in common and there's no "click." But when you do, it's like finding their wavelength, if you think of radio waves.

I didn't know Beatriz before Ilopango, but we were best friends from the first night that we had a chance to talk. It wasn't just because she was also in the Orga, or the medical skills that made her so appreciated in prison. Beatriz was a nurse. She hadn't graduated, but she had made it to her last year of nursing school and was very skilled. For several years she had been working in the camps and had been a member of the Orga's health commission. Beatriz's situation was quite complicated when she arrived. She had a false ID when she was arrested, and her cover story was that she didn't know how to read and write. But there was no way she could hide her skills, and she became the most trusted person regarding health. For instance, we had a woman with serious mental health problems, Tere, another non-political who ended up in our section. She was with us for about a year. Beatriz was the only person who could get her to bathe, or who Tere would allow to touch her when she had a serious infection.

It was around that time that we started the first—and by no means the last—restructuring of COPPES. In that first restructuring we created a bunch of *comités* to look after tasks such as security, propaganda, ideology, work, discipline, and finance, which included the Common Fund. There were five at the start, in addition to the *directiva*, and we tried to rotate the membership every four or five months. Leadership of the committees changed regularly, and those of us from the *directiva* headed as many as three or four committees during our time in prison. I like to cook but I was never in the *economato*, the commissary committee, which dealt with food preparation. But I was in the finance committee for the whole time I was in Ilopango, including being its head several times, as well as the health and education committees. All of us in the *directiva* were in the security, ideology, and discipline committees.

We felt that everybody in the section ought to be in at least one committee, and we managed to make it happen—and have everybody join COPPES—largely because of the food situation. Initially some women said, "I want nothing to do with this," but eventually they had no choice: we controlled all the basic needs—health, food, and work—and so we managed to take control and organize all of the political prisoners.

We controlled food after we negotiated through the Red Cross to get all the foodstuffs raw so we could cook it ourselves and wood to cook it with. At least we could make sure it was cooked properly. It was a major victory. The International Red Cross was our negotiating base in bargaining with the authorities for improvements. We had our demands delivered to several levels at the same time, including the Ministry of Justice, Ministry of Defense, Legal Aid, Mothers Committee, as well as the Red Cross. But we also did a lot of face-to-face negotiation in the prison office, the fastest way to get our practical demands met. It was also an opportunity to let them know what was going on, to keep up communication.

As with all bargaining positions, ours started with things we knew we couldn't get, so our list of demands went like this:

Freedom for the political prisoners.

Freedom for all the disappeared.

An end to repression of the people. . . .

Little by little it got down to basic needs, the ones the prison authorities could do something about. And they were serious. As I found out on my first day, we had a real problem with water. We just had it from 4:00 to 5:30 in the morning, and only from one spigot outside the building. We had to fill buckets every morning. And two days a week we had no water, period. Now, we knew very well that there was water available because the prison is in an industrialized area. There are a lot of factories there, and across the street was the air force base. They definitely had water, so that was one of the major points on our list.

A later demand was for a dentist to come at least once a week and to have a nurse on duty all the time. Finally, we demanded the right to administer our own medicine.

We made these demands in the first four months, practical demands to fix practical problems. They weren't a source of great friction with the authorities because in some cases, especially food and medicine, they saved the prison money and effort.

The political work was more complicated. They wanted to wash our minds of politics. Not surprisingly, our first big confrontation with the authorities was a political issue: the blackboard that we used as a bulletin board.

Although we politicals were far more orderly than the common prisoners, the authorities considered us more dangerous because we might "infect" the commons. In the beginning we received our visits with the common prisoners, but then the authorities stopped it to prevent any contact. So we received our visits in the section, and our visitors had to come all the way through the prison.

We still had contact with the commons when we were allowed outside the section, which happened relatively frequently. Some of it was pure con; we dreamed up lots of reasons to go outside, especially to see the doctors. Most of the time, the door to the rest of the prison was kept open. One of our early demands was to keep this door open so that we could have access to all of the prison, but sometimes it was closed as a punishment.

Now the bulletin board was at the entrance to the building. We wrote a lot of political things on it, and it made the authorities nervous. One day they told us to take it down, and when we refused, the guards came in with their guns drawn. We tried stopping them until one of the *compañeras* got clubbed with a gun. So they took it away. They also confiscated all our pencils and prohibited anything to come in, especially newspapers.

So we made a bulletin board out of paper, and stuck it to the wall with cornstarch paste that we cooked up in the kitchen. We wrote or drew the political slogans and messages with charcoal because we didn't have anything else. The authorities tried to divide us by offering me a "marital visit" with Sebastián in return for taking the blackboard down. I refused, so they had to think of something else.

In prison, the most effective general punishment is to prohibit visits. Your family is the only contact you have with the outside world, and their visit is the only time that you feel as though you're not stuck in prison. So it was a big deal when they cut our visits, which were already pretty limited. When I first arrived, visiting hours were on Thursday afternoons from 2:00 to 4:00 and on Sundays from 10:00 to 12:00 and 2:00 to 3:00. Sometimes the lineups to the security check were so long and the check so slow that people didn't get to see their relatives at all. For my brother Javier or my mother, who drove in their cars from San Salvador, that might be a bother, but for someone who had spent hours coming by bus from the countryside, often carrying a sack of food for their imprisoned relative, it could waste a day and a half or more. So improved visiting hours was a principal demand in our hunger strike, and we got them extended by an hour on Thursdays and continuously from 9:00 to 4:00 on Sundays. That went for everyone in the prison, as did our successful demand for more water.

On the next visiting day, around 1:00 p.m., the *celadora* gave us a list of 13 names that were not going to get a visit. She said we 13 were responsible for the bulletin board not having been taken down. The *directiva* called a meeting and told everyone what was happening. We said, "We propose that either all of us get a visit or none of us. And we don't take the bulletin board down." There were maybe 32 of us by then, and we all decided not to receive a visit. However, we would wash the bulletin board off the wall the next day. Because losing our visits was not a punishment we could hold out against for long.

We weren't powerless and without ways of making the authorities uncomfortable. We could get things published immediately outside, for instance. The Mothers Committee was an excellent way of making the authorities look bad. A mother would arrive at Ilopango and be told there was no visit.

"Why can't I see my daughter? Why can't they have a visit?"

"Because they're being punished."

"That's repression!"

Word would get out and usually get published immediately. So the authorities didn't punish us that much, and we were able to get away with quite a lot. It was crucial to COPPES that Ilopango prison did not have individual cells. If you're isolated, they can neutralize you. But if you're with a group of people it's more difficult. After a year, COPPES had gotten so strong that we could walk around the prison pretty much at will.

The work committee dealt with the handicrafts we made for sale outside the prison. It kept its own books, but the profit went to the Common Fund.

There were two ways of working. You could work on orders that you got personally: for instance, an order to embroider a blouse from a family member for pay. You could buy the material from the work committee, or you could ask Rosario the social worker or the *celadora* to buy you what you needed. Then you did the job, handed it over to your relative on visit day, and the profit was yours. The work committee also tried to find or create jobs that many women could work on. Big orders were rare, and usually it wasn't easy to sell things because the relatives of most *compañeras* were very poor. Sometimes we would give the Mothers Committee a big package of socks for children or sweaters and so on, and they would try to sell it.

Once we got a big order from the United States for Salvadoran-style embroidered blouses from a Salvadoran woman named Paulita Pike. She's an American citizen who lives in Indiana near Notre Dame University where her father works, and she was a friend of mine. Actually, she had been in the same situation as I was, working underground. She got caught but they deported her, and now she was doing a lot of solidarity work for us. One of her contributions was to find orders for our handicrafts. She'd get an order for 50 blouses, for example, and send us the money to buy material.

We made the blouses on our three sewing machines. There was only one when I got there, but the International Red Cross gave us two more. The prison also had a big sewing workshop for the commons that we could use, with a seamstress from outside in charge. The authorities didn't allow more than two or three of us to go there at the same time. Not many commons did that sort of work. In fact, it's always a big problem in prison to keep the commons entertained.

The prison had a school, from first to sixth grade. All the commons who had not got as far as sixth grade had to go. Schooling was also imposed on us politicals and we in COPPES agreed with that. There were maybe 10 or 12, and they didn't want to study, so we had to have some serious chats with them to make them go. COPPES also organized its own classes such as sewing, crafts, and English. I taught sewing and sometimes English, and I did a lot of political education. A few of us like Miriam exercised each morning, and we tried to organize regular exercise classes but it didn't work.

By now the *directiva* was composed of six of us: Esperanza, Paquita, Ana,

Beatriz, me, and another whose name I've forgotten. Beatriz was FPL and I represented the MNR, while the rest were all ERP and led by Esperanza. This was simply because the ERP was there first, and although they couldn't ignore the MNR or the FPL, they were able to dominate the early COPPES. Of course, Beatriz maintained that the FPL should be represented more heavily in the *directiva*. She said, and I supported her view, that democratic elections should be held. Obviously, she knew the FPL would win direct elections since they were the majority in the section. The ERP disagreed. They were happy with their existing majority, but if change had to come, they thought the *directiva* should be organized like the FMLN outside, with representation by organization and democratic centralism. This debate went on for months until the rising numbers of prisoners forced the issue.

In the meantime, COPPES worked quite well. Decisions were made and stuck to, and they were largely good decisions because they dealt with real needs that needed real solutions.

The *directiva* met three and sometimes four times a week. We'd set up our table and chairs and get down to it. We were all experienced in political organizations and knew how to run a meeting efficiently. Everyone came prepared to work the necessary hours, and we rotated coordinating the meeting. Everything was voted on according to democratic centralism.

Our meetings followed the regular meeting rules, beginning with an agenda that started with the most pressing items and tapered off into miscellaneous. Minutes were read from the previous meeting, and so on. In a typical meeting, after the minutes were read and the agenda approved, Paquita might present a report on the *economato*, or I might read a press release that I'd prepared to be sent out with the next visit. We all had three minutes to respond, and the discussion went around the room. The minutes were recorded in tiny writing and very condensed because all our papers had to be hidden. Periodically we destroyed them in case of a search by the authorities.

As numbers grew and we began to open up new cells for women to sleep in, our meetings migrated upward in the building. In the beginning they were in the central room on the second floor, which was also used for exercises and any other activity that required space. But we finally had to move them to the third floor, which was a pigeon loft when we finally opened it up. It had been abandoned since the nuns had left. But nobody had told the pigeons. There were thousands of them up there, and what seemed like tons of pigeon shit to clean out before we could use it. The work committee asked for volunteers, and we eventually got it washed up.

Just as the authorities' greatest weapon against prisoners is to restrict visits, the strongest tool of prisoners all over the world is the hunger strike. Methods of protest are very limited. You don't have guns or cars or access to materials like on the outside, just your bodies. But since it's passive, any kind of repression of it is cruelty against defenseless human beings. I agree with using hungers strikes when so few other options are available, but not under all circumstances. A few days ago I read that Guillermo Endara, the president of Panama, had gone on a hunger strike, and I had to laugh. It's not just that he's enormously fat, but it's foolish for someone in his position to resort to that tool.

All of the members of COPPES participated in our first two hunger strikes except those who were pregnant or had small children, or who had physical reasons not to. How do you convince everyone to participate? By talking, having a discussion. Anyone who doesn't want to join in doesn't have to. There's always a group that cannot join, so that group takes care of the ones who do.

The first few days of a hunger strike are very difficult. You just don't eat. You drink water, sometimes with four teaspoons of sugar. Or you suck on four caramels a day. And that's it. There is nothing to see if you look at yourself in the mirror. You stop shitting.

In fact, the first six days are horrible. Hunger is physical. The pain in your stomach. The headache. After that it becomes easier, so long as you don't have any physical reaction. I was lucky, I never did. But some people had horrible acidity, for example.

All your conversation, your thought processes focus on food. All the time. No matter what you start thinking about. You can start off talking about sex but it finishes with food. Or start off with politics and you end up with food. Food smells are terrible to handle. Even now as I think back to it my mouth is watering. You can't avoid the smell of cooking. And you think of the simplest things that you like to eat. You don't imagine elaborate foods, perhaps just a tortilla and cheese. God, it becomes obsessive.

All you can do is to keep busy. I would read and sew. Many of the women would sleep a lot, just staying horizontal in their beds.

Our strike was coordinated with the one among the men at Santa Tecla (in the following year they were moved to another prison in Mariona), and the Mothers Committee did a wonderful job of acting as couriers between the two, as well as calling attention to the strike on the outside.

The strike ended after 16 days, when the *línea* came through. We achieved most of the practical demands from the authorities, the ones they could actually do something about.

There would be two more strikes, one lasting 14 days and the final one 33 days. I don't remember the second one as well as the first and third. One of the most memorable things about the first one was that everyone was with it. There were about 25 of us who actually participated, out of the 35 women in the section, and at the time all of us were sleeping in that one big room. But the women who were not in COPPES—Vida, Lupita, Sonia, all of them—cooperated to keep things going and took care of the ones in the strike. The solidarity was complete.

17

Relations with the Outside

From the very first, Mother was wonderful to me while I was in Ilopango. She was always there when I needed something. At the very beginning, I asked her to bring two chickens and two pounds of hard cheese when she visited, and that's what she did, twice a week, for two years. On my birthday, she brought a big cake that I could share with the others, and at Christmas a leg of pork.

I was very impressed with her loyalty, and my image of her changed. Perhaps I did some growing up in my relationship with her. I finally accepted that despite all the problems between us, she was a good woman who was trying her best.

Visits weren't easy for her. Other families might stay all day, but Mother usually stayed no more than 20 minutes or so. It was as if she felt totally out of her element. She couldn't relate to the other prisoners at all, except for a few of my closest friends like Beatriz or Carolina. On the other hand, some of my friends couldn't relate to her either. Miriam, a trade unionist, wouldn't even say hello.

Above all, she must have found the searches humiliating. They searched everyone who came in, and she went through it twice a week for two years. I don't think she was ever body-searched by women staff, who could be pretty obnoxious. But Mother never complained or said anything about it. She took the afternoon off from work every Thursday, and then again on Sunday. Javier came every Sunday. My nana visited, sometimes coming with my mother and sometimes by bus. My brother Tono also visited a few times.

It was during an early visit that Javier told me how he learned I'd been arrested. A neighbor in the barrio saw the whole thing and called Opus Dei. I've never fully understood this because, as far as I knew, no one in the barrio knew who I was. But he said that the woman apparently said that whomever was arrested looked like she came from a "good family." After that, someone at Opus Dei called Javier.

A bit later, Javier brought me a radio. We already had several that had been smuggled in part-by-part in *embutidos*. We had strung wires together to make an antenna and could get Radio Venceremos and the national stations.[1] A group of us would sit around a little transistor radio in the square and listen to what was going on outside. The *agentes* just ignored it. Once we had the radios, it was difficult for the authorities to take them away, though one time they did a search and took some of them.

But when Javier brought me my radio, he just handed it over to me in the yard where all the visiting took place after our visits were separated from those of the commons. It was illegal, but the guards up in the turrets and the *celadoras* didn't appear to see him do it. Javier is a very successful businessman, with a great ability to get along with people. I think that little by little he cultivated a relationship with the guards at the entrance, and with the women who searched the visitors. The guards respected my brother because of who he was, but I think they also liked him. He knew exactly how to use that employer-employee relationship with people. Common Salvadorans tend to be respectful of the bourgeoisie, which Javier and Mother so obviously were. From the beginning Javier brought me *Time* magazine and *Newsweek*, which officially were forbidden. He just carried them under his arm and no one challenged him.

I was so excited to get this radio. It was a nine-band Sony and could get the international broadcasts.

And then it broke down a few hours after Javier left! That was so frustrating, because it would be at least 15 days before I could listen to it: a week till the next visiting day when I could give it to my mother, a week for my brother to exchange it, and then the wait till the next visiting day to bring it back. That's exactly how it went, but from that day till I was released I listened to the radio every day. I woke up with the news early every morning, and after 10:00 at night I listened with earphones to English programs. I knew the bands and the times of all the programs.

It was small and ran on tiny batteries we bought from the COPPES store, but it was very loud. The *celadoras* knew that it was there but ignored it. I lent it to everybody and groups of *compañeras* would sit around it wherever it was set up. A radio was something you shared during the day, but when you were going to sleep it was yours.

I often thought about books while I was held in the Guardia Nacional, once I was certain that they weren't going to kill me. All those books that I wanted to read and never had time for. The first book that I asked my mother to bring was *Don Quixote*. I'd never read it and in my school days I'd always fooled my teachers into thinking that I'd done so, going to the encyclopedia or the *Readers Digest* version. But now I had time, so my mother borrowed it from one of her friends. It was a modern edition in two enormous volumes, with wonderful illustrations.

We had a great time reading it, though we only finished the first volume. It probably looked pretty funny: there I'd sit among this group of women, reading out loud with an enormous book on my lap. We took turns reading out loud, and people came and went as we did so. After a couple of months we sent it back with my mother.

It was through books that I started to get close to Sonia, or as close as anyone ever did. Whatever books I got, she would simply devour. The Russian authors had always fascinated me, so Mother brought me those big, dense books, from *Anna Karenina* to *War and Peace*, and I'd pass them on to Sonia. She read very fast. I was amazed when she got through *War and Peace* in just three or four days. And then she wanted to talk about it! With the death of the vegetable garden, books were our connection, but not one of love and affection. Sonia could respect, but not love. She was always very alone.

I never met her mother, but her father came to *visitas* and from him I started to understand her background. The family lived in San Marcos, a workers' and lower-middle-class section of the capital. Her father was a *campesino*, a hard-working and extremely capable man who worked at anything and everything to keep his family alive. He was a bit of an electrician and a mechanic, and occasionally a carpenter. At the same time, he cared more about enjoying life than "getting ahead" so the family remained relatively poor.

Sonia was arrested in her second year of high school. She'd always had high marks, but school wasn't enough for her, so she hung out on the street a lot. Even that wasn't enough for her energy and creativity, so she also hung around her father and brother and watched what they did. Her older brother came to visit once and it was amazing how similar they were. Sonia adored and wanted to be like him, which may be why she dressed and acted so boyish. Boys got to do interesting things, and she had no interest in most girlish activities. She never wore shoes if she could help it, and her muddy footprints were always a problem on our clean floors: big, splay-toed footprints. Sometimes the ideas would just spill out of her. She wanted to be an electrician, to climb trees, to be a gardener, to use guns.

Even her sleeping arrangements were original. Her bed was in a corner, and she put up boards and a little curtain. She could close it and feel like she had her own room—or cave—when she went to bed. She also rigged up lights, an electrician's flourish with various buttons that controlled each light separately or all together. I was even more impressed when we received a complaint from the prison director: someone had stolen lights from the chapel altar. We quickly went to Sonia and made her give them back.

Sonia kept her tools in a little cupboard she'd constructed under her bed, along with other things that she stole or picked up. I never knew exactly, but I assumed she stole most of it from the prison workshop. Where else could she have got her pliers, her screwdriver, her pieces of wire, even a can of paint?

One day some of us from the *directiva* were called to the office by the prison director. Someone had painted a big *pinta*, a graffiti or slogan, in oil paint right next to the clinic. A big crudely lettered LIBERTAD POR LOS PRESOS POLITICOS—LIBERTY FOR THE POLITICAL PRISONERS—in bright red-orange paint. It was very crude. The *pintas* in our section were done slowly and carefully. Not this one. And not only was it outside our section, but it was oil paint, which is horrible to clean off. The director was furious. Our saying it wasn't an official act of COPPES didn't do much to calm her. If we didn't find and discipline the culprit, the section door would be kept locked and we would lose our freedom of movement within the prison.

We too were upset. Someone had very badly overstepped two sets of rules: those of the prison and those of the struggle.

Pintas are a time-honored weapon of all revolutionary struggles. In the city they have to be done fast; it takes planning and security, and content has to be approved by your organization. You don't just go out and do it because you get an artistic urge one evening. El Salvador has some excellent *pinta* artists. Give them some security and a few minutes and they'll do you a wonderful *pinta*. Most aren't so good, just a few seconds with a can of spray paint and away you go. But it still has to be planned and approved.

In prison, approval was even more important because of our delicate balancing act with the authorities. Our freedoms and activities were the result of negotiation. When you negotiate you have to offer as well as threaten, and what we offered was our discipline. The authorities knew we would continue to do political work, but they knew we would keep it in bounds. *Pintas* were a good example. Because of cooking with wood, charcoal was one of the few writing materials we had lots of. It also could be washed off and replaced quickly. That set up a natural limit on the activity: charcoal *pintas* didn't destroy or deface prison buildings and could be tolerated if they were written inside our section and nowhere else in the prison.

We could defend something done within the approval of COPPES, but we now risked losing a hard-won freedom because of one uncontrolled act. And this was pure Sonia—no one else had the guts to steal the paint. She readily confessed: yes, she had climbed the almond tree and stolen the paint from the prison store room. What was all the fuss about—a *pinta* was a *pinta*, wasn't it? And she'd even spelled it right, hadn't she? We gave her a stern talking-to, and that was that. We never told the authorities who did it.

The Mothers Committee was totally part of our struggle. Like COPPES they reflected the divisions in the FMLN and actually split into two factions in the early 1980s. Today they work together and coordinate their activities.

Many of those who joined the committee were looking for relatives—children, husbands, parents, even cousins—who had been disappeared. Most were (and are, for the disappearances continue and the Mothers Committee keeps up its work) middle-aged family women, not intellectuals or trade unionists or anything like that. And they were (and are) persecuted by the authorities.

It is horrible to be the mother or wife of a disappeared person. Children come from the womb, from yourself, and you are totally devoted. The Mothers of the Plaza de Mayo in Argentina are the most famous, and people ask if it's a peculiarly Latin thing about mothers, as opposed to other cultures. For me, it is more that disappearances are not common to other cultures. It was in Brazil and Chile and Argentina that it became a systematic tool of repression.

It's a very cruel torture. When you think of the worst recent crimes of humanity, you think of how Pol Pot killed and tortured hundreds of thousands of Cambodians, for example. But taking people and disappearing them from the face of the earth is something else, because the uncertainty is so awful.

Death is so certain, so absolute. You resign yourself to it. With a disappearance, you continue questioning for years and years, wondering what happened. There was an architect, Claudia, who was disappeared a month before me. To this day Claudia's mother, Doña Ana, still believes that somewhere . . . But there's no certainty because she hasn't seen the body.

Mothers used to come with photos to the prison, begging us for information, particularly if they knew you had been taken by the Guardia Nacional. Question after question after question: Did you see them at the Guardia Nacional? Did you hear them? Are there any secret places where they might be? And you really had nothing to tell them.

At the same time, they were the people most dedicated to us and worked the hardest as couriers, bringing us things, supporting us. They risked their lives to take out the *comunicados*, contact the newspapers, collect money, get food. Some of them would go all the way to Mariona prison[2] in the bus and come back with a letter in the same morning. Or if they couldn't, they'd find someone else to go back. Their dedication was absolute and their strength was admirable. Some of their husbands had been assassinated.

One incredibly active and wonderful woman was the mother of Zenaida, a *compañera* who was 17 and pregnant when she was arrested. Zenaida's mother was a market woman, about 40 years old. She visited Zenaida frequently, even though she herself had been shot during a market women's demonstration and was still recuperating when Zenaida was arrested. After that she became active in the Mothers Committee. Several months later, Zenaida was taken to hospital and came back with a healthy baby. Her mother continued to visit, but on one of those days she was arrested as she left the prison, and disappeared.

Two days later she reappeared in El Playón, just barely alive. El Playón is the name given to the lava fields of the San Salvador volcano. During the last big eruption, the lava flowed down the side of the volcano, and not into the city. You just have to see it once to understand what a disaster that would have been, for the lava covers an area as big as the city itself. There's nothing there, just an enormous barren desert, hard to walk on because the cooled lava is sharp. Nothing grows, and all that goes through it is the railway and the trails of the *campesinos*. El Playón has always served as San Salvador's garbage dump, but in the past 20 years it has become a dumping ground for bodies of political victims. And that's where Zenaida's mother was found. Whoever arrested her had tortured her, shot her four times, and left her for dead among the rocks. But she was incredibly strong and refused to die. She started dragging herself over those sharp rocks until a *campesino* walking along the railroad tracks found her. He arranged for her to be taken to the door of the archbishopric, where they found her the next morning. For protection she had to leave the country immediately.

But even after that she wouldn't let them beat her. She came back to see Zenaida some months later. I was there and it was very emotional. She was recuperating, and she was very thin and very nervous, and she had to leave the country again. But such guts.

In fact, for some of us it was far safer in prison than outside. Another *compañera*, one of the women from the Communist Party, had six brothers and sisters, and both her mother and father were elderly. All were murdered while she was in prison. Her father was a well-known trade union leader, but it didn't matter: all eight were lined up in front of their house and shot right there.

Family members, especially the Mothers Committee, were the best couriers. They carried *embutidos* with all sorts of materials: letters about COPPES activities, reports on the organization, plans for future activities, *denuncias*, statements, et cetera.

An *embutido* is a sausage, but in prison it means a hiding place. We used colón bills, soap, cornflake packages, matchboxes, and so on as *embutidos* for messages we wrote on rice paper, using the smallest possible pens. On a one-by-two-inch piece of paper we could get a full page of a letter. It is very exacting work. In a matchbox, for example: you take it apart, separate the cardboard, fold up the letters, put it inside the cardboard and paste it together. You can do the same with paper cash, old bills especially. By rubbing it carefully you can separate the paper, put the letters inside and glue the edges again. The problem then is not confusing the matchbox or bill once it's done. We lost a lot of messages that way, when couriers forgot which matchbox or bill it was in.

You can imagine how it happens: One of the women from the Mothers Committee puts it in her bra with the rest of her money, and pulls it out to pay for the bus, and gets confused and gives away the bill with the message. We also dug holes in soap, packing in written material, and covering it up again.

I frequently sent reports and *comunicados* to those in charge of COPPES propaganda in the FDR, and I kept the MNR informed as well. There was also a lot of *embutidos* back and forth between the men's prison and ours carrying COPPES documents, study materials, reflections on prison life, and personal letters. We usually said who it was for by word of mouth only. You would say to the courier taking it, "Give this bar of soap to Sebastián." Once a box of 10 soap bars ended up in their store and got sold to a common prisoner. This man was washing his clothes and found the message, which he turned in to the authorities. We were careful to change our techniques if ever they were found.

A visit from a relative was largely a personal experience, but we had other visitors who were important for everyone, and whose arrival every two weeks or so was always an event: the delegates of the International Committee of the Red Cross. Their most important role was as our mediator with the authorities, to whom they would carry our petitions and requests. They also brought us a lot of things that we asked for, including the big pots and pans we needed to cook for so many. Especially important were their incredible first aid kits, which had medicines to treat everything: ear and mouth infections, hemorrhoids, burns, skin infections, and so on. I still have some medicine from those years—I guess I should throw it out by now . . .

The Red Cross visits were public in that they saw everybody, but they were also very personal because some of them had first met us in desperate circumstances, when we were held by the security forces. They either knew or had heard of most of us.

One of their objectives is to protect political prisoners from torture and execution, and they are very successful. The secret of that success all over the world is twofold. First, their discretion is absolute. Governments let them into even the worst prisons knowing that they won't talk to the press. They keep whatever they find secret, making a report only to the government in question.

Second, whatever they bring to the politicals, they bring for everyone in the prison. Usually there were three or four Swiss delegates, generally blond and speaking fairly good Spanish. Many had a great deal of experience in other countries. The group usually included a doctor and nurse or paramedic, as well as the official delegate.

Red Cross visits followed a pattern. They would talk with the new prisoners first, and then have a meeting with COPPES. Our relationship became very familiar. They usually avoided overtly political discussion, but while our numbers were small we could talk quite freely. I remember a day that one of them, a man, dared to say that Ilopango was the most comfortable of the various political prisons he knew.

"I know political prisons all over the world," he said, "and this is the Sheraton. At least you have mattresses. They may be falling apart but at least you have them. And you have space, you have green . . ."

That's as far as he got—we almost lynched him! "Reactionary! Bourgeois!" we yelled. We accused him of siding with the government, and for a while it was quite serious. But that was very unusual.

Sometimes there were visits from foreign journalists and dignitaries. The Belgian ambassador came a few times, and some congressmen from the United States. Usually they came to see someone in particular. Esperanza, Vida, Lupita, and I were high profile, and these visitors asked for us. I often ended up doing the talking because I spoke English. A journalist from the Toronto *Globe and Mail* interviewed me while I was there, and he also interviewed my brother Javier for the same article.[3]

18

~

The Struggle Inside

The number of politicals grew from 11 to 22 by the end of my first week. When I left two years later, in May 1983, we were 96. We were all arrested under the Decree 507. Before that, political prisoners hardly existed. They just disappeared. Duarte was president of the second junta by this time, and by arresting people like us he was saying to the world, "See, we have political prisoners here, we don't disappear people."

But the fact was that for every political prisoner who stayed alive there was at least one disappearance. The decree said you could be arrested without cause. You were tried by a military tribunal under military jurisdiction rather than civil law. That meant the death penalty could be invoked. The most important proof against you was your extrajudicial confession, signed by you and by two witnesses without a lawyer or neutral witness present. The witnesses could be anyone, including those who interrogated or tortured you. Most of the confessions were obtained in the same way they got mine, through beatings or threats. All of this was completely illegal under our constitution.

Usually you were assigned a military judge to investigate your case within a month of your arrest, and he would take another declaration from you. You didn't have a lawyer, only a court-appointed "plea maker." There were 11 military judges, and who you got depended on which force had arrested you. Mine was one of the worst. I only saw him once, about 10 days after I got to Ilopango. He hardly asked me a thing about what I'd been arrested for. But I finally got to read what I had signed, and it was outrageous.

"Judge," I protested, "I want to change my confession."

"You can't," he said. "It's already signed by you."

"But it was signed under duress. It's not even my normal signature."

"Alright," he said, "I will take it under consideration." Judges could keep you up to six months while trying to prove you had "merit for detention." After

Campaign for Prisoners of the Month·

Each of the people whose story is told below is a prisoner of conscience. Each has been arrested because of his or her religious or political beliefs, colour, sex, ethnic origin or language. None has used or advocated violence. Their continuing detention is a violation of the United Nations Universal Declaration of Human Rights. International appeals can help to secure the release of these prisoners or to improve their detention conditions. In the interest of the prisoners, letters to the authorities should be worded carefully and courteously. You should stress that your concern for human rights is not in any way politically partisan. In *no* circumstances should communications be sent to the prisoner.

Ana Margarita GASTEAZORO Escolán, *El Salvador*

An official of a Salvadorian political party, she has been in custody since May 1981.

Ana Margarita Gasteazoro Escolán was arrested by members of the National Guard on 12 May 1981 at the Institute of Social Studies in San Salvador. She was then Secretary for Women's Affairs of the *Movimiento Nacional Revolucionario* (MNR), a social democratic party affiliated to the Socialist International.

Also arrested with her were Eleuterio de Jesús Cárcamo, the MNR's Secretary for Trade Union Affairs, and Rafael Barrera, a teacher.

The Salvadorian authorities originally denied that the three were being held but after worldwide expressions of concern for the detainees' safety they eventually produced Ana Margarita Gasteazoro on Salvadorian television and allowed her to speak to journalists. The arrest of the other two was acknowledged later.

Ana Margarita Gasteazoro was placed under military jurisdiction and charged with participation in guerrilla insurgency. The charges, which she has denied, were based on documents allegedly found at the place of arrest.

She was also charged with plotting against national security, working on behalf of international terrorism and using a false name. The charges apparently result from speeches she made abroad before her arrest in which she presented an analysis of Salvadorian society and the current civil strife.

Her case has been consigned to the courts but to *AI*'s knowledge she has still not been tried.

AI considers that Ana Margarita Gasteazoro is being held because of her non-violent political activities and the expression of her views.

Please send courteous letters appealing for her release to: Sr. Roberto d'Aubuisson/Presidente de la Asamblea Constituyente/San Salvador/El Salvador.

Albertino NETO, *Sao Tome and Principe*

A former commander of his country's armed forces, he has served four and a half years of a 14-year prison sentence for involvement in a "plot" to kill the head of state.

Albertino Neto was arrested in Sao Tome in February 1978 on his return to his country after a year's military training in Cuba. He was accused of complicity in an alleged plot to kill President Pinto da Costa.

In March 1979 he, his wife and five others were tried by a Special Tribunal for Counter-Revolutionary Acts. The court was composed of officials of the ruling party rather than independent judges and the defendants had little opportunity to defend themselves. Albertino Neto was convicted and sentenced to 21 years' imprisonment (later reduced to 14 years'); his wife and three other people were jailed on charges of complicity in the "plot".

The only evidence against Albertino Neto was another defendant's statement while in custody that he had tried to kill the President with a bomb and that Albertino Neto and his wife had been involved in the attempt. The prisoner concerned has since said that his "confession" was made under the threat of execution.

AI is aware of no other evidence of any attempt on the President's life, or to indicate that Albertino Neto was involved in a conspiracy. It believes that he was convicted of an offence which he did not commit because his political views were regarded by the authorities as being "liberal" and pro-Western and because his wife was closely related to a former minister regarded as an opponent of the government.

Since his arrest he has been held with other political prisoners in a detention centre in Sao Tome. He was initially held incommunicado and suffered from a severe beating which he received at the time of his arrest, when his arm was broken. He may now receive visits

from his family (his wife was released in July 1980) but is suffering from severe depression and hypertension.

Please send courteous letters appealing for his release to: Sua Excelência Dom Manuel Pinto da Costa/Presidente da República Democrática de São Tomé e Príncipe/Gabinete do Presidente da República e do MLSTP/Democratic Republic of São Tomé and Príncipe.

Bashir al-BARGHUTI, *Israel and the Occupied Territories*

Editor of the Jerusalem-based bi-weekly newspaper al–Tali'a, he has been under house and town arrest for two years without charge or trial.

Bashir al-Barghuti is one of three Palestinian editors who were first issued with restriction orders on 7 August 1980 under Article 86 of the 1970 Security Provisions Order 378. The order, which confined him to the town of al-Bireh during the day and to his house between sunset and sunrise, has been renewed four times consecutively, most recently on 12 August 1982 for another six months. The order has made it difficult for him to continue exercising his profession.

Bashir al-Barghuti is a member of the National Guidance Committee (NGC), an organization set up in 1978 by West Bank Palestinians to help coordinate their opposition to Israeli occupation. It was declared illegal in March 1982. Several prominent NGC members have been placed under house and town arrest over the past two years.

AI believes that the continuing restriction of Bashir al-Barghuti's mobility is a form of punishment for the non-violent exercise of his right to freedom of expression, and limits his political activity. It is concerned also that he is being restricted without formal charge or trial.

Please send courteous letters appealing for his freedom to: Professor Itzhak Zamir/Attorney General/PO Box 1087/Jerusalem/Israel.

Figure 21. Amnesty International's "Campaign for Prisoners of the Month" (Amnesty International newsletter, vol. 12, no. 10, October 1982)

that, you could be held for up to two years without trial. But not one of us political prisoners ever came to trial. You never got to meet your accusers and the police didn't have to tell you anything. So besides everything else you had endured, you were left wondering how you came to be arrested: Did you make a mistake in security? Did someone else make a mistake? Did someone "finger" you with a telephone call?

In my case, I had two or three theories. During my interrogation by the Guardia Nacional I was told that someone had informed on Sebastián and me. And that the police had been following me for 20 days before my arrest, since

I had got back from Mexico. I never believed that because they would have caught me with more important people if they had really been tracking me, but the rest was possible. Another possibility was that a neighbor had got suspicious of the comings and goings at our house and called one of the numbers posted by the government for fingering people. It could have been due to a security error, but also just bad luck. So many totally innocent people were arrested in that way.

I finally understood it when Lupe arrived in Ilopango. She was a big woman, a social worker by profession who had worked for the Salvadoran Social Security. She had been arrested because she was FPL and had been doing political work in the trade unions. I had never met her before and knew nothing about her. But her mother knew people that I knew, and when she came to visit Lupe, she brought messages from friends of mine in the University of Central America. That made me realize that Lupe knew people I knew before I was arrested. I spoke sometimes with her mother during visits, and from that I discovered Lupe was a good friend of the man Sebastián and I had rented the house from.

Over time I got more of the story. Lupe had been arrested just before I was: in fact, she was the person kept in the cell where I had my shower on the day of my press conference, the one who had been sleeping on the newspapers. The Guardia tortured Lupe very badly, and one day they took her out in a troop carrier to identify places that were related to the struggle. She only pointed out places she thought were empty—and that made sense, because the house where Sebastián and I were arrested was supposed to be empty, and Lupe knew it because she knew the owner. It was empty because of security problems, and Sebastián and I added to those problems when we moved in without thoroughly checking its history.

I only figured this out in bits and pieces. She told some of this to her cellmates, and that's how it got to me. Lupe and I had a difficult relationship, not because of how we were arrested but personally and politically. Sometimes we got along, sometimes not. We left prison on the same day and I never heard from her again. I wish I knew where she was and how she was doing.

We never talked much about these things directly. Nobody did—they're too delicate. Sometimes talking will bring you face to face with very ugly facts, or ugly possibilities you can't verify. Everybody has something to hide, the more so if you broke under torture and gave out information about someone. It was sometimes possible to figure out who had been broken because of the trouble they had adapting to prison. People who have been forced to finger other people often have bad dreams and insomnia because of these awful feelings of guilt. Sometimes they displayed erratic and aggressive behavior. Even though they were the only ones who knew exactly what they'd said, they had to live with the guilt and the worry that someone else would find out.

And unfortunately, information eventually does get around. People are rarely arrested alone, so stories are eventually compared through the prison grapevine or gossip. For us, one major source of information was the men's prison. About eight of us women politicals had *compañeros* there, and there was a lot of correspondence. I'd get reports saying, "You'll be getting someone new soon; don't trust her, we think she did this and that . . ."

But as a political prisoner yourself, you don't condemn someone who was broken. On the outside people hear about a person who broke and informed, and they're quick to say what a shit that person is. But if you've been in that situation, you understand what you may do when you're all alone and under a great deal of pain, when your very life is threatened. Sometimes people lose their minds under torture.

In my case, I had to deal with the fact that my arrest led directly to the arrest of another *compañero* from the MNR. Again I found this out later. When the Guardia Nacional arrested me, they went through my papers and found the electricity bills for the MNR office. It gave the Guardia the address. They raided the office and this *compañero* went to prison for 16 months.

During my time in Ilopango, COPPES never stopped changing its shape to meet new circumstances. It began as a secret organization although everyone knew who we were. The original committees included only members of FDR-FMLN organizations, and we took care of everything. Given the number of non-politicals this was logical. Most of them hadn't the experience or the discipline of a woman who had already worked in an organization. If a new prisoner was from an organization, she was immediately asked to join a committee—no ifs, ands, or buts about it. This was simple and efficient, but the rising population made it untenable. At our largest, with over 90 women in the section, there were a lot of women to be kept occupied and many tasks to be shared.

During the early months we worked out two levels to COPPES, one open and the other secret. The open level dealt with the practical side of life in prison through the committees I've mentioned: health, education, productive work, et cetera. The secret level covered the three committees that were essentially political: propaganda, political education (which included recruitment), and organization.

The open and secret structure of COPPES led to political dilemmas: Who would control what, and on what would they base the right to that control? Since all of the organizations at least paid lip service to democratic principles, there was strong support for elections.

But this has to be understood in context. Inside Ilopango we were a micro-cosm of political life outside. Mirroring the FMLN, our different organizations were constantly maneuvering to control COPPES. But the dynamics were very different inside the prison, where there was no room to move and a small number of people to struggle over. That made it very delicate. Hegemony, a word you hear a lot on the left, couldn't help but be an issue. Its literal meaning is domination or leadership, but it has a lot of historical and emotional over-tones. Everyone wants to exercise it, but no one wants to be seen pursuing it.

The main struggle in COPPES was between the ERP and the FPL, just like on the outside. The original structure, with one representative per organization in the *directiva*, was simple but clearly not very democratic given the unequal numbers among the different organizations. The FPL eventually made a stra-tegic proposal: while the two levels of COPPES should remain, the *directiva* should be elected by all the political prisoners. I say this proposal was strategic because we received a *línea* to be hegemonic, and we knew that an open elec-tion would give us the most people on the *directiva*.

After weeks of discussion, COPPES was restructured with a seven-member elected *directiva*. That was fine for us, because by this time we had a comfort-able majority of bona fide political prisoners. But it meant a loss of power for Esperanza and the ERP, who had founded COPPES at Ilopango. When the dust cleared after the elections, they found themselves with two fewer votes than they'd had in the previous *directiva*. Only Esperanza and Paquita had been elected. Each organization commanded the loyalty of its own members, and since Esperanza was her group's leader they all voted for her. But my position was less clear, and we used it to our advantage. Officially I represented the MNR and sat on the original *directiva* in that capacity. In the election, which was done by a simple show of hands, my organization's members all voted for Beatriz, the official FPL representative. But they also voted for me because I was allied with the FPL line. The FPL didn't "win" the election, but we had more members on the *directiva* than before. The organization or alliance that could muster four members won all the debates that were put to vote.

It was a victory of sorts, but also the beginning of a lot of problems. COP-PES soon split into two: one COPPES dominated by Esperanza and her group, and the other by us. We had the majority of prisoners, but the rest of the orga-nizations went with Esperanza's group.

All of a sudden there were two kitchens and two *comités de economato*, com-missary committees. The two had to meet regularly to look after the distribu-tion of food. It didn't need negotiation. Food and medicine and laundry were just divided according to the number of people. In practical terms, life mostly went on normally. There wasn't much to disturb things if there was enough food to eat, things were clean, basic needs were looked after, and there was work to do. Esperanza and I were perfectly correct with each other, and she even taught me embroidery.

The problems came when new people arrived.

Alliances and recruitment are what politics is all about. All organizations try to make themselves stronger, so recruiting people is part of organizational life. So whenever a new woman arrived in the section, each organization would try to pull her into their orbit. We always had advance warning, so two or three women from each organization would be there to meet her. The first thing was to find out if she was already a member of an organization. A lot were, but more weren't. If she wasn't already, then they tried to recruit her. Sometimes the competition was in benefits: a better bed, or a more comfortable mattress, or nicer sandals. At times it became a scramble to get there first and to trip up the competition on the way. The new woman would be overwhelmed by all the attention. When that happened, the non-politicals in the section, like Sonia, would get very confused and angry. Luckily, because I officially represented the MNR, I wasn't involved in recruitment.

COPPES never formally got back together while I was there, but we started having joint activities again toward the end of my time in Ilopango. The split was never mentioned publicly, so no one outside knew what was going on.

The balance was upset again in August of 1982 after a big arrest of the leadership of ANDES, the teacher's trade union. Ten of them arrived, some after being tortured. As a large group who all knew each other, these women were inclined to be hegemonic in their own right, even though they were from my organization. It was very difficult at the beginning. There was already an ANDES teacher in Ilopango, and she opposed COPPES because she was not elected to the *directiva*. She'd been very high up in ANDES and couldn't cope with not being important in prison. When the 10 ANDES women came in, she was the first person they looked for. We gave them their own room and immediately they got their own stove in and started cooking separately and making their own decisions separately from COPPES. Some of these women had been in the FPL for many years, but they were from another sector of the organization. They even started questioning where the *línea* came from. Who was bringing it for our side, they asked? We actually didn't know who the *línea* came from and had never questioned it. We always just accepted it when the communication arrived in an *embutido*. Eventually, however, some of the ANDES women accepted COPPES and were asked to take up posts in the *comités*.

19

The Commons and the Authorities

In the early days we politicals were treated like lepers and kept separated from the other prisoners. The authorities didn't want us to get close to the commons, of which there were just over 100 when I arrived. It's true that one of COPPES's main objectives was to proselytize among the commons, but it never worked. We got support from them, but not militancy. Most were very lumpen (in the Marxist sense), unskilled workers and peasants who were very pragmatic, very hard. We impressed them, but didn't convince them, and everything we politicals did went against the way they did things. A woman would get a sack of mangos from her family, and she would sit and eat them until she was sick of mangos or would let them spoil rather than share with anyone. That was how they conceived of life.

Prisons have their own culture, which you'll see with variations around the world. On the one hand you have the authorities; on the other are power structures among the prisoners. There are always leaders, and if a leader gets many people around her, she has a lot of weight in that prison. The authorities have to take it into account, and they compromise a lot so long as there's no disorder.

There were two or three big gangs among the commons, and each had a leader. The most powerful, Rosalía, was in the mature women's section, for people over 26. But she controlled the younger women's section too. The two or three other gangs acknowledged her power.

Rosalía was tall and good-looking, very thin, very blonde, very painted. She always wore high heels and was always tidy. Unlike so many commons, she didn't look like she came from the poorer levels of Salvadoran society. Physically she wasn't very strong, but she was ruthless. Outside, she had led a criminal gang, all men except for her. Her crime, which got her a life sentence, was the cold-blooded killing of a drive-in restaurant owner. She seduced him, found out where his money was kept, and then came in with her gang to rob him. She was in Ilopango when I arrived and I used to talk to her occasionally.

As I've described, once we politicals organized and got some power, we negotiated for better living conditions. But the commons' prison culture was different, and Rosalía wasn't interested in anything of that sort. She was interested in where her bed was, and having red rugs by her bed, and having everything cleaned for her. She didn't have to work because she had a lot of women doing everything for her.

Much of what she and the other gangs did was simply power games—power pursued in order to have more power. There was a lot of harassment to get people into one or another group, or simply molesting people not in their group. But Rosalía also used her power for very pragmatic ends. She and people close to her controlled the cigarette trade at Ilopango. The COPPES store eventually sold cigarettes, but that was only after she left, so it didn't matter. She was transferred to another prison, which was the only way the authorities could break her power, or at least shake things up.

When I got there, Ilopango was run by civilian women. Unlike the nuns they replaced, they had no experience. They did not have much of a say in our daily lives because they did not have the strength, either physically or in numbers. And what could a *celadora* do if 10 women stood together in the cell where she was supposed to be in charge and made it clear they were willing to hurt her? So long as it wasn't a total riot, she would tend to allow the prisoners to do anything they wanted.

The *celadoras* weren't armed and they were very normal women, all young women in their late 20s, even early 20s in a few cases. All had a high school education, and some were studying social work. Most were urban women from the Salvadoran *capas medias*. In the social scale in El Salvador, you have the oligarchy on top, then the bourgeoisie like my family, and the petite bourgeoisie, and then the *capas medias* that includes nurses, teachers, and some skilled workers. A few of the *celadoras* were butch like the stereotypes about women prison officers, but by no means all of them.

Most preferred to work with us rather than the commons because we were less dangerous and more respectful and easygoing. We managed always to negotiate, simply to talk to them. They often started at Ilopango thinking of us as terrorist monsters and were surprised to find we were very normal people.

Celadoras usually only stayed in a section for a while, but we got used to our *celadoras* and wouldn't want them to change. In fact we became very good friends with some. They'd bring in paper and pencils, or the newspaper, or thread or other small things we needed to work with. And we did things for them, like embroidery on their clothes.

A few *celadoras* refused to work with us. They were ideologically against us, either afraid or simply not open to us. There were two butch-looking women who couldn't stand us, and preferred working in the young women's section. But they were really repressive, horrible women, and both got seriously beaten up during a riot among the commons.

There was one social worker for the whole prison, Rosario, then a fourth-year student in psychology at the UCA. Her job was to organize sports, workshops, preventive health information, and even some entertainment. She could move anywhere in the prison but spent a long time with us. I remember her with a lot of love because she really helped us a lot. She often picked up things for us downtown, getting our sewing materials, even providing company during hunger strikes. Rosario and I became good friends, and I still hear from her once in a while. She's still in El Salvador, doing social work as a psychologist.

There were about 30 male guards, the *agentes*, who slept in their own barracks at the prison entrance. They had guns and were posted all over the prison. They weren't supposed to have anything to do with us unless there was trouble, and in fact their official orders were not to even talk to us. We politicals mostly ignored them, but we did manage to make friends with some.

We saw little of the prison administration. There weren't many, because the Salvadoran prison system has very little budget. Basically it was the *directora*, two secretaries, and the *celadoras'* supervisor who was second-in-command. She was an ex-nun who we called Señorita Daisy, because she had such a long, bitter face. Señorita Daisy was the one who made the rounds on visiting day—that is, she took all the shifts that the *directora* didn't want.

We never played tactical games like attempting to divide the different authority groups against each other, but we certainly tried to get people on our side, to make them understand the political struggle. At COPPES *directiva* meetings we'd discuss various people and say, "Let's work on so-and-so," wherever we saw some possibility of sympathy or understanding. We tried to convince them through reason, through dialogue, and through helping them whenever it was possible. We made progress with two *agentes* and one of the *celadoras*. For instance, we convinced an *agente* to bring us the newspaper every day. But if the authorities realized that an *agente* was helping us, even in such small things, he got transferred to another prison.

Ilopango is a compound with various buildings, and you could usually walk around in the big compound during the daytime. Prisoners did their washing in the big compound, for instance. But after 6:00 p.m. the doors were closed and there was no way we could get in touch with anyone else in the world. The good part was that we could do whatever we wanted in our building from 6:00 p.m. until the door was opened up at 6:00 a.m. the next day. The bad part was that the building could burn down, or experience some other disaster, before help would arrive.

After a few months we often didn't even have a *celadora* with us at night— we would let them go! If they wanted the night off, we'd chat and it would be arranged. Officially that sort of thing was up to the administration, but the prison was an administrative mess so we got away with it. Sometimes there weren't enough *celadoras* to go around and the authorities preferred to have the available ones stay with the common prisoners rather than with us. They knew that we could tear our building down if we wanted to, but that we weren't going to riot or harm each other—the type of things that the *celadoras* are meant to prevent. After about a year, we didn't have a *celadora* at all.

Most of the time, the prison was under control. But so much depends on the acquiescence of the prisoners and the tolerance of the authorities. If something upsets the balance, things can go berserk.

The commons always got excited as Christmas approached. It was party time and they would make great efforts to get drugs and liquor into the prison. One Saturday afternoon I heard someone say, "Come and look. Some of the women in Section B are naked!"

The back wall of our building backed onto the young prisoners' compound. A few windows had bars across them, and if we put two chairs up on a table we could look out on their yard. Many of our girls would stand up there and talk to the commons or look out, just to pass the time.

So I climbed up on the chairs and sure enough there were four or five girls laying in the corridor of their building, naked and having a ball, totally drunk or stoned. They were the toughest women in that section, girls who carried blades in their clothes. The two *celadoras* couldn't do anything so the party continued.

The girls had broken into the clinic and stolen all the drugs there. They'd bored a hole in one of the walls of their section and slipped out at night while the *celadora* was sleeping. (It's quite possible that the *celadora* simply didn't want to get involved.) The clinic was in a building with trees behind it, and they had climbed up a tree and broken a window to get inside. They had taken everything, all the psychiatric medicines like tranquilizers and even malaria pills, and they were just pouring them down their throats. With three or four turrets close by and an *agente* patrolling the area, it was clear that the *agentes* had been accomplices.

On Sunday I looked again, and they were still out there partying, stoned out of their minds and falling all over the place. Still the *celadoras* didn't do anything. But the party was getting bigger. We could hear a lot of banging and screaming but our view was limited, so we weren't completely sure what was happening.

My chance to see came when the authorities called me to say that there was a delivery at the office for the COPPES store. I was in charge of the store and this kind of errand was normal. So I said to Carolina, the treasurer, "Let's go see what's happening in Section B." I asked another woman as well but she didn't want to go.

I was very glad Carolina was with me, because though really sweet-looking, she was tall and strong. We went over to the office and picked up the order in a couple of boxes. Then I said to Carolina, "Okay, let's go see." At first she said no, but finally we did, leaving the supplies in a corner of the compound. Everybody except us was locked inside their sections.

But the door to Section B was open, and we just walked in.

I don't remember seeing such a horrible scene in all my life. There were about 40 women fighting among each other, pulling hair, kicking each other, half-naked. It was like a horror film, or something out of Dante. As we arrived, a woman ran out of the building with a broken bottle in her hand, looking to cut somebody.

Apparently the fight had started between the heads of two gangs, the way fights often started at the prison. One of the gangs included the women who had got into the clinic. The other was headed by a woman who was very close to the authorities. She was trying to bring the situation under control, and the other gang objected—and all of a sudden you had a riot.

Carolina took one look and said, "Come on, I don't want to see this," and tried to get me to leave. It was horrible but I was fascinated. I have no idea how long we actually stayed—15, 10, 5 minutes? A squad of guards arrived but they too were hesitant. It was crazy; there were at least 15 guards standing around and they couldn't do anything. All they knew about riot control was to shoot, but they couldn't risk killing a prisoner in a situation like this.

Separating the ringleaders is a sort of strategy that works in schoolyards, so they decided to try it here. It worked, in the sense that it calmed down the others. The guards pulled the two gang leaders outside into the prison yard, and it took six guards to separate them. The two had each other by the hair, and when they were finally pulled apart they took bunches of the other's hair with them. An angry woman who is used to violence is like an octopus. She's all arms and legs and she wriggles like mad. But when the guards finally did separate them, they threw them into the *calabozos*, the solitary cells.

Then they went back in and took all the ones that were drugged to the *calabozos*. It's amazing that none of those women died from overdoses. That night was one of the worst nights in prison, because the screaming and banging in the *calabozos* never stopped. There were four solitary cells arranged around a small caged compound. A single spigot was your only source of water. The *agentes* didn't even put the women in separate cells. They were all together, both gangs, about 10 women in total. And they went crazy. They tore off one of the iron doors and pulled the bars from the other doors. They hit each other with these bars, and they bit each other. I saw one woman after they let her out. She had an awful scar on her arm from a bite.

On Monday morning, we got up very early as usual to go out in the compound and receive our tortillas. But we were locked in and the *agente* would not let us out. Several guards had been transferred, and more *agentes* arrived later that day from other prisons to search the prison for whatever drugs were left. About 15 women were taken to the hospital, torn up from fighting or still totally stoned from overdosing or mixing drugs. Two were in comas and had to go to a psychiatric hospital.

In the end, some of the rioters were distributed to men's prisons throughout the country, where they led a separate existence confined to a single cell. Transferring gang leaders was one strategy the authorities used to calm things down. By this time, they had already done that with Rosalía, the boss of the mature women's section. But some people said that this riot had been directed by her from another prison. I don't know if that's true, but it's possible, and it's the sort of thing that she would do.

20

~

Keeping Busy

Memories come back to you in funny ways. A few days ago I was visited by a friend from El Salvador. We were sitting on my patio, and I was carving a little piece of wood. Actually it was a small stick and very delicate, so I was carving in tiny, careful cuts. I wasn't really making anything. My friend watched me do this for a while, and then said, "Ese es brete de tavo." That's jail work. He'd been in prison too and I'm sure he'd done it himself.

In jail you have time, more time than you ever had before in your life. You have time to think, or to do things with your hands—anything so long as it doesn't require money, or materials, the things you get so easily outside. But you do have time, and if you're energetic (as I am), you want to *do* things. I usually woke up at 4:30 in the morning and by 5:00 I was raring for some kind of activity or other.

Cooking was a constant activity. Once we achieved the right to do our own, we got a very good system under the *economato*. The families were extremely important to this. Each Thursday the *economato* would make a list—oil, cheese, eggs, tomato paste, lard, margarine, flour, plantains—the very basics. Then they would go around to all the *compañeras* and you would choose from the list what you would ask your family for. For instance, you might say you would ask your family to bring you flour on the following Sunday. Except for the few women who didn't have families, everyone had to contribute whatever they'd received, within reason.

I already mentioned the two chickens and two pounds of cheese my mother brought to each visit. It wasn't hard for her to drop into a supermarket on the way, but for poorer families, contributing to us required a lot more effort, and I was amazed at their generosity and sacrifice. Most had to come by bus, the way the majority of Central Americans travel. But it was common for someone's mother to show up, smiling and carrying a sack of plantains or oranges on her back, after traveling hours in various buses from the country-side. In fact, the poorer the family, the more generous they were. And the more creative.

Each Sunday the *compañeras* of the *economato* would look through the food that had been brought in and put it together with the food from the prison kitchen. Fresh produce came in weekly, or biweekly when in season, and frijoles were delivered once a month or every 15 days. Tortillas were pro-vided daily. From this, the committee would make a menu for the week. With no way to refrigerate things, we had to cook from day to day depending on what we had and how long it would last.

We took pains to make the meals as nice as possible, so we tried to put something special on the menu whenever we could. If there were a lot of string beans available, we would make *rellenos de ejotes*. They're a lot of work: you clean and cook the beans, fry them in well-beaten egg, and serve them in a sauce or soup.

You really became aware of the seasons and harvests. If the tomato crop had been good, tomatoes would appear at every meal. In the morning we'd cut them up, fry them with onion, and make a sauce that went very nicely with tortilla and coffee—a substantial breakfast. For lunch, probably spaghetti with a tomato sauce. And in the evening? Surprise—a tomato salad with lemon. Sometimes El Salvador is overflowing with avocados, so we'd have a lot of them in our diet. A luxury in most of the world, they just fall off the trees and rot during the season in El Salvador. We call stray dogs *aguacateros* because they eat avocados off the ground. But sometimes there was only rice and beans, es-pecially at the end of my time at Ilopango when conditions in the country were really bad. On Monday we'd eat well, but by Wednesday it was rice and beans, rice and beans, and of course tortillas. That was all the prison system could afford by that time. But at least we had more than many people had outside.

The work committee then distributed the work in couples. Two women cooked the day's food and two did the dishes. Since we were 96 prisoners in total at our greatest number, you either cooked or cleaned once every 20 or so days. And it was a lot of hard work, starting at 4:00 in the morning.

Main meals were cooked the same way that families all over Central Amer-ica do it, over a *polletón*. It's a long table made of mud, like a clay oven, and built into the surface are mounds with a hole in the center where you put the pot or the frying pan. The mound is hollow and you stoke it with wood. In our first negotiation with the prison, they agreed to supply wood for cooking, but it didn't always come. Sometimes our families had to truck in a load of wood from the market, paid by the Common Fund.

We had three *polletónes*, and some enormous pots we got from the Red Cross. We had an electric cooker, but it was used only for children's meals and when someone was sick and needed special food, or for tea and coffee during the day.

The trick to cooking for so many people is essentially to get the quantities right. Not everyone can do it, and with such large quantities it's a tragedy if it comes out wrong. Which it inevitably did on occasion. Burnt rice, or over-salted sauces, or spaghetti cooked so long it got mushy. The work committee had to make sure that a *compañera* who knew how to cook was matched with someone who didn't—or didn't like to. That way one would help the other, or supervise her. We tried to put together couples who liked each other, but occasionally we tried matching two women who didn't get along in hopes that they'd talk and get to know each other if they cooked together. It never worked!

Luckily there were enough people who knew how to handle this kind of work, and some were very good cooks. Whenever Beatriz or Paquita or I cooked we generally were given a difficult menu because we knew how to do it. For example, *chiles rellenos* are a treat and the *compañeras* loved getting them, but it's no treat to cook them for 96. I used to hate it. And although I was a good cook, I have to admit to a lifelong insecurity about frying rice traditional Central American style. We fried it in our huge low-rimmed pots with grated carrots and onion, if we had them, and a few bouillon cubes bought from the store. Then you throw in the water. But fried rice is something I never learned in Opus Dei club cooking class, and I'd look everywhere for Beatriz to calculate the water for me.

Less traumatic was making pancakes for breakfast. It's not so bad for three or four people at home, but for 96 it's endless work. I used to dread hearing we had received a load of flour or powdered milk, especially if we had a lot of eggs and the honey harvest was good—I knew I'd end up cooking pancakes.

Kitchen duty started around 4:00 in the morning. After stoking the *polletón*, you lit the fire and put water on for coffee. Next, you heated the beans made the day before, and perhaps started frying bananas.

Breakfast was served at 6:30. We clanged a piece of metal, everyone lined up, and two girls served. But for the cooks, work was just beginning. You had to start working on lunch, which was the main meal. So the work went on all day.

The morning was the worst part, and the worst part of that was cleaning the noontime rice. You had to pick stones and bad grains out of the rice by hand, slow, painstaking work because the prison bought the cheapest rice possible. And you cooked beans every day, like everywhere else in Central America. If we were doing *chiles rellenos*, we'd start peeling the peppers. God, peeling peppers for 96 . . . ! Or during orange harvest, peeling 96 oranges. It was a long hard day for two people. It went faster if your friends helped clean the rice or some other task. We didn't listen to the radio much while we were on kitchen work because we weren't supposed to even have radios, and we had to conserve the batteries. Sitting and chatting while we worked with our hands was the best way to make time go by.

Our diet was much better than that of the commons, but they didn't resent it. It didn't come into their heads to share food, so the poor ones or the ones that didn't get visitors didn't eat very much. Once or twice they tried to get a bit organized like us. But it never worked for long, and they always went back to the basic *rancho* of fried beans and two tortillas.

Some of the *compañeras* in our section didn't like the idea of sharing very much either, but COPPES controlled the supply of basic raw food, so they had to comply. The ones who received more had to share more, of course. Everybody saw the benefit in the long run, but sometimes it's very difficult to share, especially if your family has brought something that was only for you.

In the beginning, COPPES made sharing work because we were very few and we had time to talk it through with people. But with bigger groups you have to establish more rules about what's personal and what's for the community. After four or five months, we agreed that certain things were not shared. Say a *compañera*'s family had a few orange trees, and they brought her a sack of oranges. What would she do with a sack of oranges? Obviously she could share, and it wasn't hard to convince her of that. But if she got a box of chocolates, she wouldn't want to share it with everybody, and we understood that. Then you just shared with your close friends.

I remember a few special delicacies that came in, like when Beatriz's aunt brought cooked crayfish that had been caught that morning. Or what we call "June plums" that my nana brought from the family's orchard. In times of scarcity, even common things like tomatoes were a treat. Mother brought me a pound of tomatoes during one of those periods. I made it into a little salad with garlic and lemon and shared it with Beatriz and Miriam and one or two others. It couldn't have been shared with everyone, so it was no big deal.

I had lots of ideas for productive activities. Some were *locuras*, crazy notions that didn't work out, but one that worked was our bee project. Only three of us politicals participated, but it got some of the commons interested, and we worked together.

It happened like this. A young widow named Mabel was arrested six months after I arrived at Ilopango and we became very good friends. Mabel came from one of those European families that had been in El Salvador for generations yet remained European by marrying people from the Old Continent. Her grandparents were Swiss, and her mother had married a Swiss. Until a year before her arrest she had lived in the same neighborhood as my brother Javier, and her kids had played with his. So I'd heard about Mabel, and later on I learned that her mother and my mother had grown up together in San Miguel. The bourgeois network again! She looked completely Swiss: blonde, pale, with a very sweet expression and always beautifully dressed. She was a little older than me but seemed very naive. She became excellent at crafts like knitting and embroidery. So it was strange to find out what she was in prison for.

Mabel was a kidnapper. It had been big news when a member of the Bustamante family was kidnapped.[1] The Bustamantes are one of *las catorce*, the 14 oligarchy families reputed to control El Salvador's economy. There was a lot of speculation that it was a political kidnapping. After all, Guillermo Antonio Bustamante was a logical target and sure to get quite a ransom. The demands duly came, threatening to cut off his nose or ear if a huge amount of money wasn't paid.

Then the police made three arrests: an ex-military man named Guillermo Roeder, his lover, and Mabel. It turned out to have been a plain mercenary kidnapping with no political objective. Roeder was Bustamante's best friend and a good friend of Robert D'Aubuisson. He had left the military for the security business, selling guard services to people with something to protect. He was rumored to have maintained his connections to the military and worked with the death squads on the side. A complete bastard.[2] His lover was Mabel's best friend, which is how Mabel got mixed up in it.

Actually, it was pathetic how inept the kidnappers were, especially Mabel. If there's one thing you shouldn't do if you're in the business of kidnapping, it's work with someone as naive (and, as it turned out, uncommitted) as Mabel. After the snatch, they kept Bustamante in the house that Mabel and her friend had shared after Mabel's husband died. It was supposed to be empty as the two had moved again, so when the neighbors noticed strange comings and goings they phoned the police. The cops arrived, freed Bustamante, and raided Roeder's office. Mabel told me later that they had played backgammon all day in the office as they waited out the negotiations for ransom.

They were taken to the Media Luna prison downtown, where Mabel immediately told the police everything. The other two had coerced her into the kidnapping, she said, by threatening to kidnap her first cousin. The other woman wasn't pleased about that, obviously, and threatened to kill Mabel.

A new prisoner was always of interest, but people were especially curious because the kidnapping had been so sensational. I already had a connection through our families, so I went to Section C soon after she arrived. The two of us got along very well from the start, but what was more interesting was that the commons loved her. Whenever I visited her in the cell she shared with eight other women, she was always surrounded by four or five women—prostitutes, thieves, murderers—telling her their stories and listening to her gentle voice. Because they accepted Mabel, they accepted me, and I visited quite frequently. I heard horrifying stories there, both past and present. Meanness and violence were part of their lives. They had far too much time on their hands and tended to sit around smoking and letting out their hate and resentment, and Mabel's personality provided a sort of soothing balance. It's an amazing testament to her personality that she never had any trouble while she was in prison. I got to know a lot of commons through her, in a depth that would otherwise have been impossible.

Eventually she became religious and helped redecorate the prison chapel. After a year and a half, she testified for the prosecution in the trial of the other kidnappers and was set free. She married a Swiss soon after and moved to Switzerland, where as far as I know she has lived happily ever after.

Since Mabel's co-kidnapper had threatened to kill her, the authorities had to keep them completely separate, so Mabel was with the mature prisoners and the other woman with the younger ones. They even had different visiting days. Mabel's family came on Tuesdays. During my trips to the office for the store, I met her family, and it became a habit for me to visit with them. I would always find a reason to go to the office, even if there wasn't an order or any other real business. Like most visitors, they brought food for their daughter, and they started bringing lunch for me also. Mabel's mother taught both of us to knit during visits, and I taught Mabel to embroider. But the most important result of our friendship in prison was the bees.

Mabel's family had an enormous coffee plantation in one of the conflict zones, where the guerrilla was fighting the army, and it was almost abandoned. One day about 10 months after I was arrested, Mabel's mother and I started talking about their farm, and she mentioned some beehives that had been left unused. Now, we were always looking for projects, and if we could make a good proposal for something productive, the prison authorities could get help from the Ministry of Agriculture. So when she mentioned that if we wanted the hives she would bring them in, I got very excited.

A few days later I took some other *compañeras* to talk with the *directora*. By then we had a good sense of what would be acceptable to her. In Salvadoran law (if not in practice), the prisons are supposed to improve the prisoners' lives and teach them new skills for when they are released. The prisons are also supposed to provide work, but it is usually labor like folding paper bags that is unpleasant and very badly paid. Above all, the project had to benefit the whole prison. That was fine with us, since COPPES deemed it important to maintain contact with the other prisoners as much as possible. With that in mind, we proposed that each section choose two volunteers to take care of the bees, and that the duties would rotate to give more people a chance. We told her that we could get the hives for free and that the prison's costs would be almost nothing, just for bottles with corks for the honey.

As we had hoped, the *directora* liked the idea. She contacted the Ministry of Agriculture, and after a few weeks the ministry sent an expert to give weekly beekeeping classes. By that time Mabel's mother had already trucked in the boxes from her farm. The course was the ministry's standard one: a little theory of bee health and behavior, bee diseases, and how to identify the different bees, then the practical work of setting up the hives and maintaining them.

The bees had to be at least 100 yards from people, so we set up the hives outside the main prison walls in a ravine. The prison grounds were surrounded by a high fence and were quite extensive. Back when the nuns ran the prison, it had a farm with a pigsty, chicken coop, and fruit trees. But that was long abandoned when I arrived, and the grounds were off limits. Now, however, those of us who worked with our bees were allowed out of the main compound, accompanied by a *celadora*. I often thought about escaping as I walked to and from the hives. It might have been possible to climb over the fence or find a place to break through it. It also seemed possible to escape from the chapel, where the windows looked out on the streets of Ilopango. But I knew that if I got caught my case would be much worse, and I always kept the hope that I might be freed legally. So I never tried it, and neither did anyone else working with the bees.

At first the prison tried to obligate the prisoners to participate. Predictably, that didn't work. But our proposal about volunteers from each section worked well, although the initial enthusiasm dropped off and the routine set in. Most of the women who started out in the bee project continued all the time that I was there, as I did.

And why not? Beekeeping is not exactly fun, but it was nice to get out of the compound once or twice a week, and the work (mainly cleaning the hives) wasn't hard. The rules of safe beekeeping are pretty uncomplicated: cover your head, don't wear bright colors, and above all don't wear T-shirts or other clothes that cling to your skin. Most of us observed those rules, but not Sister Lidia.

Lidia's title of "Sister" was honorary, as she was a Protestant who converted while in prison. She was about 45, a tiny, thin woman with a big behind.

I always thought that from the rear she looked like an ant—maybe a soldier ant, because she was in prison for murder. Sister Lidia had been a street vendor, one of the thousands who park their big baskets by Salvadoran roads and sell everything from cheap makeup to costume jewelry. A particular Guardia had taken to hassling her, and since she couldn't complain to the police about a policeman, she'd decided that the only solution was to kill him. Which she did and received a life sentence. In a funny way it was remarkable that she had a sentence at all. Most of us, whether common or political, were in prison awaiting trial. The Salvadoran justice system, if you can call it that, takes its time.

Sister Lidia had already served 12 years when I arrived, and always said she was quite happy there, paying her debt to society and accepting the Lord's will. Well, she may have accepted God's rules, but she sure didn't accept the rules of beekeeping. She was very tidy, always dressed and made up very carefully. She invariably wore tight clothes, high heels, a lot of makeup, and a lot of perfume. Her hair, which went down to that big rear end, was always worn loose. A beekeeper's nightmare.

"Doña Lidia," we would tell her over and over again in our most respectful manner, "you can't wear high heels down here. You can't wear makeup. And your dress! If you anger the bees you'll need loose clothes to protect you from their sting. Please, Doña Lidia . . ."

But it did no good, and she often got stung. Yet she never complained, even the time the bees got into her hair and she was stung 21 times. Though badly swollen, she accepted the pain and went on dressing the same. She was one of the most faithful beekeepers, as if she was doing penance.

Another of the commons who worked diligently was Doña Eva, who was the same age as Sister Lidia and came from the same section. But that was the end of the resemblance. Where Lidia had been a street vendor and was in prison for a sudden act of violence, Eva was upper-middle class and had committed fraud worth over a million dollars. After her false check scam was discovered, she'd hidden in a false ceiling in her house. The police arrived, and suspecting that she was somewhere in the house, they announced loudly that they would arrest her mother if she didn't give herself up. And so she landed in Section C.

It may sound funny, but Eva was quite a decent sort of person, and apart from the bees, she also cooked for the children in the prison. There were a lot of them, since the Salvadoran justice system doesn't like to separate mothers from their kids and most Salvadoran women over 20 are mothers. The first political to have a baby was Ana, one of the women arrested with Esperanza, then Delia and Carolina. Others came in with kids, like Doña Angela who arrived with three. We cleaned up a separate cell for them so that they wouldn't bother us during the night and furnished it with cribs and whatever else we could get. The cooker was downstairs in the kitchen but they got priority for it.

There was often a sort of family atmosphere in our section, with kids scurrying around and mothers nursing babies. The rest of the day they were outside in the main compound. What else could we do with them? Many of the commons also had kids and they mixed. There was sometimes some talk about "the other kids"—should this group play with another group?—but that's normal, like in any neighborhood. At their most numerous, there were 8 or 9 mothers and 15 kids. The oldest was a boy about seven or eight years old, who actually went out to school.

Eva kept herself busy cooking for the children while she waited for her sentence. I don't know how she managed it but she was released after six months. It probably involved graft and lawyers.

Sometimes on my way to or from the bees, I'd meet and say hello to Ilopango's other million-dollar prisoner, one who stole even more than Eva and came from even higher up in Salvadoran society. Señora Rengifo was also in her mid or late 40s but absolutely stunning, one of those bourgeois Salvadoran women whose only job is to take care of herself and look elegant. She was accused of stealing $5 million from the state in collaboration with her two adult children. Her scam worked like this: El Salvador's most important product is coffee, and to ensure the various producers don't destroy each other (and therefore the national economy) with cutthroat competition, the government is the sole exporter through the National Coffee Institute. Most small countries that are dependent on a few products operate the same way. The producer ships its own coffee but is paid by the institute on the basis of receipts. Señora Rengifo's scam was to submit receipts worth millions without actually shipping the coffee.

Like Eva, she wasn't in prison long—rich people rarely are—and while she was at Ilopango she had all sorts of special privileges. I think this happens in other countries too, where you can buy special treatment from the prison system. It's so unjust. You don't have to look any further to see why there is struggle. Señora Rengifo didn't even have to sleep with the other common prisoners; the authorities gave her a separate room in another part of the prison grounds. I think it was almost a suite, with its own living room. Her chauffeur arrived three times a day with meals cooked at her home. She was given total freedom of movement within the prison, and a guard to watch over her wherever she walked. Not that she had any problems: the common prisoners couldn't relate to her at all and didn't go near her as she walked around the grounds dressed immaculately in her fine clothes. She often sat in the orchards near the bees, where we mostly met.

You're probably expecting me to say that she was a friend or acquaintance of my mother?

Well, you're right. Señora Rengifo had known me since I was a child, although she wasn't a family friend and was a different generation from my mother. So they didn't know each other well and Mother never came to see her when she visited. I was one of the few people Señora Rengifo ever spoke to in Ilopango, and even then she was very distant; mostly, I suspect, because she was terrifically embarrassed to be there. In any case, she wasn't there long. I believe she simply arranged to pay back the $5 million and the state called it quits. Easy, if you've got $5 million—

The ministry's bee expert taught us until the first harvest. By then we had learned all we needed to know, and he stopped coming. That first crop was incredible: we harvested some 180 bottles of honey from six hives. It was easy to sell and the prison helped us sell it. The profits amounted to about 100 colones (40 dollars), which was significant. The politicals' share went to the Common Fund. I don't know exactly what happened to the commons' share; I think the *celadoras* managed their money and it went into improvements for the different sections. Eventually we had 16 hives at work, and after the bees started up, the commons started raising chickens as well.

21

~

Discipline

I don't usually use the word "whorish" to describe women, but Estela fit the description. She was about 25 and tough-looking, with tight clothes and too much makeup. When she arrived in the section, she told us that she was a member of the ERP, and so a bed was provided for her in the cell with Esperanza and other ERP *compañeras.* That was standard when a woman affiliated to a political or guerrilla organization arrived; she was given a bed in the same area as other compañeras from her organization.

But we had doubts about Estela from the start. Some of it was her manner, but most came from the fact that no one—least of all the ERP women—knew her or anything about her. It was possible that she was bona fide because, like all guerrilla organizations, the ERP used compartmentalization and false names as part of their security measures. On the other hand, the total lack of information was very suspicious. The organized Salvadoran Left (not to mention the country itself) is small enough that most people are known in some way or other. Our communications with the male politicals in Mariona prison and with our organizations outside the prison walls were very good, and they often sent us information about new prisoners, sometimes even before their arrival. But we knew nothing about Estela. This put Esperanza and the *compañeras* in a delicate position. They were pleased to increase their numbers and therefore their influence in Ilopango, but not at the cost of a security problem.

I'm sure that Esperanza quickly sent a secret message to the ERP asking them to double-check on Estela. However, before any information came in Estela was exposed as a plant. It happened one afternoon about a week after her arrival, when a woman in the ERP cell complained that Estela had stolen letters from her. COPPES was still unified at that point, so the six of us on the *directiva* got together and decided to search her things. We got someone to call Estela to the plaza on a pretext and keep her there while the six of us went to her cell.

The accusation was true: we found not only the stolen letters but papers she had taken from other *compañeras* hidden in her pillow.

It was obvious that Estela had been planted by the police, so we all agreed that she had to be kicked out immediately. No waiting, no explanations: we picked up all her things, put them outside the door to the section, and told the guard to take them away. Then we escorted Estela to the door and told the guard to take *her* away. He did so, quickly. End of problem.

COPPES usually solved problems regarding individual women quickly. If you are organized and can make a credible threat of force, you have the leverage to solve things—usually without resorting to force. The prison authorities knew that we kept order in Section A, and since their main interest was to keep the prison quiet they let us run it on our own terms.

What a contrast we were with the common prisoners in Sections B and C, where there was a great deal of physical aggression between the women. A lot of them carried blades and weren't afraid to use them. Among other lessons, my two years in Ilopango taught me what women—some women at least—are capable of doing.

The worst incident, outside of the Christmas riot, was the day I saw a common prisoner named Emilia batter another woman, Rosario, bloody in less than a minute. It happened near the children's kitchen in Section C, in a common area called *maternales* where the children and mothers had their dinners. Despite the name, there was nothing maternal about *maternales*: it was nothing more than a concrete hallway with a few ratty chairs and tables.

Emilia was one of the women who hung out in the cell of my friend Mabel, the failed kidnapper. She was 30 or older, a big strong woman whose appearance would be called "butch" in English. Personally, I found her interesting to talk to, and she had a good sense of humor. But there was no forgetting that she was extremely tough. The crime that landed her in Ilopango was a horrible act of premeditated assault: after finding out that her common-law husband had another lover, Emilia took revenge by throwing boiling water on both the other woman and her child. I could never get over the idea of her doing that to an innocent child, especially since she had children herself.

One day Rosario arrived at Ilopango. She was an expensive prostitute by Salvadoran standards and reminded me of the prostitutes I'd seen in Vancouver during the 1978 Socialist International Congress. Streetwalkers with mink coats standing on street corners a couple of blocks from the Hyatt Regency. They'd made a strong impression on me because I had never seen anything like them.

Rosario looked after her appearance very carefully, anticipating the time she would get out and back to work. She dyed her hair, went to bed with curlers, and kept her nails perfectly manicured. She never did anything to bother anyone, but somehow Emilia decided she didn't like her. Every time she saw Rosario, Emilia would insult her or say ugly things about her to anyone who was standing nearby. Sometimes she even threatened her.

When I went to visit Mabel in Section C, I often found Emilia there. She would sit around and talk all day with us, but unlike Mabel and her gentle way of talking (she really was the most unlikely kidnapper you ever saw), Emilia's stories were cruel and violent. She sometimes even talked about murder and cutting people up. And along with the stories she told, Emilia would often say under her breath how much she hated Rosario. You'd hear her mutter, "All she does is SIT AROUND and DO HER NAILS. Fucking PROSTITUTE..."

Even if you didn't catch all the words, you knew who and what she was talking about. But since Emilia wasn't addressing anyone in particular, conversation would go on for a while. Then Emilia would say softly, with that hard look on her face, "One day I'm going to GET her," and she'd add, still under her breath, "Yeah, and BEAT HER UP and DISFIGURE HER."

You couldn't tell if it was just talk or if she meant it. There was a lot of violent talk among the commons.

Then one morning at 6:00, I had dropped by to see Mabel on my way to pick up the tortillas for Section A's breakfast. There were a few people hanging out in the cell and we were chatting as usual when Rosario walked by with her hair in curlers.

With no warning at all, Emilia jumped up, grabbed Rosario by the hair, and bashed her head against the nearest concrete pillar. Then she dragged her shrieking to the next pillar and *BANG* into that one, and then the next and the next until she had smashed poor Rosario's head on each one of the hallway's six pillars. She was much stronger than Rosario and in such a fury that none of us could stop her. It only lasted a moment before the guards arrived, alerted by the screaming and hysterics, but it took six of them to pull her off.

They punished Emilia with 10 days in the *calabozos*, the isolation cells. When she came back she said no more about it and resumed her prison life as if nothing had happened. A very hard woman.

Rosario was taken to hospital and returned to prison after a few days, terribly bashed up. She also refused to talk about it, but somehow she didn't seem the same. There was something about the way she looked at you, a sort of vagueness in her manner. I think she actually suffered some kind of brain injury. She was released after a couple of months, and I never heard any more of her.

We in Section A never had an incident like that, where someone was actually hurt in a physical fight. It might have been possible; some of us were also pretty tough, especially those who'd been in the mountains and had military training. You had only to look at Esperanza, for instance, to know you didn't want to mess with her. Though pretty, despite the scars on her face, she walked and carried herself with all the authority of the guerrilla *comandante* she was. Yet she was also gentle and soft-spoken and had an aura of calm about her. The only evidence of tension was the way she smoked, with those thin little hands constantly working at lighting up or butting out a cigarette.

Serious discipline problems of any kind were rare in Section A. Part of this was due to the simple fact that we weren't criminals. Despite whatever acts we'd committed in opposition to the government (and I was far from the only person in prison for entirely legal activities), most of us had never done anything seriously illegal. But the order we kept in Section A was also due in part to COPPES's discipline committee. It was composed of senior women whom everyone trusted, and we lived up to that trust: whenever a problem arose we dealt with it quickly and resolutely.

The discipline committee was originally composed of the same women as the *directiva*, with representatives from each of the main political and military groups: Paquita, Esperanza, me, and so on. But as time went on, other women were appointed to the committee because of the respect people had for them. When the ANDES leaders were arrested, for instance, some of them were immediately brought into the discipline committee in recognition of their part in the struggle outside the prison walls.

Sometimes, when the authorities dumped a non-political person in our section, we could see that she was going to give us trouble. There were three or four such cases, and in each of them we did the same as we'd done with Estela. We just put her things at the door and told the authorities, "We don't want this woman in here. She's a common delinquent, not a political prisoner." And they'd take her away.

The discipline committee didn't have a set activity or schedule of meetings like other committees, because discipline was not a constant issue. We had most of the minor problems that you'd expect when adults are stuck together in groups, and someone had to be responsible in each cell for getting people to turn the radio volume down, for example, or quit smoking in the cells after 10:00. The biggest part of the job was simply reminding people to be considerate of others.

"Reminding" is a good word to describe what the discipline committee did most of the time. When people didn't want to work, or pretended to be sick, or didn't want to stand guard, you had to talk to them and explain why order was important and what COPPES was trying to achieve. Punishment rarely entered into it. You had to do the same thing when someone got depressed: find a way to talk them out of their depression and back into participating in our community.

I had to talk to a few of the girls who wanted to get something going with the male prison guards. In fact, it was a fairly constant problem. Although some of these girls had been active in political or military organizations, they were still just teenagers with their hormones in overdrive (the guards, of course, were only too happy to oblige). We weren't about to kick one of these girls out of the section for this kind of infraction, so it meant being vigilant and calling it to their attention whenever we discovered something was going on.

However, there were other issues that were a lot more complicated because they weren't about being considerate or remembering the proper prisoner-guard relationship. One was lesbian relationships.

As everyone knows, homosexuality is both prevalent and heavily repressed in prisons everywhere. Ilopango was no exception. In the common prisoners' sections the lights were kept on at all times, partly for safety but mostly to discourage sexual activity between the women. We politicals had quickly gained the right to turn our lights off at 10:00, but even with us lesbian relations remained an issue that had to be handled carefully.

I had only been in Ilopango a few weeks when two young *compañeras* were brought into Section A. When I say young I mean *young*; they were high school students, aged 14 and 15, respectively. I'll call them Magdalena and Patricia. One was a bona fide political who had participated in an urban militia organized by the guerrilla. The other had been arrested simply because of association; one of her brothers was involved politically, though I'm not sure how or with whom.

They were two normal teenagers from lower-middle-class families. Magdalena was blonde and blue-eyed, which is the epitome of beauty in El Salvador because such coloring is rare. She was a sweet-natured, enthusiastic kid. Patricia was darker and perhaps a little less sociable than Magdalena. But she was also full of life, just bursting to learn how to use makeup and all those other fascinating things that adult women do.

These two kids had been tortured during their month-long detention in the Guardia Nacional headquarters before they were passed on to Ilopango. Although they hadn't known each other before they were arrested, the Guardia had kept them in the same cell. That was lucky. Imagine how much harder it would have been if they'd been isolated during that ordeal. At least they'd had someone of their age to hold onto when the beatings were over.

And that was basically what the problem was when they arrived at Section A. They had got used to sleeping together in the Guardia Nacional headquarters, and they didn't want to give it up. They asked to have cots right next to each other, a request that was granted immediately. The very first night, Patricia went to Magdalena's cot and they slept together the rest of the night. Inevitably in such close quarters, it was noticed immediately and eventually ended up before the *directiva*.

Rules are usually made to deal with situations as they come up, rather than in anticipation of their occurring. This was the first time the question of lesbian relations had come up in COPPES, so we didn't have a ready-made rule for it.

As always in our meetings, the talk went around the table as each woman got her chance to speak. I think Paquita had the chair, and one by one the *compañeras* spoke against letting the girls get away with sleeping together. The prison's rule was one person to a bed, and the *directiva* agreed this was a good rule. Sleeping together might lead these girls into temptation and, in the time-honored revolutionary jargon, this could result in a "typical bourgeois deviation." Not that the bourgeoisie would have disagreed: in El Salvador anything to do with sex is bad.

As each of the women spoke, I listened to how clear and set their attitudes were, and quickly decided I hadn't strong enough reasons to speak in the girls' favor. I didn't think women sleeping together was wrong, but the majority of the *compañeras* obviously did. It was clear to me that I was the only one who saw it differently, so I shut up.

After a half hour's discussion the group decided that the rule would be "no physical contact, and one person to a bed." To be fair, part of that decision arose from a feeling that COPPES had enough problems without this one. There were beds enough for all so there was no need for people to double up, especially if it would create problems with the prison authorities.

My own decision, to keep my mouth shut and let the majority decide, was basically a survival scheme. I'm open and liberal about most personal things, partly because I lived in Europe for many years. Nowadays there are openly lesbian revolutionaries (admittedly they are mostly in the refugee community in Los Angeles or Canada or Nicaragua). But the Salvadoran mentality is very conservative when it comes to values and principles.

Abortion and homosexuality are important issues in Europe and the United States, but in the context of El Salvador's struggle for basic human rights and economic justice they seemed secondary. So even before I was arrested I had decided there were some issues I would not take a stand on. I justified my strategy with the thought that we could deal with those issues after change came to the country. The consensus of COPPES was that it was wrong to allow lesbian relationships within a revolutionary movement, and I would abide by that consensus.

Unfortunately, my willingness to bow to the *directiva*'s decision didn't mean I was saved from having the problem dumped in my lap. Magdalena and Patricia slept in my cell and I was in charge of its discipline, so it was up to me to call the matter to their attention. That was doubly hard because, quite apart from my opinion on the subject, Magdalena was one of my closest friends. It was like my relationship with Titina so many years before. Magdalena admired me and wanted to learn all she could from me. I was almost the age of her mother, and in some ways she was like my child. She used to love to braid my hair, and I taught her to sew. Patricia was a little cooler, but we got along fine.

Yet now the *directiva* had given me the task of forbidding them to sleep together. As I walked down the stairs, I prepared myself for what I thought was going to be a difficult task. In El Salvador the suggestion that a woman is a lesbian is a terrible insult, about as humiliating as you can get. But when I got together with the two girls, the word never came up. I simply told them that the rule in prison was one person to a bed and therefore they couldn't sleep together. We were living in a group and there was little space, and we had to have discipline and order in our lives. Magdalena and Patricia were sad but they accepted that we had to have rules. So they agreed, and I secretly heaved a deep sigh of relief and thought that was the end of it.

Then, two weeks later, it blew up again. It was after breakfast on a Sunday morning, always an exciting time as everybody rushed around getting ready for *visitas*, taking out our best clothes and putting on makeup and getting things ready to send out with our relatives. I remember the moment clearly: I was pressing my blouse when a tattletale sidled up to me with "Magdalena and Patricia are taking a shower together!"

My heart just sank and I put down the iron. Why, oh why did people have to bring me these things? And why did these two girls have to do it so openly that I had to get involved?

Everyone was buzzing about the scandal of Magdalena and Patricia daring to be in the shower together. *Sí*, and on a Sunday! The girl who tattled was pulling me by the arm and insisting that I come and look.

I went down the stairs to the shower stalls to see; the two girls were definitely taking their shower together. But I didn't say anything, just went back to pressing my blouse and getting ready for *visitas*. I believe in telling people what they need to know privately, not making it public. Besides, I needed to figure out what to say. The moment arrived a few minutes before visiting hours started, when the two had finished dressing. I walked over and took them aside, saying I wanted to talk to them.

Now, you have to picture this. Taking them aside doesn't mean much when you're sharing a cell with 30 women. If Ana Margarita was talking in a corner with Magdalena and Patricia, it was pretty clear what was going on. Everyone was aware, and the two girls were aware that everyone else was aware, and they got upset. Which made it even more public.

The trouble was that I couldn't think of any way to approach it except straight. Despite my personal feelings, I couldn't appear to contradict the *directiva* by saying, "This is how I feel but the rules say . . ." So I did it the *directiva's* way, explaining to the two of them that the closer they got physically, the more, um, temptation they were in.

"Temptation of what?" they wanted to know. They still didn't get it. So I had to say it. I couldn't just say, "You're doing something wrong," and not give any reason at all.

"Temptation that it might become a lesbian relationship." There, I'd said it.

They reacted angrily, especially Magdalena. How dare I insult them! How dare I humiliate them! I, who she admired most in the prison—how dare I think such a thing of her! It was as bad as I'd imagined it would be, and I couldn't blame them. Nor could I back down.

Patricia was released from prison only three weeks later, and there was never another incident as public as that one. But I never really patched things up with Magdalena. For a month afterward she wouldn't even talk to me, not even to say good morning or good afternoon. That was very common in prison. When you lived together in such a small space and couldn't physically remove yourself from a problem, the best thing you could do was pretend the other person didn't exist. Sometimes such resentment was so thick in the air that I imagined you could take a knife and cut it into pieces.

Eventually Magdalena relaxed enough to speak to me, but we were never friendly again. A year later her parents managed to get her released from Ilopango. I don't know where she is now.

It only happened a couple of times that somebody just said, "The hell with you and your discipline committee." The worst of these incidents involved Sonia, whom I mentioned earlier. She was an amazing kid and one of my favorites, but at the same time she had serious conduct problems. She'd push and push to be allowed to join in a project, and although you'd have reservations from past experience you'd say, "Okay Sonia." And for a while things would be fine. But then she might decide to sneak out of the section and climb a tree when she was supposed to be teaching a crafts class, and you'd look and look for her while the class waited. Or she might suddenly stop an activity altogether because she didn't like the way someone acted. And she had a horrible temper. She would start cussing and screaming, and when that happened it was difficult to deal with her.

I talked with her frequently about acting responsibly, but it did no good. She was so difficult and so wonderful and such a source of laughter that I couldn't help forgiving her most of the time. But the truth was that she kept getting us into problems like the oil paint *pinta* and the light bulbs she stole from the chapel.

Just before my first Christmas a plastic jar full of *chicha*—Central American moonshine—was discovered in a closet in Section C. The closet was where the *celadoras* kept all the prison's Christmas decorations, and it was normally locked. With Christmas approaching we wanted to put up our decorations, so two prisoners and a *celadora* walked over to Section C and opened the closet. They were surprised to find that the lock was broken, and even more surprised to find a plastic jar among the decorations. The jar was full of *chicha*, busily fermenting.

Moonshine is taken seriously by prison authorities everywhere, and they set up strict rules and procedures to prevent the prisoners from making their own alcohol. In Ilopango, one of those measures was to forbid us to eat or receive pineapple; it ferments fast and you can therefore easily make it into *chicha*. So we weren't allowed pineapple, or fresh sugarcane, or anything else with a high sugar content.

The *celadora* immediately marched back to Section A and accused us— that is, the politicals—of making *chicha*. That was a serious charge, and it could have been tough for COPPES if our group had been involved. But when we saw the jar we knew that it was one of Sonia's projects. She had brewed it using fruit from the nance tree in the section's courtyard. The tree dropped its fruit from time to time, and every morning Sonia would get up early and pick up the nances, stroll over to Section C, open up the closet, and put them in the jar. The lock on the door hadn't been a problem; she'd just broken it and gotten on with the job.

Just as she'd done with the *pinta* that caused so much trouble, Sonia didn't even try to deny it.

"Sure, I was making *chicha*," was her answer. As usual, she couldn't see that she had done anything wrong. It was just another project. She could just as easily have been making candied fruit.

After confronting us, the *celadora* went to inform the prison administration. All we could do was wait, knowing that Sonia was going to be punished quite severely. There was no way for COPPES to defend her. The broken lock was not that big a deal. We would have been able to negotiate something with the authorities, some sort of internal discipline that would satisfy them. But negotiating over alcohol was not possible, and by that time negotiating *anything* to do with Sonia was difficult because she so often got into trouble.

Her punishment was 10 days, including Christmas, in the *calabozo*, the isolation cell. Christmas! It was terrible. The isolation cells were grouped around a little courtyard that I described before, really no more than a cement cage with barbed wire hanging over it, empty and featureless except for a spigot and a drainage hole. The cells themselves were three feet wide and six feet long. No bed. A hole in the corner as a toilet. And that was all. The door to each cell had a small shutter for the *celadora* to look in at you, and at the top of the cell was one foot of space with thick iron bars that let in a little light. The isolation compound neighbored our sewing workshop, and we often heard screams and pounding on the cell doors when common prisoners were punished there.

At first Sonia took the *calabozo* in stride. Soon I got permission to go and see her. I brought her books and food every day, and that both distracted her and made her a little more comfortable. But after a few days all her restlessness and energy took over. You couldn't get her to sit still very long at the best of times, and now she had only two square meters and bare concrete around her. She climbed to the top of the cell and managed to wrestle one of the bars out of the concrete. Then she set about sharpening it and scraping a hole in the wall. By the 10th day she was just about berserk, doing whatever she could to make a racket. When the guards finally came to take her out she was insolent to them. An argument started and she hit one of them. Result: she had to stay in solitary for another couple of days.

The episode was also painful for us as an organization. It was the first time a political prisoner had been sent into the isolation cells. Section A had no drug or alcohol problems, and left to ourselves, we would have dealt with Sonia's little contravention of the rules without the authorities ever knowing.

After Sonia got out of the *calabozo*, she was harder to deal with than ever. Punishments like that never improved her conduct; in fact, they just made her worse. Sometimes she would refuse to eat, in protest of something or other. Other times she fell into moods where she said no to everything. No to doing her cleaning. No to wearing her shoes. No to washing her clothes, so she started to stink.

Sonia was in my cell, so she was my problem. At the same time, Section A's population expanded to almost 100, well over double its capacity. Such numbers meant that COPPES had to be increasingly strict with discipline and rules. The arrival of the ANDES women and the splitting of COPPES into two factions complicated matters even more for someone like Sonia. She was sensitive enough to feel the unspoken stresses and contradictions, but she couldn't understand the conflicts they created.

Talking to her sometimes helped, and sometimes didn't. For instance, I often tried to explain what COPPES was about and why we did what we did. Why we were in the struggle and what part we played in it. Some of it made sense to her, but it upset her greatly that human beings are not consistent between what they say and what they do. COPPES politics made her furious.

All of a sudden she would explode. Once we were sitting upstairs sewing, and something she'd been brooding over for a few days came out.

"Why are you and Esperanza so fucking polite to each other," she demanded, "when the truth was that you work against each other all the time. You hate her and she hates you!"

"We don't hate each other," I explained, trying hard to keep my temper. "Personally, Esperanza and I get along quite well—she taught me to embroider, right? But we represent different organizations and we have different opinions on what's best for COPPES."

Sonia couldn't accept that.

"It's all goddammed hypocrisy!" she screamed, and stormed off.

Sometimes she stopped seeing me as Ana Margarita and just saw me as a figure of authority. At such times the tension between us got very heavy indeed. I could often defuse it with books or games or projects like the vegetable garden, but sometimes I just didn't have the energy or patience to make the effort. And then she said I was hateful and did anything she could to bother me and disrupt the cell. She was so hard to reach. Plus, I have to admit that physically she still intimidated me, with her size and violent temper, as she had on that day by the storeroom. I tried never to let her see it.

The tension between us rose and fell for almost a year. Then came the final straw. The incident was touched off by her transistor radio, which she started to keep on after 10:00 p.m., when the lights were turned off. After lights out we usually had two hours before it was time to be totally quiet. And everybody would be quiet. Some people went straight to sleep, while others talked quietly until the cell grew silent. Although I was in charge, I hardly ever had to say when it was time for that silence; everyone could feel the energy level diminishing and it felt right to be in bed and quiet.

It was the moment when we were finally, totally alone with ourselves. Often I would hear women cry, and because I was in charge I had to get up and console the person who was crying. Usually it was because she felt alone and was suffering from the simple fact of being there, away from her family and her life. And there was much I didn't hear as I slept. A lot of stories came out of that blackness, the result of so many women being in the same space and the same situation. Things were heard and misunderstood, and sometimes things were invented. Maybe that same day, or the day after someone would come to me and say I heard so-and-so masturbating, and I would have to talk to whoever it was. Whatever the problem, it hardly ever required more than a talk.

But Sonia was clearly pushing it, abusing the quiet and the feelings of the other *compañeras*. After three nights of this, I got up to put a stop to it.

"Come on, Sonia," I said quietly, bending over her. "Turn off the radio, put out the cigarette and go to sleep. It's time, lights are off."

She got up from her bed and held the cigarette close to my face.

"What if I don't want to?"

The cell was absolutely quiet as everyone listened. I felt the heat of the cigarette on my cheek. Even now, almost 10 years later, I can feel it when I think back to that moment. I slowly lifted my face and replied in the same quiet tone, "You'd better do it." It was a showdown. I wasn't about to get physical with her, but I couldn't allow such continued abuse of discipline.

I straightened up. "This is the last time I'm telling you."

As I turned to go back to my bed, she leapt up and kicked me. I fell and she jumped on my back, screaming and punching and kicking. I screamed too, and all of a sudden the entire cell was in an uproar as the *compañeras* tried to separate us and the *celadora* came out of her room to intervene. They finally pulled Sonia off and the *celadora* hustled her off to solitary.

I was in a state, shaking and trying to calm myself, but the *directiva* of COPPES immediately called a meeting. Although the organization had divided, this incident was so important that both factions met.

The meeting didn't last long. What should we do? One thing was clear; we could not defend Sonia anymore. There had never before been any physical violence in Section A, much less against one of the *directiva*. There was lots of violence in the prison—beatings and threats and stabbings—but that was among the commons. This was the first time there had been violence among the politicals. There was no other solution: she would have to leave the section. It was very painful to me. A couple of days after the incident, the *directiva* of COPPES officially asked the authorities to transfer Sonia to another prison on the grounds that she wasn't a real political prisoner.

Meanwhile they kept her in the *calabozo* for 15 days, and again I went to see her in the isolation cells. We talked, but she really didn't understand why we were having her thrown out.

It was terribly sad the day she left. I felt especially bad because despite everything I really liked her. When the guards came for her, they didn't have to drag her away. She was a very proud little girl at that moment as she said, "The hell with you. I'm leaving."

Although Ilopango was the only women's prison in El Salvador, women are frequently kept in special cells in the jails of smaller towns. It must have been terrible for Sonia to be by herself, all that vitality and imagination with nothing to entertain her. I heard through the grapevine that she continued causing trouble and was moved from prison to prison. The last I heard of Sonia was that she was set free five months later under the same amnesty that got me released. I was glad to know that, but never heard any more of her. It would be wonderful to know where Sonia is and what she is up to. Such a bright and creative kid, and so restless. I can only hope the two years in prison didn't permanently harm her.

Section A was a quieter place after she left, and there were no more discipline problems, at least not on the same scale. Despite the division in COPPES, life followed its routines and the section continued to function as smoothly as could be expected. Then in April, the news of a murder and suicide in Managua changed the face of the Salvadoran opposition forever and shattered the certainty that had kept me going for so long. Ironically, that same event also brought COPPES back together.

22

~

A Strike, a Murder, and a Suicide

The third hunger strike was held during the visit of Pope John Paul II to El Salvador, deliberately using his visit to publicize the strike. The pope paid no attention to us when he arrived on March 6, even though he had to pass the prison after landing at Ilopango air base. It wasn't a surprise. This pope tends to support the authorities, except those in Communist countries. He doesn't make any waves with capitalist governments.

At the time, US president Reagan was certifying that human rights were getting better in El Salvador. They weren't, but the US Congress had forced him to certify every six months. So we were drawing attention to that as well.

This third strike was especially important to me. It was very long, lasting 33 days. But this time there were only 12 of us, and since it came after the split, only one COPPES of the two participated. Actually we were 40 people altogether: 12 women in Ilopango and 28 men in Mariona prison, which had also split. In Ilopango we carefully selected the strikers to represent different sectors of Salvadoran society: students, teachers, market women, MNR, *campesinas*, et cetera. All were from my cell.

This was two years after Bobby Sands died in the hunger strike in Ireland.[1] The *línea* was to go all the way but no deaths, only to take it "as far as you can."

Once again, the first few days were horrible. The craving, the pain in your stomach, the headache. Then it became easier. As always we tried to take our minds off the discomfort, and the boredom. Reading was a big part of this. One of my strong memories is of reading *One Day of Life* by Manlio Argueta, the story of repression in a village in El Salvador, a book eventually banned by the government. Every afternoon we read it, crying as we shared the emotion, and we were doubly sad when the book ended.

During hunger strikes we had a series of special activities. Three times a day there were little political *actos* to keep up our moral. We had a COPPES song that we'd sing along with other songs, and there were *consignas*, slogans supporting the strike. The kitchen was controlled a bit more strictly, and the *compañeras* made an effort not to talk about food. They washed our clothes, and gave us priority in the bathroom, and for water. A certain quiet was maintained to let us sleep. This was kept up by everyone, because even the people who weren't in our *línea* were respectful of what we were doing. Some of the supporting *compañeras* kept us company. It was hard for me that my friend Beatriz had left by that time. (I need to mention here what eventually happened to Beatriz, if only briefly. After some very tough times, including a second imprisonment in Ilopango, she became a refugee in Australia. With no papers or professional qualification, she had to start all over again, but she finally qualified as a nurse. The special bond between us has remained, despite the distance. When I first had cancer two years ago, she felt it and called me on the telephone from Victoria.) As the strike dragged on, my mother was extremely worried, more than by the previous strikes. But it was almost funny because my sister-in-law Judy and other friends of my mother were sending her articles about Gandhi and how he went for 60 days without eating anything. If Gandhi hadn't died, why should I die? They were trying to help my mother, obviously, but also to help me, to say, "It's okay, you can to do it." My aunt from Los Angeles came to visit, and every time she saw me she would cry.

As the strike continued, it achieved its aim of drawing publicity, especially against Reagan's policy. You evaluate that by the newspaper clippings and official visits it generated, the help we received, how far the knowledge got. It's not easy to get something like that into the local press. But our connections in the news agencies told us that the news had gone out on their wires. So we were very happy with the result.

But still the strike went on.

Thursdays and Sundays were visiting days, the only days we would get communication from the outside. On the 33rd day, a Thursday, we still hadn't received a message, so that meant there was no *línea* to stop. That was disappointing but no problem. It simply meant we had to go on. Then someone arrived with the news that the strike had stopped at Mariona. That was good to hear, but we couldn't stop until we got it in writing or from the hand of someone of absolute trust. Finally, 15 minutes before the end of visiting hours, a mother brought in an *embutido* with a written message from Sebastián saying that they'd stopped. They were worried that it wouldn't arrive in time, because if not, we'd have had to go on for three more days.

It was finally over. But you can't start eating normally after a hunger strike. What you need are tiny bits every hour, because your stomach has shrunk, so you start with little bits of broth, with bread soaked in it. Alicia and some of the other ANDES women did all the cooking for us. They used their stove to make broths and vegetables and boiled chicken, all chopped up. The first normal thing I ate were jocotes (sometimes called Spanish plums, which they look like), and the fresh fruit made me really sick. It took maybe a week to recover. I don't think there was any permanent damage, at least not that I'm aware of. I'm pretty strong, and I've recuperated well from my cancer and chemo so far.[2]

What felt nice was the solidarity all around us. There was a lot of unity, even from Esperanza and the others. It happened every time there was something like that, any important event or big dates to celebrate—the divisions were forgotten for a moment.

A few weeks later, only a month before I was set free, came the deaths of Ana María and Marcial. That brought one of the most painful moments I ever experienced in prison, like my whole world had just fallen apart. Before, I'd been in a "mystical" state—I don't really know of an English term for this, but it's a mixture of the sense of discipline and being obedient, absolute faith in a process, and absolute faith in my leaders.

First of all, Comandante Ana María, the second-in-command of the FPL and the person in charge of the FPL's political activity, was cruelly, horribly assassinated in Nicaragua. Her real name was Mélida Anaya Montes and she had been secretary-general of ANDES, leading them in their most successful strikes and campaigns. I believe she became the FPL's second-in-command during its 1976 congress. It wasn't public, obviously; everything about the FPL was clandestine. But we knew Comandante Ana María existed, and it was quite something to know that a woman was a top leader in an organization that was so "manly" and led mainly by men. It wasn't until 1981, after the formation of the FMLN, that the real names of the various organizations' leaders were announced publicly.

Her death happened on April 6th. Like most of the FMLN leaders, she lived in Managua. Some come and go between Nicaragua and El Salvador, especially if they are in their organization's military wing, while others live there more or less permanently. It's just too dangerous to live in El Salvador.

The initial information was that the CIA had killed her. That meant she was a martyr, and her death was something to take pride in. We make all such deaths our own, and we celebrated it (in the Spanish sense of *celebrar*, like with a Mass) with a lot of ceremony.

Ana María's death made us into one COPPES again. The ceremony held in her honor was the first activity we had all participated in for almost a year. We held it outside the section. All the organizations had something to say. There was a minute of silence, and songs and speeches and chanted slogans. People who'd known her shared their memories, especially the ANDES women who'd known her as a young teacher. They talked about her dedication, how she got to be secretary-general of ANDES, and her participation in the big strike of 1968, one of the biggest teachers' strikes ever. How she went into the FPL and joined Marcial. What an incredible woman she was.

It was very formal, very quiet, very serious. It was also painful and very emotional. I'm better at organizing formal public things than speaking at them, so I didn't speak. Overall the ceremony was a positive thing, because the FMLN came together in commemoration of this woman's death. It was a moment when Esperanza and I shared the same space, the same songs, the same *línea*.

Then five days later my whole world fell apart. It was in the evening and I was just falling asleep when the woman in the next bed got up and touched my arm. Now that was a surprise in itself because Miriam hadn't talked to me for quite some time. We were in the same organization, we worked together, and we had slept in adjacent beds in the same cell for months. But I had said something one day that she resented, and so for months she hadn't addressed a word to me.

And there she was saying, "Margarita, Margarita, the radio is saying that Marcial is dead, that he committed suicide!" I got up in shock, trying to understand it.

"Impossible," I told her. "It's the CIA. They're trying to create confusion." All the women in my cell turned toward me to say something. I was in charge and they wanted me to take a stand. So I did. "It's not true!" I told them.

Then suddenly Esperanza appeared in front of me saying, "You have to believe it." It was true, she said, the details were coming to light. Marcial had committed suicide because his closest colleague had killed Ana María. With an icepick. It was too horrible to think about, one of those things you never expect to be faced with in life, but Esperanza told me I had to be realistic. She was very strong.

I said to her, "Esperanza, until I hear something officially from the radio, I'm not going to believe it." And I still didn't believe the worst of it when we listened to the radio that evening. We used to get two stations from Nicaragua. Radio Sandino, the national AM station, said nothing while Radio Nicaragua International had only a short notice that Comandante Marcial, first in the line of command of the FPL, had died. So that much at least was true. But I refused to believe the rest of it.

The next morning was a visiting day, and as always there was a lot of excitement as we ironed our clothes and got dressed up for it. There were never enough chairs for everyone to have a place to sit, so usually a *colectivo* was put in charge of distributing chairs. But this time there was a bit of a struggle over chairs and benches to seat everyone's family members.

When the visit was over, I sat in my cell and turned the radio dial to find Radio Farabundo Martí, the FPL's station. It came on air at 10:00 a.m., and sure enough it announced that Marcial had taken his own life. And that Marcial's closest colleague, who he'd brought up and had been the organization's head of security, had killed Ana María. All of this came out in the radio report.

My world was coming apart, crumbling. I was floating in limbo, questioning many things but not very clearly. And that was dangerous, because to survive in prison I needed to believe in my organization. To the outside world, the FPL had always looked totally together and focused, and even for us working in El Salvador it looked like a block of granite that nothing could shake. But it now became clear that the FPL had deep internal divisions. Ana María's *línea* believed the time had come for negotiations, while Marcial still held that prolonged military struggle would eventually wrest power from the government. Later on I realized that much of what went on in the prison reflected this conflict, even though we had never talked about the divisions within the organization.

Marcial and Ana María's deaths opened my eyes to disobedience. In an instant, I went from being obedient in the religious sense to being a more critical, open-eyed human being. I never believed Marcial was the intellectual author of the murder, but we don't know. All I can talk about is how it affected me.

Their deaths brought me to understand that no human being is perfect. Obedience has to be based on respect, on trust, on knowledge—it has to be a learning process, not simply thinking someone is always right. Organizations are not infallible.

There is a particular kind of obedience you have to accept when you're clandestine and dealing with compartmentalization. You can't know personally the people whose orders you are obeying. The orders come and you don't know who they're from. But because you understand the strategic objectives of the overall organization, it's what you want and why you are willing to follow orders. It's a conscious process, an exercise of judgement: you are aware of why it's done and you accept it because it's necessary to achieve the goals.

But there's another aspect to obedience, which is idealization of human beings. That's what I'd had for my superiors, and which we usually have in relationships. That's what I lost when Ana María and Marcial died, not the belief in compartmentalization or obedience to "This is what we have decided to do and these are the measures we have to take." In all the time I was in the FPL, I never had to question an order.

People ask extreme questions like, "What if they'd told you to kill your brother?" but I was never forced to make a decision like that. It just doesn't fit in my head to carry out an order like that, to be a "good soldier," whatever that is, with that absolute obedience and discipline. A more realistic question I had to deal with was lesbianism in prison, which I discussed earlier in relation to Magdalena and Patricia. Homosexuality is something I accept and respect. I believe everybody has the right to choose the partner that they want as long as there's no pain or coercion. But in the moment, when it became an issue, I decided to put away that belief and that respect. I put it away because I wanted to survive and the majority did not think the way I thought. I don't mean physically, but to be part of the group.

Figure 22. Mélida Anaya Montes, a.k.a.
Ana María (Wikimedia Commons)

Figure 23. Salvador Cayetano Carpio, a.k.a. Marcial
(AlfredoMercurio-503, Wikimedia Commons)

A Strike, a Murder, and a Suicide ⁓ 223

I've been asked if I ever received an order I thought was badly thought out and was going to lead to a disaster. Sometimes I got orders that made me think, *I wouldn't do it this way*, but we would discuss them, or at least the method. Because the method was ours, decided by the group. One of the orders that confused me was for the Ofensiva Final. I had an intuition that things were not going to work, but I enthusiastically fulfilled all my tasks of providing four or five houses with their basic needs. I didn't think it was crazy. I don't think I ever got an order like that.

The deaths of Ana María and Marcial left me badly shaken. I went through many changes in prison, but this was the biggest, an immense process of change that lasted from a month before I got out of prison until a month after I got out.

I will never give that kind of obedience again.

23

~

Freedom

Two or three weeks later we started to hear about a possible amnesty. It all came from the US Congress's demand that President Reagan get a report every six months on human rights in El Salvador. Coming on top of our hunger strike, this created pressure on the government to consider a general amnesty. Eventually El Salvador's president Duarte created an amnesty commission.

The first I heard of it was during a visit by Javier. I started insisting that the family get a lawyer to reactivate my case, but Javier said, "No, there's no need. The amnesty is going to come." So with all this talk and rumors, there was great excitement, partly due to our fraying nerves. There was also controversy as the organizations each tried to find a *línea*. Initially the ERP was the most extreme. They announced that they would not accept the amnesty since it was just a show being put on by Duarte, and anyone who left the prison would be committing treason. But at some point their *línea* changed.

On May 18, five weeks after the death of Marcial, the first woman received her *carta de libertad*, her letter of freedom, and was released under the amnesty. That was Vida, if I remember right; someone arrived with her *carta* and she was free. Just like that.

The two COPPES *directivas* held a meeting about what to do. It was possible that the authorities might try to use the amnesties to make personal deals with us, and we needed to avoid this. The eight of us decided to hold a theater event to illustrate this risk to the *compañeras*, with someone playing a person being offered her liberty. Lupe volunteered, and she was the right person, partly because she had experience in popular theater and enjoyed acting, but also because of her general condition. She'd had a lot of ups and downs throughout the two years we were in prison, and had been criticized. At times she'd be very strong and work hard with COPPES, then she'd get depressed, and stop working and talking to people. So she was the right person. Esperanza couldn't play the part because no one would have believed her. She was too strong and too consistent. I didn't say much at the meeting. I didn't have much interest in theater, but I agreed with the idea. It didn't take much organization and only the eight of us knew what was going on.

As we'd planned, Lupe left the section during daily chores. After about 40 minutes one of us asked loudly, "Where's Lupita?" and someone else said, "She's gone to the office. She has a visitor."

"A visitor? On Tuesday?"

A visitor out of normal visiting hours always caused rumors and speculation. Everyone was out in the yard by this time, and suspense was building up.

Finally she came back and went straight to her best friend. She said a lawyer had come with her mother, offering her a letter to sign stating that she would give up her ideology and so on. "And I'm going to sign it!" she said aggressively—she really was very good at acting. Then she went up to her bed, with a group following her. One woman said, "Don't do it, Lupita. It's a bad example." But many girls with less consciousness were getting very excited, because if Lupe could do it, maybe they could too. There was disorder and optimism, and some even started packing their bags.

As the tension built up the *directivas* called a COPPES meeting to ask Lupe for an explanation. It was one of the big meetings we used to hold with everyone, where we would sit in a circle on the floor. Lupe sat down and answered that yes, she would give an explanation, and started talking again about this lawyer and the offer she'd been given.

The situation almost got out of hand. Some of the girls started insulting her, saying that they knew that she had always been weak, and she had never been politically solid, and that she was a traitor. Some begged her not to do it, arguing it was a bad example. We in the *directiva* participated a little, but essentially it was the others who kept things going. Finally Lupe brought the act to an end and said it was theater.

Some people were angry. How could she do that to them? The *directiva* explained the exercise, and we discussed it with the group for an hour or so.

As it turned out, there was no pattern in the releases in the first few days. All of a sudden a *carta de libertad* would appear and the person would leave. Four women had left by Sunday the 22nd, when Mother and Javier came to visit me. I think Lupe left that morning, a surprise because she was so obviously political, known to oppose the government. But the next person had no political involvement at all.

Javier had bad news. He had talked to the amnesty commission because a cousin's husband was on it and was told that neither I nor Esperanza would be included in this amnesty. We were the only two whose cases were judged too serious to be set free. The shock was driven home later that day when another visitor confirmed it. To make it worse, this person told me that Sebastián was to be included in the amnesty. That was a second shock, because it had been a source of strength for me to know that Sebastián was also inside. We'd been in constant contact by letter, and it had helped keep me together. Now all of sudden he was not going to be sharing the ordeal. You might think this a strange reaction, but it had made a sort of sense: I was "married," I was with a man. But now, where would he be? How were we going to work together, as we had worked together during these past two years?

So that night I decided to break down a little bit and cry. In fact I cried quite a lot. But then I took hold of myself and said, "There's nothing I can do about this." So I forced myself to think of five more years in jail and began to revise my list of projects. I still had a lot, mostly manual. I was in the middle of knitting a blanket, and I had just bought wool to knit sweaters for my nephew, my niece, and my nana. There were the bees. And something I had started many times but never kept up: a diary. I told myself, "Okay, you're going to write at least once a week. It will be very valuable when you leave. You've managed to write letters, so now you can stick with a diary."

I wrote these projects down on paper, telling myself I was going to be in prison indefinitely and I simply had to keep on with my activities. When I finally went to sleep I was sad but okay, and slept fine, resigned to my destiny.

The next morning, it was my turn to cook with a girl called Cristi. We were good friends and because I was a good cook the *economato* had given us something complicated to cook, and since it was the day after the visit we had good food to work with. As usual we were up at 4:30, and we worked without a break. The main meal was a stew with rice, which meant frying every little bit of meat that we'd received. By noon we had the stew ready, and Cristi and I were carrying a heavy pot of stew between us when a girl came running up and said, "Margarita, Margarita—Rafael is at the gate!"

My heart went *THUMP!* and we put down the pot. Rafael was Sebastián's code name. I said, "No, it can't be," but she insisted it was the man that she had seen in my photographs. "Come on," she said. "Come on and look!"

It's funny to say this now, but my immediate reaction was anger. The fact that she had seen someone outside meant that she had disregarded something I had called her attention to a number of times. The prison was built of prefabricated concrete slabs which sometimes didn't fit together perfectly. Once we politicals had won the right to walk around the grounds, we had discovered a space between a post and a slab where it was possible to see all the way to the

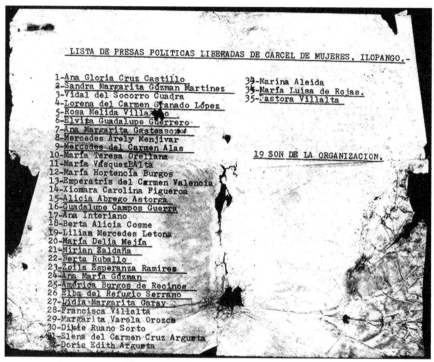

LISTA DE PRESAS POLITICAS LIBERADAS DE CÁRCEL DE MUJERES. ILOPANGO.-

1-Ana Gloria Cruz Castillo
2-Sandra Margarita Güzman Martinez
3-Vidal del Socorro Cuadra
4-Lorena del Carmen Granado López
5-Rosa Melida Villa..o
6-Elvita Guadalupe Guerrero
7-Ana Margarita Gasteaso...
8-Mercedes Arely Menjivar
9-Mercedes del Carmen Alas
10-María Teresa Orellana
11-María VásquezBAlta
12-María Hortencia Burgos
13-Emperatris del Carmen Valencia
14-Xiomara Carolina Figueroa
15-Alicia Abrego Astorga
16-Guadalupe Campos Guerra
17-Ana Interiano
18-Berta Alicia Cosme
19-Lilian Mercedes Letona
20-María Delia Mejía
21-Mirian Saldaña
22-Berta Ruballo
23-Zoila Esperanza Ramires
24-Ana María Güzman
25-América Burgos de Recinos
26 Elba del Refugio Serrano
27-Lidia Margarita Garay
28-Francisca Villalta
29-Margarita Varela Orozco
30-Dixie Ruano Sorto
31-Elena del Carmen Cruz Argueta
-Doris Edith Argueta

33-Marina Aleida
34-María Luisa de Rojas.
35-Pastora Villalta

19 SON DE LA ORGANIZACION.

Figure 24. List of liberated prisoners from Ilopango
(Courtesy of Museo de la Palabra y la Imagen)

street. The field of vision was only about six inches, but it was outside. The women used to sit in single file, sometimes as many as four or five in a row, knitting and sewing and talking while they peered through this little space. I hated that spot. I did not want to see the street or be reminded of the outside, and I thought it was masochistic for these women to sit there. That was very puritanical of me. All they wanted was to see a bit of street life: people walking by or cars passing on the highway. A tiny bit of contact.

This particular girl spent a lot of time there. I had mentioned it to her several times and here she was telling me that she'd been there again. At first I thought she was inventing stories, but all of a sudden she convinced me. So I left the pot on a table and followed her, wiping my hands on my apron.

It was true. I could see Sebastián standing at the gate with his sister. The excitement was like madness, with everybody saying, "Ah, Ana Margarita will be set free!" But I thought he'd only come to say goodbye.

Then a guard started walking through the prison from the gate with a letter in his hands. The excitement was too much for me: I ran up as close as I could get and said, "What do you have there? What do you have there?"

Typical guard: "Well, it's lunchtime and there is no one in the office so I cannot tell you. You'll have to wait until two in the afternoon."

I got very angry and said, "You can't do this to me," and everyone else had gathered and was screaming, "You have to give it to her!" And he finally said, "Yes, it's your *carta de libertad*. Go and get ready." But he wouldn't let me see it, because it was addressed to the prison authorities.

So I went to the cell and started to gather my stuff. Women started packing my things, and the excitement was such that I couldn't think. Almost since the day I arrived at Ilopango I'd kept a list of all the things I would take with me. There was a little pot Beatriz had given me, a blouse that I had embroidered, some gifts from people, books I wanted to take—all things with sentimental value. A little table with a secret drawer. But it was such a crazy, emotional moment that I forgot about the list and took the stupidest things instead. A set of sheets I didn't need, clothes . . . It took five minutes, and in my memory it's a blur.

So I left, and once you are out of Ilopango you can never go back. That's one of the prison rules.

By the time I got to the office, Javier had arrived, and he was waiting with Sebastián and his sister. She had gone to the commission to pick up Sebastián's *carta de libertad* and had asked if they had mine also. It was there, so she took it. She'd called Javier and here he was.

Javier drove us to my mother's apartment. Sebastián had never met my mother before. She'd known that there was someone in my life but had never met him. My nana had gone to visit him in Santa Tecla several times, but never my mother. It was too much to ask her. She was cool with him but always very courteous and didn't show what she felt.

It all felt unreal, and I had a funny reaction: I wanted to shut myself up in a room with no windows. I went to a bedroom, a very bare room, and Sebastián and I sat there and talked for several hours. I felt safe and didn't want to leave.

But we couldn't stay at my mother's apartment. The MNR had been in touch with Javier and they had agreed that the safest place was the Spanish embassy. Nothing in the amnesty said we had to leave El Salvador, but our lives were in danger if we stayed. I was too well known. So Javier drove us to the embassy, an enormous house in San Benito, the suburb where Javier also lived. So we went from prison to a mansion in a single day.

We weren't the only amnestied "guests" there. Two other MNR members, Carlos Molina and Mauricio Domenech, had been released three days before me and had gone there immediately.[1] They left soon after we arrived, having fixed their passports and other papers already. Sebastián and I had no papers at all, so we had to stay in the embassy for a few days until we could get our passports.

As it turned out, the ambassador was on vacation, so we had this whole mansion almost to ourselves. Once again, I had the same reaction, and I chose a room with the least number of windows possible for Sebastián and me. The embassy had enormous grounds we could have walked in without danger, but we didn't.

Sebastián was sweet and tender with me, but tensions between us surfaced over small things. I wanted to lie in the sun a bit and swim in the embassy's pool. Sebastián thought that wasn't appropriate: I was not on vacation. That was his years of seminary training coming out. He was very disciplined and self-contained. It wasn't that he wouldn't let me, but he didn't approve and at that moment I needed his approval. With a little support from him I would have enjoyed swimming and being in the sun. It wasn't until two or three months later in Cuba that I got to jump into the water—it felt marvelous.

But it covered a bigger problem. Sebastián had never been a member of the MNR and the MNR was looking after us because of me, not him. All communication went to me, so it was my "show" and he didn't like it at all. There were no confrontations, but I could see his resistance developing as days passed.

We were there five days. We never went out, but a lot of people visited us. Journalists interviewed Carlos and Mauricio and me, because we were FDR people. Sebastián was always on the sidelines.

Although we considered going to other countries—Canada, Spain, even Sweden—Sebastián and I settled on Mexico. Both the FDR and the FMLN had infrastructure in Mexico City as well as Managua, and the MNR's main office was there, so it made the most sense. But first there were some details to take care of. The terms of our amnesty papers required us to go before the commission and promise not to get involved in anything else. I refused, and Javier and I had a big fight over this, and in the end he signed for me. I still have the document. I think Sebastián's sister signed for him.

On the fourth day, Javier took me out for my passport picture. Everything scared me—cars, construction noise, everything. I still have the passport picture, and I look scared to death. Javier didn't show any nervousness as he drove us. He's very cool, but also a speedy person who does things fast, even relaxing.

The following day the Mexican ambassador arrived. The rules were that Sebastián and I had to present ourselves at the Mexican embassy in order to receive our passports, so the ambassador took us himself. Then we left directly for the airport, along with Mother and Javier.

All of my people from the MNR were waiting at the airport in Mexico

City: Guido, Héctor, Vera, and David.[2] Vera and Guido got permission to go to the ramp of the plane so they could help us through customs and immigration. They organized a seafood dinner at a restaurant and it was a beautiful "homecoming" for me. It was harder on Sebastián, though everyone tried to make it comfortable for him. I think he had a good time, but although he knew some of them from university days, basically they were strangers to him and he was a curiosity to them. But it was a celebration. We had beer and wine for the first time in two years, and such happiness.

Things started to fall apart on our third day in Mexico. I said, "Sebastián, I want to talk with you about Marcial and Ana María. I need to talk about this."

By now he had got in touch with people from the Orga and received a report about what had happened in Managua—a "flat" report giving the Orga's official line. He was willing to accept it 100 percent, or at least unwilling to show me any doubts. Again, that was his discipline and obedience coming out. But my question was, "Obedience to whom? Now that we don't have Ana María and Marcial, who will we give this absolute obedience to?"

He got very upset and said I was a traitor for my questioning. And that exploded into another issue: he said I was dominating him and trying to decide his life for him. The MNR was looking after him, and my link with the MNR gave me a position of power. That was true, but only because I had demanded that whatever the MNR did for me, they would do for him too. He wasn't really questioning that, though; he was questioning my attitude. I was sure of myself. I had traveled all my life, but it was only his second time on an airplane. Getting through airports, dealing with luggage, finding taxis—I knew about these things, so I managed them for both of us. And Mexico City is overwhelming, especially after you've been confined for two years, so Sebastián felt lost. It was easier if I took over when we bought clothes or took the subway. But he didn't like it. He felt I was usurping his position, his role as a man. And it didn't help if I tried to explain that it wasn't true, that it was just easier.

About three weeks later he was suddenly ordered to Managua. We parted as comrades. I asked what would happen to our relationship, and he replied, "We have to do what we are ordered to do." Then he was gone.

I missed him, but it gave me more space to get on with my own work. There was a lot of it, mostly press conferences and interviews about my experience—after all, I was still a vice president of the Socialist International. It was hard, despite what I said earlier. After the isolation and limited horizons of prison, I was paranoid, scared of people in the subway, of traffic and crossing a road with 10 lanes on it, and the potential violence. I'm a tough person but at that moment I wasn't psychologically strong enough to handle it. The MNR could never understand that, but sometimes organizations only work to the extent that they sacrifice individuals.

In June the MNR sent me to London. It was a fine trip. London was beautiful in the summer, and the work was fun. There is an FMLN presence in almost every city in Europe so I was meeting with all the Salvadoran leaders. There was also solidarity work to be done with trade unionists, teachers, human rights groups, and so on. Nonetheless, Sebastián and I spoke by phone every week.

Meanwhile another problem was brewing. The ERP wanted me expelled from the MNR, accusing me of double membership in both the MNR and the FPL. They made a complaint about me at the FDR-FMLN level, or possibly to Ungo directly. The charges clearly stemmed from Esperanza, and it was plain that my activities had been reported on constantly in prison. (Shortly after, in August, we heard that Esperanza had been killed. I never found out exactly how, because the ERP doesn't talk about it. They only published a little obituary note saying that Comandante Clelia and another *comandante*, a man, had been killed in action or an ambush. But I've never been able to get details. Her sister, Mercedes del Carmen Letona Pérez, was the longtime director of Radio Venceremos and a very high *comandante* in the ERP. I met her once after I got out of prison. It was like seeing Esperanza again: strong little arms, wiry, tense.)

Ungo called me in and asked if the charge was true. I said no. I had been adopted as a member of ANDES after I was arrested, so of course I had participated with them. I admitted to taking positions in prison that agreed with the FPL *línea*—of course I had, what else could I do? I was alone, the only MNR member in Ilopango. I hadn't received communication from the MNR every week. I accepted responsibility for what I had done. But no, I wasn't a member of the FPL.

Ungo accepted what I said and that was it: he took a stand with the ERP and defended me. I was not alone. The ERP charges concerned several people, and he defended all of us.

But Ungo wasn't stupid, and I don't think he ever trusted me again. He was extremely honest, a straight man.

After that, the MNR decided I shouldn't see Sebastián for a time since it would be taken as confirmation of my double membership. They didn't actually prohibit me, but every time I had to travel and there was a possible route through Managua, another route would be arranged. Finally in July I was invited to the 25th anniversary of the Cuban Revolution in Havana. The itinerary took me through Managua, and I insisted on stopping off to see Sebastián on the way back. The MNR disagreed but I ignored them and arranged my own *contacto* with Sebastián. We agreed to meet in a public park in Managua—just like our old clandestine meetings.

The trip to Cuba was marvelous. I went with a group of FDR-FMLN leaders like Roberto Cañas, Fermán Cienfuegos, and Mario López, all of us arriving on different flights. The Cubans treated us as one of the most important delegations. Fidel acknowledged me as an ex–political prisoner and embraced me. I met other people there like Maurice Bishop.[3] I also went into a Cuban hospital for a thorough examination. I don't ignore the problems that Cuba has, but I respect Fidel and what the country has achieved despite its isolation.

I finally arrived in Managua in the middle of September. We'd arranged to meet in the Parque de las Madres near the Metrocentro shopping center. I walked into the park, and Sebastián came about 30 seconds later. I said, "Well, what's going to happen to us?"

"Have you thought about it?" he replied.

"I'd like to hear what you have to say first," I said.

Again, he answered with a question. "Are you sure you want me to talk first?"

By that time I knew it was impossible for us to go on, although I wasn't clear in my thinking. But it was already clear and final in his mind. He told me the relationship was over. He had decided that it was impossible and had already informed his organization. I should do the same with mine, he said.

And that was it. Nothing more to discuss.

I was in a state of shock, which continued as he told me not to watch him leave the park. Then he walked away. I did too, but as I was walking to the house where I was staying in Managua I saw him get into a car with a woman. Two weeks later I learned that he was already with another *compañera*, one that he considered more militant and more disciplined than me.

I know where Sebastián is now. He's married and happy, and I'm happy for him. But at the time, seeing him with another woman so soon was painful, and I shed a few tears over it as I walked.

Still, my personality has its survival mechanisms. For me, when something is over, it's over and I say, "Okay, life goes on." When I got back to the house I decided to leave immediately and flew back to Mexico the next day.

Epilogue

~

A na Margarita moved to San José, Costa Rica, in 1985, where she supported herself as a translator and Spanish teacher. In 1989, she moved to
the village of Puerto Viejo on the country's Caribbean coast. There she opened
the Café Coral, a bakery and café where she served a mixed menu of North
American health foods, cakes and breads, and pizzas. Her small business was
popular and prospered, and she became deeply involved with the village's economic development. Friends who had known her for years thought she was
the happiest she had ever been, particularly when she began living with Adolfo
"Smokey" Stewart, a local man who also became her partner in the bakery. The

Figure 25. Ana Margarita in Café Coral (Courtesy of Andrew Wilson)

only shadow in her new life was cast by breast cancer, which led to a mastectomy in 1990.

In 1991, as the war in El Salvador was winding down, Ana Margarita was invited to be a delegate at the first open congress that the MNR had held in many years in San Salvador. As the political space continued to open in the country with the peace accords in January 1992, the party approached her to run as an MNR candidate in the 1993 elections. Though skeptical about the political situation in El Salvador, and happy with her life in Puerto Viejo, Ana Margarita was considering the party's offer when her breast cancer recurred.

She spent her final days at her mother's home in San Salvador, where her brother José Francisco, a Catholic priest, gave her last rites and communion. Ana Margarita died on January 30, 1993. She was 42 years old.

JUDY BLANKENSHIP AND ANDREW WILSON

Acknowledgments

～

We are grateful to the following people, some of whom have been involved with this project since the late 1980s.

In El Salvador, huge thanks to Ana Margarita's sister Eva María (Tito) and her brothers Javier, José Francisco, and Ricardo Antonio (Tono). Although we only got to know them in the past few years, they helped immeasurably with finalizing the book. We also thank them for their warm welcome when we finally met them and their families in San Salvador at the 2019 launch of the Spanish edition of this book.

Also in El Salvador: Carlos Henríquez Consalvi, director of the Museo de la Palabra y la Imagen (MUPI), though better known as Santiago, the legendary Farabundo Martí National Liberation Front (FMLN) radio broadcaster. It was Carlos who propelled the Spanish translation and publication from the moment he heard about Ana Margarita's story. Thanks also to Tania Primavera Preza of MUPI for the many hours she lived Ana Margarita's life and mourned her early death while transcribing and editing the memoirs in Spanish, *Díganle a mi madre que estoy en el paraíso*. Iván Montecinos very graciously provided photographs he took of Ana Margarita.

In Costa Rica, Diana Avila, poet and dear friend of Ana Margarita, made several useful suggestions for the book. We also remember with great affection the late Adolfo "Smokey" Stewart, Ana Margarita's last partner and source of loving care in her final years.

In the United States, Erik Ching, professor of history at Furman University, brought enthusiasm and profound expertise to the task of providing this book's introduction. We were delighted to make contact with Eva Gasteazoro, Ana Margarita's first cousin based in New York and editor and translator extraordinaire. Eva not only shared her memories of Ana Margarita but dropped everything to help "capture Ana's voice" in the rushed final stages of the Spanish version. Ana Margarita's California cousin, Elizabeth Fujimori, loved Ana Margarita as a sister from the year Ana Margarita spent in Los Angeles as a child with her family. Elizabeth supported the idea of this book from day 1, helping us fill in some biographical blanks and providing photographs of Ana

Margarita at different ages. In Texas, *cantautor* and professor Juan Carlos Ureña was helpful with his memories of the Havana Youth Festival, which he attended at the same time as Ana Margarita, and in reading parts of the manuscript.

Both of us thank Wendi Schnaufer, senior acquisitions editor at the University of Alabama Press, for her dogged support in bringing this edition to English-speaking audiences. She is now an honorary member on our list of Ana Margarita's friends. Kelly Finefrock, project editor at the press, did a great job copyediting a manuscript that over the years generated a fair number of inconsistencies.

Judy adds: I thank friends and acquaintances everywhere who have supported the Ana Margarita Gasteazoro Fund for Women's Education, created upon Ana Margarita's death in 1994. Now called the Cañari Women's Education Foundation, the nonprofit provides university educations for indigenous women in Ecuador. All royalties from this book will go to a similar scholarship program in El Salvador.

Many thanks also to my walk/talk/book friends Nancy Henry, Maya Muir, and Joanne Mulcahy, who read and gave suggestions on the manuscript or talked about the project on long walks. A special thanks to Dagoberto Flores, whom I met in a Central America solidarity group in Portland in the 1990s and who remembered my mention of Ana Margarita and years later initiated the Spanish translation.

Thanks to my partner, Michael Jenkins, whom I met in Costa Rica right before I knew Ana Margarita and began to record her life story. I can hear him still on the original tapes, banging pots and singing in the kitchen as he prepared our dinner. Today, he is still *a mi lado* and preparing dinner every night.

Thanks to my other partner, coeditor Andrew Wilson, who paid me the best compliment after our very long and harmonious collaboration on Ana Margarita's book: "What shall we work on next?"

Andrew adds: I am deeply grateful to my wife, Claire Bolderson, who is not only the first and best reader of anything I write, but for 21 years has been remarkably tolerant of the "other women" in my life, Ana Margarita and Judy.

JUDY BLANKENSHIP AND ANDREW WILSON

Notes

〜

PREFACE

1. Don W. Lewis, "U.S. Military Assistance to El Salvador Negates Benefits of Economic Aid," *Los Angeles Times*, May 16, 1988.

INTRODUCTION

1. Erik Ching, *Stories of Civil War in El Salvador: A Battle over Memory* (Chapel Hill: University of North Carolina Press, 2016).

2. Leigh Binford, *The El Mozote Massacre: Human Rights and Global Implications*, 2nd ed. (Tucson: University of Arizona Press, 2016); and Mark Danner, *The Massacre at El Mozote* (New York: Vintage, 1994).

3. For example, the investigators failed to uncover the internal purges within the Forces of Popular Liberation (FPL) between 1986 and 1990 that may have cost upward of 1,000 lives. Geovani Galeas and Edwin Ernesto Ayala, *Grandeza y miseria en una guerrilla*, 2nd ed. (San Salvador: Centroamérica 21, 2008).

4. United Nations Commission on the Truth for El Salvador, *From Madness to Hope: The Twelve-Year War in El Salvador* (New York: United Nations Security Council, 1993).

5. Joaquín Chávez, *Poets and Prophets of the Resistance: Intellectuals and the Origins of El Salvador's Civil War* (New York: Oxford University Press, 2017); Charles Brockett, *Political Movements and Violence in Central America* (New York: Cambridge University Press, 2005); Jeff Gould, *Solidarity under Siege: The Salvadoran Labor Movement, 1970–1990* (New York: Cambridge University Press, 2019); and Leigh Binford, "Peasants, Catechists, Revolutionaries: Organic Intellectuals in the Salvadoran Revolution, 1980–1992," in *Landscapes of Struggle: Politics, Society, and Community in El Salvador*, ed. Aldo Lauria and Leigh Binford (Pittsburgh: University of Pittsburgh Press, 2004), 105–25.

6. On the US role in the civil war, from competing perspectives, see Russell Crandall, *The Salvador Option: The United States in El Salvador, 1977–1992* (New York: Cambridge University Press, 2016); and Brian D'Haeseleer, *The Salvadoran Crucible: The Failure of U.S. Counterinsurgency in El Salvador, 1979–1992* (Lawrence: University Press of Kansas, 2017).

7. Ana Guadalupe Martínez, *Las cárceles clandestinas de El Salvador: Libertad por el secuestro de un oligarca* (Sinaloa, Mexico: Universidad Autónoma de Sinaloa, 1980); Nidia Díaz, *I Was Never Alone: A Prison Diary from El Salvador* (New York: Ocean Press, 1992); and Lorena Peña, *Retazos de mi vida: Testimonio de una revolucionaria salvadoreña* (Querétaro, Mexico: Ocean Sur, 2009).

8. Diana Sierra Becerra, "Insurgent Butterflies: Gender and Revolution in El Salvador, 1965–2015" (PhD diss., University of Michigan, 2017); Jocelyn Viterna, *Women in War: The Micro-Processes of Mobilization in El Salvador* (New York: Oxford University Press, 2013); Ilja Luciak, *After the Revolution: Gender and Democracy in El Salvador, Nicaragua,*

and Guatemala (Baltimore: Johns Hopkins University Press, 2001); Karen Kampwirth, *Women and Guerrilla Movements: Nicaragua, El Salvador, Chiapas, Cuba* (University Park, PA: Penn State University Press, 2003); Karen Kampwirth, *Feminism and the Legacy of Revolution: Nicaragua, El Salvador, Chiapas* (Athens: Ohio University Press, 2004); Julie Shayne, *The Revolution Question: Feminisms in El Salvador, Chile, and Cuba* (New Brunswick, NJ: Rutgers University Press, 2004).

9. Anonymous member of a Salvadoran elite family, email correspondence with the author, March 11, 2020.

10. Betsy Morgan, and Caroline Cargo, eds., *Mothers in Arms: Conversations with Women Ex-Combatants from the Late War in El Salvador/Madres en armas: Conversaciones con mujeres ex-combatientes de El Salvador* (Philadelphia: Jamie Moffett, 2010), 92–93.

11. Andrew Wilson states that Ana Margarita Gasteazoro told him that Fidel Castro said this. Andrew Wilson and Judy Blankenship, phone interview by the author, March 11, 2020. Subsequent quotations from Wilson and Blankenship, as well as details about the origins of this book, are from this interview.

12. Héctor Lindo-Fuentes, Erik Ching, and Rafael Lara, *Remembering a Massacre in El Salvador: The Insurrection of 1932, Roque Dalton, and the Politics of Historical Memory* (Albuquerque: University of New Mexico Press, 2007).

CHAPTER 1

1. Ana Margarita's mother, Ana Marina Escolán de Gasteazoro, died in August 2016. See the obituary published in *La Prensa Gráfica*, www.laprensagrafica.com.

2. Alfredo Cristiani was president of El Salvador between 1989 and 1994.

3. Verified in 2018 by email with Titina's husband, Juan Mendoza, and with Marjorie Melville.

4. See Penny Lernoux, *Hearts on Fire: The Story of the Maryknoll Sisters*, centennial edition (New York: Orbis Books, 2012).

5. Thomas Melville and Marjorie Melville, *Whose Heaven, Whose Earth?* (New York: Knopf, 1971).

CHAPTER 2

1. Charles W. Koch, "Jamaican Blacks and Their Descendants in Costa Rica," *Social and Economic Studies* 26, no. 3 (1977): 339–61.

CHAPTER 3

1. For more on Eric Anthony Abrahams, see Paul Henry, "Anthony Abrahams, Dead at 71," *Jamaica Observer*, August 8, 2011, available from the National Library of Jamaica, https://nlj.gov.jm.

CHAPTER 4

1. The Second General Conference of Latin-American and Caribbean Bishops, held in Medellín, Colombia, in 1968, focused on the poor and oppressed in the region.

2. Instituto Salvadoreño de Comercio Exterior, now part of the Ministry of Foreign Affairs.

3. T. L. Pearcy, *The History of Central America* (Westport, CT: Greenwood Press, 2006), 106.

4. Before he was assassinated by Nicaragua's national guard, Augusto Sandino was a

revolutionary who between 1927 and 1933 led a rebellion against the US military occupation of Nicaragua. The Sandinista movement took its name from him.

5. Soviets were workers' councils set up by Russian revolutionaries in the late 1800s. After the revolution, these became the basic political organization of the Soviet Union.

6. The Unión Nacional Opositora (National Opposition Union, UNO) was a coalition of the Christian Democratic Party, National Revolutionary Movement (MNR), and Nationalist Democratic Union (UDN).

CHAPTER 5

1. Héctor Oquelí was assassinated, along with lawyer Gilda Flores, while in Guatemala on National Revolutionary Movement (MNR) business in December 1990. See "Report N° 28/91, Case 10.518, Guatemala (Héctor Oquelí and Gilda Flores)," Inter-American Commission on Human Rights, 1991, https://www.cidh.oas.org.

2. Omar Torrijos was a populist military commander who ruled Panama from 1968 to 1981.

3. Anastasio Somoza (1925–1980) was president of Nicaragua from 1967 to 1979, when he was deposed by the Sandinista Front. He was the last of a dynasty of dictators that had held power in Nicaragua since 1936.

4. The Chilean president Salvador Allende was overthrown by a military junta on September 11, 1973. Before democracy was restored in 1990, some 200,000 Chileans went into exile. See Thomas C. Wright and Rody Oñate Zúñiga, "Chilean Political Exile," *Latin American Perspectives* 34, no. 4 (2007): 31–49.

5. COMADRES, "History: Timeline," Comité de Madres de Reos y Desaparecidos Políticos de El Salvador, accessed April 10, 2020, www.comadres.org/enghistory2.htm.

6. Servicio Informativo Ecuménico y Popular, "ILPES conmemora 36 aniversario de muerte de Raúl Castellanos Figueroa," SIEP, October 20, 2006, https://ecumenico.org.

7. Marianella García Villas, "El Salvador: Campesinas y campesinos conmemoran la Masacre de La Bermuda del 14 de marzo de 1983," *Resumen Latinoamericano*, March 15, 2017, http://www.resumenlatinoamericano.org.

8. This is one of Fidel Castro's most famous speeches, pronounced as his legal defense after attacking the Moncada Barracks in Santiago de Cuba.

9. Yasser Arafat was president of the Palestine Liberation Organization, which at that time was based in Beirut.

10. Argentinean-born Ernesto "Che" Guevara was a key military leader of the Cuban Revolution. After serving in the revolutionary government, he left Cuba to assist liberation movements overseas. He was captured and executed in October 1967 in Bolivia.

CHAPTER 6

1. Ana Margarita later identified the leader as Costa Rica's president Luis Alberto Monge but did not wish to name him while he was still alive and she was a resident of Costa Rica.

2. Rubén Zamora has been a prominent politician, civil servant, and academic in El Salvador for several decades.

3. A long-time member of the National Revolutionary Movement (MNR), Italo López (1932–1986) was a distinguished poet, academic, and publisher. Ana Margarita's reference is to *El Salvador: Entre el terror v la esperanza*, a book published by the Editorial de la

Universidad Centroamericana while López was its director. Rodolfo Campos, ed., *El Salvador entre el terror y la esperanza: Los sucesos de 1979 y su impacto en el drama salvadoreño de los años siguientes* (San Salvador: UCA Edit, 1982).

4. The *New York Times* reported in 1984, "Where once some 70 manufacturing subsidiaries or sales divisions of American corporations operated, now only about three dozen remain." Fred R. Bleakley, "Americans in Business in El Salvador: Juggling Risk, Fear and Returns," *New York Times*, March 25, 1984, www.nytimes.com.

CHAPTER 7

1. In the end, there were three successive juntas. The first lasted from October 15, 1979, to January 5, 1980, with two military men, Colonels Adolfo Majano and Jaime Abdul Gutiérrez, and three civilians, Guillermo Ungo, Mario Antonio Andino, and Román Mayorga. The second junta ran from January 9 through December 13, 1980, with the two colonels and José Antonio Morales Ehrlich, Héctor Dada, and José Ramón Ávalos. The final junta ran from December 13, 1980, until May 2, 1982, with José Napoleón Duarte as the junta's president and with three other members: Gutiérrez, Morales, and Ávalos.

2. José Napoleón Duarte (1925–1990) was mayor of San Salvador from 1964 to 1970, president of the governing junta from 1980 to 1982, and president of El Salvador from 1984 to 1989. A founder of the Christian Democratic Party, he won the 1972 presidential election but was denied office due to electoral fraud.

3. Major Roberto D'Aubuisson (1943–1992) co-founded the Nationalist Republican Alliance (ARENA) in 1981. Director of the country's intelligence service as well as a politician, he commanded death squads during the 1970s and was implicated in many crimes, including the assassination of Archbishop Romero in 1980. See Marjorie Miller, "Roberto D'Aubuisson, 48; Reputed Head of Salvadoran Death Squads," *Los Angeles Times*, February 21, 1992, www.latimes.com.

4. Guatemala's civil war lasted from the early 1960s until the mid-1990s. During this deeply unequal war, the country's military carried out a policy of genocide against the indigenous Maya populations in rural areas, along with systematic human rights violations and terror against civilians. See Comisión para el Esclarecimiento Histórico, *Guatemala, memoria del silencio* (Oficina de Servicios para Proyectos de las Naciones Unidas [UNOPS], June 1999), http://www.centrodememoriahistorica.gov.co/descargas/guatemala-memoria-silencio/guatemala-memoria-del-silencio.pdf.

5. The Coordinadora Revolucionaria de Masas was an effort to coordinate the different mass organizations. It lasted for most of 1980, before the creation of the Farabundo Martí National Liberation Front (FMLN).

6. Felipe González of the Spanish Socialist Workers' Party (PSOE) was prime minister of Spain from 1982 to 1996.

7. Like the Armed Forces of Anti-Communist Liberation–Wars of Elimination (FALANGE) mentioned earlier, the Mano Blanco (White Hand) was one of El Salvador's death squads, along with Unión de Guerreros Blancos (White Warriors Union) and the Ejército Secreto Anticomunista (Secret Anti-Communist Army).

CHAPTER 8

1. The colón was El Salvador's currency at the time. It was replaced by the US dollar in 2001.

CHAPTER 10

1. Marcial and Ana María were leaders of the Farabundo Martí Forces of Popular Liberation (FPL), Joaquín Villalobos was leader of the People's Revolutionary Army (ERP), and Fermán Cienfuegos was leader of the National Resistance (RN).

CHAPTER 11

1. Rafael Guidos Véjar, the distinguished Salvadoran sociologist and academic.

CHAPTER 14

1. Manlio Argueta's novel was published in 1980 and is one of the great pieces of literature to emerge from Latin America's struggles in the 20th century. It recounts 24 hours in the life of a rural family in Chalatenango, with brutally frank observations of the conditions that Salvadoran peasants suffered in the 1970s. Manlio Argueta, *One Day of Life*, trans. Bill Brow (New York: Vintage Books, 1991).

2. Jacobo Timerman was an Argentinean journalist and editor. In April 1977 he was kidnapped and tortured by the country's military and spent 30 months in prison despite there being no charges filed against him. His book about his prison experience became an international bestseller. Jacobo Timerman, *Prisoner without a Name, Cell without a Number*, trans. Toby Talbot (New York: Knopf, 1981).

CHAPTER 15

1. The official term is *instructora*, in line with the prison's putative rehabilitative mission, but the women who guarded female prisoners in Ilopango were more commonly called *celadoras*.

CHAPTER 16

1. Decree 507 created a legal definition for political prisoners in 1980. See Margaret Popkin, *Peace without Justice: Obstacles to Building the Rule of Law in El Salvador* (University Park, PA: Penn State University Press, 2010).

CHAPTER 17

1. The guerrilla radio station Radio Venceremos was run by the People's Revolutionary Army (ERP) and broadcast throughout the war beginning in 1982. The other major guerrilla radio station was Radio Farabundo Martí, run by the Farabundo Martí Forces of Popular Liberation (FPL). See Carlos Consalvi, *Broadcasting the Civil War in El Salvador: A Memoir of Guerrilla Radio* (Austin: University of Texas Press, 2010).

2. About nine miles away.

3. Oakland Ross, "Politics Splits Salvador Siblings," *Globe and Mail*, May 31, 1983; Adam Hochschild, "Inside the Slaughterhouse," *Mother Jones*, June 1983.

CHAPTER 20

1. See "Salvadorans break up extortion ring. Police say former army officer masterminded series of kidnaps," *Boston Globe*, February 11, 1982.

2. Tim Golden, "Former Salvadoran Soldier Plunges from the 'High Life,'" Knight-Ridder Newspapers, November 7, 1985.

CHAPTER 22

1. Robert "Bobby" Sands was a militant in the Irish Republican Army who died in Northern Ireland's Maze prison while on hunger strike. During his strike, he was elected to the British Parliament but died on May 5, 1981, after 66 days of refusing food. He was 27 years old.

2. From an interview recorded with Ana Margarita in 1990, seven years after the strike and during her first bout with cancer.

CHAPTER 23

1. Carlos Molina and Mauricio Domenech had been disappeared in late October 1982, at the same time as two other National Revolutionary Movement (MNR) members—labor leaders Jorge Herrera and David Elias Guadrón—and Luis Menjivar of the Popular Social Christian Movement. See Richard J. Meislin, "5 Key Leaders of the Opposition Reported Kidnapped in Salvador," *New York Times*, October 23, 1982, www.nytimes.com.

2. Guido Véjar, Héctor Oquelí, Vera Matthias, and David Elias Guadrón.

3. Maurice Bishop was a Grenadian lawyer and politician. Prime minister in the People's Revolutionary Government of Grenada from 1979 to 1983, he was deposed in a coup and executed on October 23, 1983, shortly after Ana Margarita met him in Cuba.

Index

~

Cienfuegos, Fermán, 12, 104, 233
Claramount, Ernesto, 45
Colegio Externado de San José, 11–12, 37, 66, 79, 80–81, 137
COMADRES (Committee of Mothers of the Disappeared), 55, 121, 161, 168, 170–73, 179–81
Comandante Clelia. *See* Letona, Ana Mercedes
Comandante Luisa. *See* Letona Pérez, Mercedes del Carmen
Comintern, 42
Communist Party of Costa Rica (Partido Vanguardia Popular), 53
Communist Party of El Salvador, 26, 41–42, 48, 50, 51–55, 180
Consalvi, Carlos Henríquez, xxvii
Coordinadora Revolucionaria de Masas (CRM), 74, 242n5
COPPES (Committee of Political Prisoners of El Salvador, created in Santa Tecla prison), 2, 121; bee project, 198, 200, 201, 204; Common Fund, 155, 161, 162, 165, 166, 167, 168, 171, 196, 204; COPPES store, 55, 101, 166, 167, 176, 179, 181, 190, 193, 197, 200; *directiva* (steering committee in Ilopango), 161, 165, 166, 168, 170, 171, 172, 178, 187, 188, 191, 205, 208, 210, 211, 212, 216, 226; discouraging relationships with guards, 209; *economato* (cooking committee), 168, 172, 187, 195, 196, 197, 227; expels police informer, 205, 206, 208; first action in Ilopango, 154; garden, 163, 165, 166, 177, 215; hostility toward lesbian relationships, 209, 210, 211, 223; hunger strikes, 158, 165, 173, 218; maintaining discipline, 205; relations with common prisoners, 154, 164, 169, 171, 176, 189, 190, 191, 192, 198, 200, 203, 204; restructuring, 168, 186; splits in two, 187; struggle for hegemony within Ilopango, 187, 188
COPREFA (Press Committee of the Armed Forces), 97
Costa Rica, 51–52, 118
Crater (drop-in center in Guatemala), 16, 18
Cristiani, Alfredo Félix (Freddy), 12

Cuadra, Vida, 152, 154, 159, 160–62, 163, 165, 174, 182, 225
Cuba, xvii, xix, 17, 29, 31, 51, 52, 60, 66, 122, 230, 233; Cuban Revolution, 8, 10, 17, 26, 48, 54, 60, 232; International Youth Festival (1978), 48–63

Dada, Héctor, 71
Dalton, Roque, xxviii, 41
D'Aubuisson, Roberto, 67, 70–71, 74, 199
death squads, xix, xxii, 51, 56, 66–67, 81, 84, 108, 118, 199
Decree 507, defines political prisoner status, 158, 183
Díaz, Nidia, xxiii, xxv
disappearance, as a tool of political terror, 64, 67, 111, 121–22, 126, 179, 183
Domenech, Mauricio, 229
DRU (Unified Revolutionary Direction), 73, 74
Duarte, José Napoleón, 69–71, 73–74, 183, 225
Dueñas, Ernesto Regalado, 26

Ellacuría, Ignacio, 37
El Mozote massacre, xx–xxii
El Salvador: civil war (1980–1992), xvii; first junta (1979), 70, 153; general amnesty for political prisoners (1983), xvii, 217, 225, 227, 230; *las catorce* (oligarch families), 7, 199; oligarchy, 7–8, 12, 17, 26, 37, 68, 92, 94, 190, 199; presidential election (1977), 44; second junta (1978), 71, 121
El Salvador: El Pueblo Vencerá (film), 91–99
embutido (hidden message), 122, 180, 188, 219
Endara, Guillermo (president of Panama), 173
ERP (People's Revolutionary Army), 26, 41, 70, 111, 152, 154, 172, 187, 205, 225, 232
Esperanza (pseudonym). *See* Letona, Ana Mercedes
Espinosa, Martín, 35, 104

FALANGE (Armed Forces of Anti Communist Liberation–Wars of Elimination), 67
FAPU (Unified Popular Action Front), 66–67

Oquelí, Héctor, 47, 61–62, 71, 118, 122, 231
ORDEN (Nationalist Democratic Organization), 36, 70, 96–97, 102, 116, 151
Orga. *See* FPL
Ortega, Daniel, 61
Osorio, Oscar, 39

Palme, Olaf, 46
Panama, 39, 52, 60, 74, 173
Pancho, Mónica (pseudonym used by Ana Margarita), 75–78
Papo (photographer), 91, 97
Paquita (COPPES member), 152–55, 171–72, 187, 197, 208, 210
Parra, Isobel, 56
Paz Zamora, Jaime, 62
Peña, Lorena, xxiii
Pétry, Irène, 76
pinta (graffiti or slogan), 178–79, 213
Playón (lava fields outside San Salvador), 180
PNP (People's National Party, Jamaica), 28–30, 40
Policía Nacional, 81
political prisoners in Ilopango, 151, 154, 158–59, 169, 171, 182–83, 186–91, 198, 204–5, 209, 213, 216, 227
Poma, Roberto, 27, 41
Pope John Paul II, 218
Popular Forum alliance, 67
Prieto, Emilia, 53, 56
Prisoner without a Name, Cell without a Number (Jacobo Timerman), 141
PRTC (Revolutionary Workers Party of Central America), 51, 54
PSOE (Spanish Socialist Workers Party), 75–76
Pueblo Armado, El (music cassette), 89
Puerto Viejo, Costa Rica, xii–xiii, 98, 235, 236

Radio Farabundo Martí, 89
Radio Rebelde (Cuba), 10
Radio Venceremos, 176, 232
Reagan, Ronald, xxi–xxii, 75, 218–19, 225
Recinos, Héctor, 121, 122
Red Cross, 155, 167–68, 171, 181–82, 197
Richard (Ana Margarita's boyfriend), 48, 51, 100–101, 106

Rodríguez, Silvio, 56
Roeder, Guillermo (kidnapper), 199
Romero, Archbishop Oscar Arnulfo, xxi, 37, 72, 73, 74, 75, 156
Rosalía (prison gang leader), 189–90, 194
Rosario (social worker in Ilopango), 171, 191

Samayoa, Salvador, 104
Samuel (pseudonym), 119–23
Sandinista National Liberation Front (FSLN, Nicaragua), 52–53, 58, 61, 68, 92, 113
Sandino, César Augusto, 41
Sands, Bobby, death of, 218
San Sebastián (Spain), 23
Santa Tecla, 2–3, 66, 87, 106, 108, 112, 124
Santa Tecla prison, 2, 121, 158, 173, 229
Seaga, Edward, 29, 31
Sebastián (Ana Margarita's lover and FPL mentor), 2–3, 100–110, 114, 119, 121–30, 137–46, 170, 181, 184–85, 219, 227–33; background, 83; begins relationship with Ana Margarita, 107; comes to live in Ana Margarita's house, 101; last meeting with Ana Margarita, 233; recruits Ana Margarita, 83; released from prison, 227; tortured, 128, 130
Señora Rengifo (common prisoner), 203, 204
Silva, Héctor, 12, 118
Sister Lidia (common prisoner), 201, 202
Sister Marian Peter. *See* Melville, Marjorie
Social Democratic Party (Germany), 42, 46, 63
Socialist International (SI), 46–48, 61–62, 74–76, 104, 206, 231; Socialist International Congress (Madrid, 1980), 75; Socialist International Congress (Vancouver, 1978), 62
Socialist International Women, 47, 76
Somoza, Anastasio, 53, 67, 113
Sonia (COPPES member), 162–65, 174, 177–78, 188, 212–17; arrives in Ilopango, 162; confused by COPPES internal politics, 215; discipline problems, 178, 212, 214; expelled from COPPES, 216, 217; garden project, 163; makes *chicha* (home-brewed alcohol), 213; physical confrontation with Ana Margarita, 216